Tim Crooks was brought up in Surrey vicarages and educated in independent schools. He excelled at rowing and sculling on the Thames, served an apprenticeship with BSA Motorcycles, raced motocross bikes and, as a member of the GB rowing team for eight years, earned a string of medals, including an Olympic Silver. Tim has worked primarily as an engineer and teacher, and also as an artist blacksmith and landscaper. He is married with children and grandchildren.

When he was a teenager, his emotions – especially anger and depression – puzzled him. Years later, he was diagnosed with bi-polar disorder and the broad knowledge of the disorder now qualifies him to write about the illness, his life, and his sport.

To anyone confused by their emotions, for those who have to put on an act at times, to try and appear normal during daily life, and for anyone suffering mental illness.

It is also for those interested in sporting lives, links between instability and performance, in the origins of motivation and drive, and for everyone, because by sharing our experiences, we build knowledge, but crucially understanding.

Tim Crooks

DRIVEN BY DEMONS: BIPOLAR OLYMPIAN

AUSTIN MACAULEY PUBLISHERS
LONDON * CAMBRIDGE * NEW YORK * SHARJAH

Copyright © Tim Crooks 2025

The right of Tim Crooks to be identified as author of this work has been asserted by the author in accordance with sections 77 and 78 of the Copyright, Designs and Patents Act 1988.

All rights reserved. No part of this publication may be reproduced, stored in a retrieval system, or transmitted in any form or by any means, electronic, mechanical, photocopying, recording, or otherwise, without the prior permission of the publishers.

Any person who commits any unauthorised act in relation to this publication may be liable to criminal prosecution and civil claims for damages.

All of the events in this memoir are true to the best of author's memory. The views expressed in this memoir are solely those of the author.

A CIP catalogue record for this title is available from the British Library.

ISBN 9781035870769 (Paperback)
ISBN 9781035877331 (Hardback)
ISBN 9781035870776 (ePub e-book)

www.austinmacauley.com

First Published 2025
Austin Macauley Publishers Ltd®
1 Canada Square
Canary Wharf
London
E14 5AA

ACKNOWLEDGEMENTS

When I started writing, I was encouraged and helped by Ken McKellar, a Kingston Rowing Club friend. He chased me along for copy, spoke regularly, made a superb contribution, but had cancer and has most regrettably died.

I asked a number of people to write a short piece for the book, which they did. Later, while taking advice about my draft, I was advised to take these pieces out because they broke up the flow of the narrative. Thank you so much, however, to the following, listed in the order in which they arrive in my story, and whose input I have largely included: Guy Tod, Tim Bucknall, Anthony Robinson, Donald Legget, Christopher Woodhouse, Glyn Locke, Patrick Delafield and Hugh Matheson.

There was a period when I had difficulty shaping the book into its final form and I reached out to a number of friends to help. I cannot name them all, but thank you for reading my drafts and advising, or for simply humouring me when my greatest need was self-confidence.

Those who have helped significantly have been John Reader, Graham Davidson, Hugh Matheson, many of my other crew-mates, and David Reynolds with his publishing experience. Others who have helped or contributed in any way, know that I am grateful, and I'm sorry that I can't name you all.

The one person who has contributed more than anyone is Annie, who has not only put up with me for years and years, but has supported me endlessly in writing this book.

Table of Contents

Foreword: Racing Your Hero	12
Introduction	15
Chapter 1: Boating	18
Chapter 2: Good Fortune	22
Chapter 3: Boarding School 1957–61	31
Chapter 4: Meanwhile at Home	34
Chapter 5: What Next?	39
Chapter 6: What in God's Name Was Wrong?	42
Chapter 7: Radley College January 1963	44
Chapter 8: Finding My Sport	52
Chapter 9: The Rugby Term	55
Chapter 10: The Die Was Cast	59
Chapter 11: The First Eight	65
Chapter 12: Motorbike Madness	70
Chapter 13: Last Year at Radley	74
Chapter 14: 'The BSA'	80
Chapter 15: Leander Club	86
Chapter 16: The New Challenge	93
Chapter 17: The Grand Challenge Cup	103
Chapter 18: 'The Grand' Again	109
Chapter 19: Mood Crash	116
Chapter 20: Towards Munich 1972	122
Chapter 21: Germany	129
Chapter 22: The Lubrication Laboratory	134
Chapter 23: Not All Bad	137
Chapter 24: Aiming for Montreal	142
Chapter 25: Out of the Pit	153
Chapter 26: Summer 1974	156
Chapter 27: World Championships 1974	166
Chapter 28: The Second Season	177
Chapter 29: Montreal in Sight	184

Chapter 30: 1976 Olympic Season	188
Chapter 31: The Even Bigger Challenge	201
Chapter 32: Superstars and Early Regattas 1977	208
Chapter 33: The 'Diamond Sculls' and Lucerne 1977	212
Chapter 34: Deja Vu	219
Chapter 35: The 1978 Season	228
Chapter 36: The 'Diamonds' and Lucerne 1978	235
Chapter 37: The Boston Marathon on the River Witham, Lincolnshire	245
Chapter 38: Training Camp and New Zealand	250
Chapter 39: Six Months in Sydney	252
Chapter 40: A New Career	256
Chapter 41: Out of the Woods? Not Yet	264
Chapter 42: Fire and Muscle, and That Race	270
Epilogue	276
Glossary of Rowing Terms	281
Appendix	283

Tim Crooks has done great service in explaining his bipolar illness. As a doctor specialising in some aspects of adolescent development, I have been very aware of psychiatric and psychological problems associated with stress of all kinds, including sport.

In the 1960s, mental illness was not discussed in public or in rowing. Even now it carries a stigma and is considered different from 'physical illnesses'. It may be poorly understood and difficult to treat, but is an illness in the same sense that heart failure is an illness. The organ of origin may be different but that is all.

A colleague of mine had the same condition as Tim, and he maintained some medical practice while receiving treatment. When recovered sufficiently he gave a fascinating lecture, and I was struck by his remark that 'he had no idea that this disease makes you feel so very ill.'

Professor Christopher Woodhouse FRCS

Foreword: Racing Your Hero

While Tim was winning a silver medal during 1976 in the British Eight at the Montreal Olympics, I was a youngster, aged 14, learning to scull and row. Tim went on to race as Great Britain's single sculler in 1977; I watched him win the Diamond Sculls at the Henley Royal Regatta.

He came 4th in the World Rowing Championships and he won the BBC's UK Superstars competition. He was my hero. A bit of a maverick, slightly wild but very talented. He was the one I wanted to be like.

Tim won the 'Diamonds' again during 1978, but gave up being Britain's sculler later that year, but our paths crossed a number of times in the early '80s. The National Sculling Coach, Mike Spracklen, was putting together a crew of eight single scullers early in 1981 to compete in the Eights Head of the River Race held on the Tideway in London.

To this day, it feels odd—we wanted to go afloat in the eight but were short of one person and Tim happened to be running past. Mike, knowing that Tim was fit, shouted out, "Do you fancy a row, Tim?" Then, I couldn't believe it. I was rowing with my hero.

With a few training sessions under our belt, we went on to win the Tideway Eights Head of the River Race, beating the National Rowing Squad eight by almost ten seconds. The drinking session at Vesta Rowing Club was legendary.

Two years later, I met Tim in the final of the single sculls event at Marlow Regatta, my hometown and club. There are not many times you get to row with, drink with and race against your icon of the rowing world. Tim had given up competing for Great Britain 5 years before and I was a strong, confident young man aged 21, but was still scared of racing a retired 'old' man.

Sitting on the start, after a bad night's sleep, I wondered, '*how I'd perform against this formidable man, but in the race, I pulled out to an early lead and won by four lengths.*'

A fortnight later, we met again in the final of the Diamond Sculls at Henley Royal Regatta. I was flowing with confidence after our previous meeting, especially as Tim had already raced that day during the morning in a quadruple scull and had won that event, the Queen Mother Cup.

He'd elected to row the quad sculls first, which he felt he had a better chance of winning at his age of 34 and I thought that my race against him in the afternoon would be a walk in the park but also my first Diamond Challenge Cup win.

Our race started, and just 45 seconds into the race, I was leading by 1½ lengths—with a similar feeling that I'd had at Marlow. But this is where it changed. I didn't continue to move away—the distance stuck. It stayed like this for the next 5 minutes.

As we approached Remenham Club, support for Tim by the Kingston faithful spurred him on. Some people in the sport can push hard for 10 strokes, some for 20—but the reports I heard afterwards were that Tim said he had closed his eyes and burned for 50 strokes. When he opened his eyes, he led the race.

I couldn't believe what I was seeing. How could this be so different to 2 weeks earlier? I had given everything and just been overtaken against all odds. As I was faltering I sensed that he was starting to pay the price for his commitment, and a few strokes later, we were level.

At this point, he stopped rowing. My thought at the time was, *Thank God for that* as we were in front of the General Enclosure and were in the final stages of the race. Within fractions of a second, I was a length in the lead. People said later that I stopped at this point but I argue I went to a very light paddle, knowing that the race was won.

Tim was gasping for breath and bent over—I can still see his face clearly in my mind as he looked round at me—then suddenly, he seemed to jump 10 feet in the air and back to life. He started one of his bursts again. The race was not over.

We both picked up the pace, but fortunately for me, he couldn't maintain more than 10 hard strokes. We paddled across the finish line physically and mentally exhausted. People still talk about that race to this day and I learnt a valuable lesson to never underestimate your opponent.

We were both happy to have a victory at the 1983 Henley Regatta. I could say, however, never race your hero.

Sir Steven Redgrave, CBE

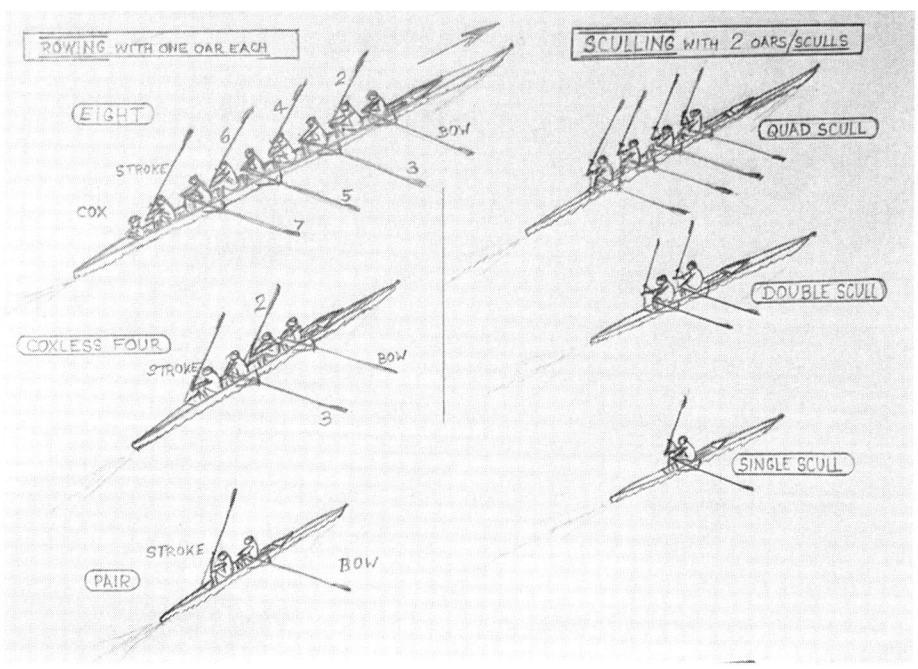

Racing boat types

Myself racing at the Henley Regatta

Introduction

Mental difficulties were not spoken about during the 1960s and 70s, and my mind has been a mystery to me for most of my life. It has become clear recently that as a schoolboy I was subconsciously using sport and other activities in attempts to control worrying feelings which disturbed my peace of mind. I was simply trying to get by.

In this book I describe how I used sport and other stimulating activities to avoid depressions, and these generally promoted higher, more manic, moods, however there were also torments and nightmare low moods which I couldn't avoid. There were plenty of great times, which I considered normal, but my moods were unstable and could suddenly collapse, leaving me weak and depressed.

Undiagnosed mental illnesses can lead to addictions, crime and sometimes death. Few who suffer survive unscathed.

The sport of rowing suited me, made me feel good and gave me so much that there has been an element of addiction in my relationship not only with sport, but with commitment to practical activities, pressure and risk. My mind could usually be rescued, even on the worst of days, but I came to know that if I'd been in the black pit of serious depression before any challenge or liberating excitement then, given a short respite, my destination would again be the pit.

I was unpredictable, and was frightened of the feelings in my head, which made me fear the future. I had no long term ambitions as I never knew how I would be, and this affected how I lived my life. The fear of falling into the pit drove me subconsciously to do crazy things to keep my mood up. It pushed me from one thing to the next, minute by minute, day after day, and was quite often mentally exhausting.

My plunging mood could be saved by immediate action, whether acceptable to others or not, and hence the unpredictability. The distant future might well not have existed.

I was well loved and supported by many, but was too often an angry man, and am very sorry to all those I alarmed or hurt in any way. There are many causes of anger, and I see it in others, but have learned that factors which can cause it, but do not excuse it, include fear, upset and mental exhaustion.

During 1978 I walked away from top level sport because an extended episode of serious depression took first my spirit, but then my athletic ability away, and it became impossible for me to go on with it. Fifteen years later, during 1993 I was diagnosed with bipolar disorder, treatment helped, and the illness can be improved by medication along with understanding of it and management, but it cannot be cured. My quality of life improved, I was by then married, had children, and continued working in a variety of professions, including teaching and landscaping, until the children had left home and I retired during 2014.

Following the decision of my wife and I to divorce in 2017, and our separation, I started to write this book, but soon ground to a halt because I still didn't understand myself at that time, nor my behaviour and school rebellions as a younger person. Two courses of action on my part opened my eyes to the past, however, first a psychiatric assessment in Harley Street, the results of which were most enlightening, and the second was the decision to research the illness of bipolar disorder in depth.

Within weeks this new self-knowledge was allowing a window in my mind to slowly open. It was as if my monochrome memories were acquiring vivid technicolour, and I began to understand where my motivation and drive had come from all those years earlier.

When I came back to my desk, I wrote from a different perspective, and the slow-motion re-run of my past was an emotional rollercoaster. On some days I finished feeling uplifted and satisfied, but on others was depressed and debilitated, shocked at how faithfully my mind had followed the depths of the bad times. For months I wrote down the memories. They poured out, including some that had been long forgotten.

This draft acted as the source material for my book, and then it was condensed, amended and fashioned into the chapters that follow. There were delays that included moving my dwelling place five times in five years, during which many good folk helped and advised me, but Annie and I found we missed each other too much to go on being apart. It was Covid that finally threw us together and during the summer of 2022 we had our second happy wedding.

Further delays to the book were caused by physical health problems and accidents. A wheelchair, Zimmer frame, crutches, and my rowing machine helped. The show went on and a publisher was found.

I'm now well, living happily in Dorking with Annie, family members nearby, boating on the Thames, and making music in retirement. A lucky man indeed.

Writing this book has led to self-understanding, and finding myself has been a joy. I very much hope that others who relate to my story will be helped in their journey.

Chapter 1
Boating

It's fun, you can spend years working at this sport of rowing, it's satisfying with others in crews and it can be continued into later life. The common aim is to make the boat go well, and the challenges are for the individuals to learn a good rowing stroke, to get fit, and to row perfectly in time with each other.

You can get the 'rowing bug', that's when you're at your very happiest, spending time with others, taking exercise in the fresh air with the elements while blending as a team in a boat.

Or you can be on your own in a boat with two oars or sculls, paddling along, just doing your thing and taking a stroke whenever you feel like it, or you can race along as fast as you can. But it's rewarding to scull for miles, allowing the boat to glide effortlessly between strokes while finding out what exactly makes the boat run further each stroke, and to have another sculler alongside is useful as you can see what works for you and what doesn't. It's very much about your boat going faster than the boat next to you in the instant that your sculls lift out of the water, the result is travelling further before the next stroke. Bigger steps on the water from one stroke to the next wins races.

Rowing and sculling were a gift from my grandfather who had been a champion in his day. What a gift.

A rowing eight carries nine, it's two feet wide and nearly sixty feet long, the captain of the boat is the coxswain, or cox, who steers the boat but for everything else, uses their voice to control the eight human power plants.

During 1974, twelve years after I'd been introduced to racing boats, I was rowing in the British National Squad Eight. Nearly all of us had been in the 1972 Munich Olympic Rowing Team and this eight, put together by National Rowing Coach, Bohumil 'Bob' Janousek, had been together for about two months but hadn't raced as a crew internationally.

One Sunday morning during our last two-minute flat-out training row, we were tired, but were on form and were rowing as one. Suddenly, we had speed with ease and were flying. We were working on water but flying. It was sensational. In sporting terms, we were in a psychological state of 'flow' where each member of the crew contributed an exceptional performance and each stroke sent us for miles. It felt so relaxed but the boat was going faster than ever. Such a buzz.

The top races are two thousand metres long, about a mile and a quarter, but there's a problem in going flat out because it's an endurance race. Off the start in a race, it's maximum power, that's a must or you get left behind. Everyone in your crew does it and if absolute maximum power is delivered far into the race, there's a good chance you'll be leading.

That's good you might say, but it's not. Muscle action produces lactic acid and if the acid builds up faster than the blood can carry it away, it reduces muscle efficiency and causes pain. It's important fairly soon after the start for the crew to settle to a pace which can be maintained.

It goes like this. Blast off the start flat out, but if you go too hard for too long, you'll be in pain and you're done in, you can't contribute your full share any more but you have to keep going somehow, you've messed up. It's awful to have to carry that acid and pain all the way.

Through the middle part of the race, the whole crew have to row just below full power, but if the boat slows much, it's heavier to pull, so the boat speed *must* be kept high. You need all eight to be on form and doing it right. It's a challenge and a fine balance for everyone to keep their movements fast but relaxed to keep the boat going for the distance. If the boat slows, some of the crew, maybe everyone, will be done in and the crew can fall apart before the end.

Imagine a race.

On the start, six eights to race two thousand metres. The racing lanes are marked with buoys and the crews are getting straight and ready. We need to produce our best. We're ready, and we're off, flat out, stretching out for powerful and long strokes.

We're moving well and we've settled to a rating of thirty-eight strokes per minute, but there are crews ahead of us. Cox keeps driving us along, encouraging and giving orders that we're familiar with. We'll do a big burst of power half way along the course for ten strokes to try to improve cohesion and move up on our opposition, but to keep our speed high over the rest of the course, we'll have a number of smaller pushes.

Cox might tell us to take the beginnings of our strokes faster and harder, or other reminders, but before a burst when we really push on, we'll always be given three strokes warning, so that when the change comes, we all commit to it together. We go. Everyone focuses, works harder and 'thinks quick' about catching the water efficiently at the beginning of the stroke.

We do it *together* and the boat speed increases. You trust your crewmates, you get to know that they *will* do it. We *all* have to do it otherwise the boat doesn't speed up, and it's harder for those who do push hard.

Fatigue is building but when you're tired, you can still do more. It's essential to concentrate on rowing technique and the balance of the boat while driving yourself to deliver the goods. There are eight individual mental battles being fought about absolute limits.

The finish is five hundred metres away, the last quarter of the race, nearly a minute and a half. Cox gives our three-stroke warning, we jump on it, legs driving, and go for the finish at well over forty strokes per minute, the pain is coming.

Two crews are left behind and we're in a bunch of four, sprinting for the line. The crew on our left is leading us by nearly half a length, the one on our right is just in front but we're going well. Suddenly, I realise that we've gone through a window in the sky and we're flying.

We have that 'speed with ease'. It's magic and it doesn't come in every race. It doesn't come often, but when you've got it, you know it, and you're catching up.

Listen to cox, we're on our knife edge of perfection with senses tuned, peripheral vision, balance and feel, so many factors in all of our minds. A fantastic rhythm. Don't look round to see how we're doing, look straight, keep the balance, and focus on making the boat go. God, it hurts, pushing on, it's good, just a few more big ones, still flying, going well, pain, but flying, still flying, and cox shouts, "Wind down." We've finished.

It was dead close but we won. It's sensational and so worth the effort. Satisfying, rewarding, epic even.

Those who go rowing are sometimes considered to be nutters, but even normal people can take to the water and eventually, prove to themselves and to others that they're complete nutters as well.

An eight racing with myself sitting six from the bow (Leander Club winning on the Thames Tideway in 1973).

Chapter 2
Good Fortune

A boy in the bath, running the hot tap
my feet are feeling this
using my hands to paddle the water
clockwise is good today
pushing the water even faster
with tricks to make it go
catch, accelerate, push it round
it's really going now
learning about this resistant fluid
is a challenge, really fun
measured forces, don't tear it at all
use full, flat hands
more finesse for whirlpool speed
I turn off the tap, it's *hot*
this game's absurd, funny really
but useful skills for the future

I had to pack it in eventually when Mum kept asking me to keep the water in the bath. She always said I'd be good at something as I'd see to it that things were done properly, and she could see that I had drive as well as perfectionism. She asked me sometimes to clean the bath as she knew I'd do a proper job. Absolutely the business when finished.

We had German girls to stay with us, for a year each, to help in the home until I was old enough to go with Mum and elder brother Steve to church on Sundays, I have many happy childhood memories of the grandparents' big property in Kingston and lazy summer days in our vicarage garden. Dad mowed the lawn with the faithful green Atco mower while Mum brought out tea and cake.

Our 'German girls' sometimes sang German lullabies at bedtime, we had trips out, picnics and summer holidays in Cornwall. I loved those grown-up young women and I was sad when each one had to leave. Many years later, Dad told me how damaged some of these girls were after the war, and particularly about one of them, who had been flung down and raped by a Russian.

The girls' time in Cobham was very much a rehabilitation. Aleksandr Solzhenitsyn, an ex-captain of the Soviet Army is reported to have said, "All of us knew very well that if girls were German, they could be raped and shot. This was almost a combat distinction."

Our Dad was born in a vicarage in Ireland, he read Psychology and Music at Trinity College, Dublin, but then Theology, and after being ordained he worked as Dean of Music at Kilkenny Cathedral. He came to England during 1943, became a naval chaplain, he travelled widely, and in Sicily was issued with a 500 cc Norton motorbike to fulfil his duties which included dispatch riding.

The following year, he went ashore on Juno beach on D-Day from an American tank landing craft after the Canadians had fought their way ashore earlier.

Dad on the Norton in Sicily.

D-Day transport.

Some months later, he was appointed chaplain to Admiral Ramsay, the senior naval officer on mainland Europe at the RN headquarters near Paris where he courted an attractive WRNS communications officer. Crooks was seen riding a motorbike with his 'Wren' hanging on round his waist and he taught her to shoot beer cans off a wall with his Smith & Wesson service revolver.

She'd worked as a cipher officer during 1943 aboard the Queen Mary steaming across the Atlantic with Churchill to the Québec conference and during February 1945, again with Churchill, this time aboard HMS Renown through the Mediterranean to the Yalta conference. Aboard ship, the communications team would hear Churchill shuffling along the gangway and then, "What's up, girls?"

After the war, the Wren and the Irish cleric were married. She was the daughter of John Tann who rowed at Thames RC (Rowing Club) and during 1914 as a single sculler[*] had become the amateur sculling champion of Great Britain.

---

* See Glossary

He went on after the First World War and rowed in the Thames Rowing Club eight during 1919 to win the Fawley Cup in the Peace Regatta at Henley. That was the top event for non-services eights and the Australian army eight won the King's Cup for crews of services personnel. Thereafter there was one top eights event, the Grand Challenge Cup.

My elder brother Steve was born during 1947, I came two years later, and in 1952, we moved from the vicarage in Dock Street in London's Whitechapel to the village of Cobham in Surrey.

Our Dad was to be vicar in the parish of St Andrews, which was superb after the dirt and grime of bombed-out London, the village was small and there were very few cars in those days. Steve and I went to a nursery school where Steve got on better with the schoolwork than I did, and in the long run, I was happiest when involved in practical activities.

Later on, I was very committed to making things, particularly structures and mechanisms with Meccano. It seems that from a young age, I needed a passion to keep my brain occupied.

*

Dad played practical jokes and one day while driving us all, he pointed out a low-flying aircraft sign, shouted, "LOOK OUT," and swerved, using his hand to bang on the outside of the driver's door. Mum was shocked but we were in tears in the back.

On holiday while driving down a steep hill in Cornwall, Dad stiffened up, stamped hard on the floor a few times and shouted, "NO BRAKES, NO BRAKES." Dad laughed but we were wrecks.

We loved him. He was my hero. He used his BSA 250 motorbike for his work around the parish and they loved it at the local school when he turned up to take assembly on his motorbike with his black cassock blowing in the wind.

Some years later, Dad showed us his brand new motorbike, a 350cc Triumph twin, the T21, it was beautiful and a lot faster than the single cylinder BSA. We had burn-ups on his motorbike, bonfire burn-ups in the garden, sometimes with petrol, and he could enjoy a good fart when Mum wasn't around, but he took care to teach us the dangers of petrol which he'd learnt in Ireland.

The class divide. I was about seven years old when we had two small rooms off the hall in the vicarage knocked into one to make a visitor's washroom and I got to know Harry, the builder, who was a man with many skills. I told him that Dad had been in the navy and asked him if he'd been in the war.

He said he'd been in the army in the First World War, and with a pause and a fixed look at the wall, he said, "The Somme—it was terrible." He was still looking at the wall and I hurried inside to ask Mum what the Somme was. I could never understand why Mum always seemed to look down on Harry and she had said that he was an *ordinary man,* but she was shocked by what he'd said and made him a cup of tea straight away.

The finished building work, which had involved knocking a wall down, plastering, plumbing and electrics, was creative and quite superb, and in my mind, he was absolutely *not* an ordinary man. Mum looked down on Harry but it was one of those topics never spoken about and I was confused by these secrets which adults kept. This was a 'no-no', one of many.

My temper wasn't good Our family was very close and mealtimes were special. One breakfast time, we were seated at the kitchen table but I was blamed for damage to the stair carpet.

[I HATE UPSET, WHAT'S GOING ON? I CAN'T STAND IT]

Walking powerfully to the door,

[WHAT'S THIS TERRIBLE FEELING?]

I slam the door
just as hard as I can
and the pots and pans in the cupboard rattle

[THIS EMOTION, I'M ANGRY, WHERE DID IT COME FROM?]

the pots and pans and jars are shaken.
I'm shaken.
I open the door and the family's shaken.

[IT'S A TERRIBLE UPSET, WHAT'S HAPPENING?]
They're all shocked. Everything's ruined.
I'm ashamed at what I did.

That incident played on my mind, and as is evident, is not forgotten.

Another time, Grandfather told me to do something and I kicked him on the shin. My reaction had been sudden and inexplicable. I never wanted to hurt him and when I told my parents what I'd done, Mum was shocked but Dad reacted with a stifled laugh.

"Did you really?" Dad unwittingly encouraged me in the Stubborn Glory of Defiance. My temper and anger worried me from an early age as it was a dark side to my nature which was unacceptable. I was moody too and felt ashamed and confused, my self-confidence suffered but to talk to anyone about this sort of thing was out of the question.

We were lucky at home to be financially supported by our Mum's parents. We had our home, the vicarage, through the church, and Dad's contribution to our lives was huge in other ways. Mum was an only child and through her, we were given so much, including education in independent schools.

Soon after the First World War, Grandfather had taken control of John Tann Ltd, the family business which had been started in 1795 by his great-grandfather, making lockable wooden chests. The company had moved on to making high quality steel safes, strong rooms and strong room doors, respected the world over.

John Tann, Amateur Sculling Champion of Great Britain 1914.

The Tann family.

Strong room doors manufactured by John Tann Ltd.

Strong room doors manufactured by John Tann Ltd.

Naval Chaplain Crooks

WRNS Officer Tann

The Crooks family, Exhibition Road. 1955.

Chapter 3
Boarding School 1957–61

At the age of eight, I followed brother Steve to Feltonfleet Prep School. I had new activities, playing the piano, carpentry lessons and new sports. The school rules were strict and at the beginning, I went along with it all but then rebelled and misbehaved.

After breakfast each day, we had to queue up to use one of the six toilet cubicles, on our return, we had to announce loudly to the duty prefect; tick or cross, which referred to our success, or not, in producing a big one. Apparently, Matron needed to know.

After a year or so, I reported whatever I wanted but made sure to keep my average up. How dare they presume to make public what I held as private. I was increasingly resentful of the strict regime.

My academic progress had never been good and increasingly, I became a naughty boy. My sense of humour was an asset though and I was remembered by some (many, I hope) as a likeable rogue.

My poor behaviour led to the slipper rather too often but at least we didn't have to take our uniform grey shorts down, and six of the best on the backside was pretty shocking but the pain didn't last long. I got the slipper 14 times while at prep school, the most common reason being 'ragging in the dormitories', running around after lights out, bouncing on beds and generally misbehaving.

I had recurring dreams. I had wings and was being chased by a monster but wasn't quite strong enough to fly up and away, but through supreme effort, running and flapping my wings, I avoided being caught. During my teenage years, my dreams would be different.

After a few terms, my parents and the headmaster must have discussed my behaviour and agreed that creative activity kept me out of trouble. It was arranged that I could keep my box of Meccano under my bed, and after checking in with Matron, could spend time making things in peace and quiet. I often had bad feelings in my head but found that I could dispel them through action, and in particular at school through bad behaviour.

Those bad feelings, though I didn't know it at the time, were warnings of approaching depression and these were much more frightening than any possible punishments for bad behaviour. When my mind felt bad I was presented with two options, the fast approaching depression or some weak punishment for misbehaviour, the obvious choice was to avoid depression and take the punishment.

Warning feelings would arrive, my mood was falling, and often I couldn't help myself. I didn't wilfully misbehave for no reason, but a force greater than my will was driving me. It has become apparent that I was not in control. Instinct took over to save my mood. The instinctive action could be to play the fool, interrupt, take risks, rebel, flick pellets; *anything, and never mind the consequences.*

At school during the summer terms, we played cricket but swimming was my favourite sport. Some of us used the 25-yard rifle range with. 22 rim fire rifles, Steve and I were good shots because Dad had taught us target shooting at home with an air rifle. Dad and his friend, Barry, had got up to all sorts of tricks in Ireland when they were lads, with petrol, rifles, girlfriends and motorbikes.

During the winter we played rugby and football. I was quite good at rugby but soon found the game frustrating due to repeated lack of progress and all the stoppages. Football was more satisfying to start with but my skills didn't develop well and my main talent was to hoof the ball up the pitch in the general direction of the opposition's goal, so I ended up playing in defence.

I found ball games frustrating, there was too much chasing and standing, simply watching others playing. Piano players had to play the hymn during morning prayers at some stage, and when my turn came, I messed up most verses and everyone sang on without accompaniment.

It was public humiliation, and yes, we had to take the knocks but I'd already had a few years of 'troubles'. There were many times when I didn't feel good and more recently, I've referred to these feelings as demons, but there was no alternative to absorbing the knocks and getting on positively.

I recognise now that poor academic results and many disappointments confirmed to me that I was failing, but I never considered admitting to myself that I was a lesser person, so I pressed on regardless, driven and often running from one thing to the next. I was living in denial and getting on purposefully with enthusiasm and humour while my self-esteem was being gradually crushed.

[SOMETHING'S WRONG, I FEEL BAD. WHY? WHAT'S WRONG?]

The headmaster called me to his office before the end of the summer term in 1961, I was 12 years old and he explained that there was doubt as to whether I could pass my 'Common Entrance' exams to join Steve at Radley.

Grandfather was to pay the fees for Radley College, an independent boarding school for boys in Oxfordshire with a reputation for its rowing. The headmaster at prep school was telling me that I was to go to another school first for a year 'for coaching', so that was how I left Feltonfleet a year early.

It seemed that not only was I badly behaved, I was thick as well.

Chapter 4
Meanwhile at Home

When I had started at Feltonfleet Prep School as an eight-year-old in 1957, Mum was going to produce a baby, and as her time approached, towards Christmas, Dad took Steve and myself to Ireland to stay with one of his sisters. Our journey took us by train and ferry, and we set out into the stormy Irish sea in the dark.

Our cabin faced forward below the ship's bridge, we were battling straight into the wind and a huge swell. Our grandstand view of the floodlit bow was fabulous. We'd always loved small boats and had sailed, motored and rowed in big swells on the sea before but this was on a *grand scale*.

Every time the bows came down, a shudder came through the ship and we watched solid walls of water flying up and outwards on both sides of the bow before being caught by the wind and thrown in a tumble on the foredeck.

We knew that Mum had a battle to fight, what sort of battle I didn't know, Dad would have been worried but he made the best of this time with his boys who were having the excitement of their young lives. For us, this was majestic and the naval chaplain was at home on the sea. A tumult for all the family, four of us with the forces of nature, five really, the baby fought too.

We had a good visit with our cousins in Dublin, and on our return to the vicarage in Cobham, as if by magic, we had a sister—a dark-haired Deborah Jane. Two years later we gained a young brother, a fair-haired Christopher, so there were four children, two plus two with a nine-year gap in the middle.

The aircraft produced by the Vickers factory at Brooklands near Weybridge flew over us in Cobham every two minutes when they were being test flown. The two planes in production during the mid-1950s were the Viscount, a small airliner, and the Valiant, one of the three Cold War V-bomber jets.

The aircraft produced by Vickers were flown from the short runway within the Brooklands race circuit to Wisley airfield with its long runway for the test flying. Dad knew one of the test pilots and we visited the factory at the Brooklands race circuit where Mercedes-Benz World is now.

While we were walking on the concrete banking of the circuit, which was almost complete at that time, the pilot, Dickie Rymer, asked if we'd like to fly in a Viscount airliner.

[CRUMBS, YES]

Just the four of us in a Viscount. We took off and during the flight, we were each allowed to take the controls.

[GOLLY]

I flew a Viscount.

Dad and I were in the garden a few months later and a Valiant jet bomber had been circling for hours, doing some crazy dives and pulling up hard. Dad suddenly said, "Quick, on the motorbike." I didn't know what the rush was about, but Dad told me later that he'd realised that the pilot was probably trying to get his wheels to lock down and was circling to use up fuel.

Riding hard the country lanes
Dad guns the Triumph twin
we park not far from the runway's end
a *ROAR*, she's coming, *NO WHEELS*
the blast overhead, just feet away
slow-motion, right overhead
she's lining up beside the runway
to beach her belly on grass
slowing and holding off, so close
now gently, gently, down
grass and earth spews out each side
the dark brown furrow ploughed
she overtakes the convoy on the runway
fire trucks driving on tarmac
now it's quiet, eerily silent
she charges on but slowing

stable and safe, a mile away
her silhouette turning left
she softly sets her right wing down
all smooth and —-[OH MY].

My neighbour, Ian White, a year older than me and known as Prof, introduced himself after he'd seen me playing with gliders in our garden. He showed me his control-line plane powered by a noisy engine with a propeller which flew round in a circle on the end of a pair of long wires.

He controlled it from the ground, it could do aerobatics but he needed someone to launch it into the air for him. I was excited because this became my job, it could be dangerous with that vicious propeller going at about 15,000 rpm, and it was all new to me.

After a year or so, I started making my own balsa wood planes with an engine of my own and I flew mine in the vicarage garden on short control-lines. Prof's more adventurous planes, which he designed himself, we flew in a field on longer control-lines, and with my all-absorbing hobby, I was happy.

When I was 12 I made a control-line scale model of the WW2 twin-engine American P-38 Lightning with a fixed undercarriage. For take-offs I used a sheet of hardboard on the lawn with bricks under the end to launch it skywards, the sound of those two unsilenced and unsynchronised engines going in circles was *grand/shocking/epic* but oddly, no neighbours complained.

A real P-38 Lightning.

Family and two of my other model planes.

As children, we were very sheltered, we were not included in discussions about anything important of course, it seemed that adults had many secrets and I resented being kept in the dark.

- Money never spoken about
- Family illness seldom spoken about. 'White lies' were told.
- Sex avoided completely.
- Class differences not spoken about.
- Religion at school, we learnt that there were wars between people of different religions. The Roman Catholics had been our enemies historically, so to me, they were the baddies, but religious people are supposed to be good and to love their neighbours, so there was something wrong there.

Each of these topics seemed to be a 'no-no'. There were too many questions. *The world was weird and our comfortable life was unreal.*

The biggest secret of all was sex, it seemed that almost any contact with girls and women was base or wrong, and nakedness was an odd one, which seemed acceptable in some art forms but in real life—shock/horror. Pictures of women showing bare flesh in adverts were ignored by most adults, but real life displays of naked flesh were definitely not spoken about.

Televisions were a new invention and Mum's parents had a small black and white set, and when we watched, if there was flirting or (God forbid) a kiss, Granny would say, "Oh, aren't they *SILLY*, turn it off." Grandfather would comply and we knew it was a serious 'no-no'.

Our family of four went to see the pantomime *Dick Whittington* and Dick, who became the mayor of London, was played by a tall and beautiful young woman. Her never-ending legs were displayed in sheer black tights and she strode around the stage, playing the part of a man in a most provocative way.

The tradition of having the leading man's part played by a 'principal girl' in theatre wasn't explained, and afterwards, the four of us agreed that the show had been good but we drove back home in silence with the elephant in the car.

Attitudes passed on through books and TV often told of unhealthy relationships between men and women. There were images of frightened women being chased, or of being overcome and held down by men and it seemed that to *do anything to a woman* was wicked. Adults had brainwashed me completely.

Chapter 5
What Next?

Having left Feltonfleet a year early 'for coaching', I was due to go to a different school in September. During the summer holidays at home, I made an old-fashioned soap-box cart crudely put together and based on the one belonging to Dennis the Menace in the Beano comic.

Prof and I needed a hill to go down, we found a wide road on a hill and had some successful and quite speedy runs, but Prof had an epic roll-over crash (driver error but I got blamed).

We walked home with Prof holding his bloodied head and after that, I added a steering wheel, which operated the loop of rope attached to each end of the front axle as well as a crude brake on a back wheel. Recently, I asked my elder brother Steve what he'd thought of my various hobbies, he said he thought they were all a bit nuts.

I stayed on a farm for a week with a school friend and helped with the animals, which was novel for me and one day, my friend's older sister and I were alone, she pulled out the front of her jeans and said, "I'll show you mine if you show me yours."

I knew there was good in it somehow although girls didn't have one, so it didn't seem like a good deal, but I didn't know how to relate to girls at all and said no. At the time, I was 12 and didn't feel horny but she was 14 and maybe she did.

A friend of mine said years later, "Didn't you take her up on it—that was a pretty good offer."

Prof let me have a ride on his motorbike, a big heavy pre-war Matchless 350cc single, in his garden. I went in the hedge a bit. Big bike, small lawn.

350cc Matchless similar to the one I rode.

Little did I know how significant motorbikes would be in my life, or that years later, I'd buy a bike almost identical to that one but with the bigger 500cc engine and a sidecar bolted onto the left hand side.

September 1961 and Mum dropped me off at my new school, Hawkhurst Court near Billingshurst, and one of the boys told me that the school was a crammer. There were fewer pupils in each class and the lessons were more engaging, I think the move had given me a knock and my behaviour was better.

The following summer (1962), I was told that I was to stay on for an extra term until Christmas to give me a better chance in my exams. A pop song at the time which was on my brain all that summer was Brian Hyland's 'Sealed with a kiss' and I realised much later that this was in a minor key, which matched my mood.

Towards the end of term, I caught a stomach bug and was put into bed in the sick bay to recover, my stomach was bad but my head felt full of stress, negative thoughts and padding. It was unfamiliar and frightening. I certainly wasn't looking forward to the extra term leading up to Christmas, and when I was out of bed for the last two days of term, my head was in a very bad way. This was depression, not that I knew it at the time.

Grandfather had taught my brother Steve to scull from Thames RC at Putney before he started at Radley; now, it was my turn, and after a few outings in a heavy training boat, I went out in Grandfather's sleek, light racing boat. This was the boat which he had used to win the Wingfield Sculls over fifty years earlier and it was a challenge to stay upright in such an unstable craft.

The Thames RC boatman, Dick Phelps, who, I'd been told had won the Dogget's Coat and Badge for Professional Watermen, and was a Queen's Waterman also, was the man who helped me with the boat onto the water.

I could *not* understand why such a hero of rowing and sculling had been put in this position, he even called me sir, and I was just a kid, but this was in the days when working men had to help 'gentlemen' like us. There's a large and very grand painting of Dick Phelps wearing his red Dogget's coat and badge on the wall now in Thames RC. When Grandfather's boat was built in 1911 by Edwin Phelps, a relation of Dick Phelps, it had cost just eleven pounds.

My final term at Hawkhurst Court was mainly about preparing for my exams and there was hack-about football, but at home just before Christmas, there was relief all round when Dad announced that I'd passed my exams and could join Steve at Radley. Mum then said that the school policy was to let younger siblings in even if they weren't quite up to the mark.

[OH NO, SO MAYBE I DIDN'T PASS AT ALL.]

Chapter 6
What in God's Name Was Wrong?

At the end of 1962, the family were all pleased that I was to go to Radley, to start in the new year. During my teenage years I became frightened of falling moods, and of these 'demons' which plagued me. I became increasingly driven to be active to avoid them, although there was no understanding of it at the time. My mind was telling me something and instinct drove me to act. This lack of understanding has been a feature of my life, until recently.

When making a start at writing this book during 2017, quite soon, I ran into difficulties. I'd begun by relating how Grandfather had taught me to scull, then the rowing and sculling at Radley, but I found that I was glossing over events which were important.

Despite continued attempts to write, I simply didn't understand the young Tim Crooks or the motivations for much of my behaviour, and writing ground to a halt.

After some preliminary research, I was in touch with a Harley Street psychiatrist, I told him about my schooling, my sport and the diagnosis of bipolar disorder, which I'd had aged forty-four. I told him that I'd started writing my book and that I wanted to know whether I would have had learning difficulties at school. He suggested that I should have an 'Age-adjusted Educational Psychiatric Assessment'.

Five minutes before the appointment, I rang a doorbell and was welcomed by a psychiatrist who ushered me in, and when she had finished her assessment, she said that I would not have had any learning difficulties. She also informed me that I have a particularly high IQ. I was dumbstruck and was looking at the floor.

After a few moments, she said, "That's good, isn't it?"

I looked up. "Yes, but I don't understand. I've had failures, difficulties and confusions all my life. I mean, I'm the one who still gets confused and missed the point."

She went on to say that I would have been gifted as a child and that if intellect wasn't recognised, then boredom could lead to various serious difficulties. The full and detailed written report which followed, included:

"High potential children do have learning needs which, if not recognised and met, can lead to underachievement, mental health difficulties and poor behavioural compliance. If high potential children are not provided with engaging, challenging material, they become bored and look for other things to occupy their minds, or they lose motivation."

"It is quite possible that Timothy's unrecognised very superior set of intellectual abilities played into his troubles at school. Also, that rowing has been the activity through which he has actualised his abilities and experienced a term used in the psychology of learning as 'flow'."

"Flow is the optimal psychological state that people experience when engaged in an activity that is appropriately challenging to one's level of skill, resulting in immersion and focus on a task. Flow results in deep learning and high levels of personal and work satisfaction."

When I'd read the full report, I felt confident about its validity, not particularly because of the news about my IQ, but because the aspects of my character which may have been affected during my schooling were not just *applicable* to me, they were *central to my character.*

It was only after this assessment that I researched in some depth my illness of bipolar disorder, diagnosed twenty five years earlier, and my feelings and motivations as a young man became apparent.

Equipped as I had become, both with understanding of myself and knowledge of bipolar disorder, I was able to write my story from a very different viewpoint after a delay of only two or three months.

It should be borne in mind that most of my life was navigated without this information, and my story can be fully told because my motivations and drive are only at this late stage understood.

Chapter 7
Radley College
January 1963

With snow all around during the 'Big Freeze' in January of 1963, Mum drove Steve and I to Radley near Oxford, I was in the back of our estate car with two trunks, two tuck boxes, Steve's French horn and my new trombone, as yet untried. On arrival, I went to a common room for junior boys while Steve went to his shared study. Both of us were in Crowson's Social, one of the eight boarding houses at Radley known as Socials.

We all had to wear gowns including prefects who would sometimes come into our common room, 'Social Hall', and shout, "FAG," and there was instant chaos. The last boy to get to the prefect had to undertake the task, whether it was polishing army boots, putting up a notice, wiping up milk; it could be anything.

In the dormitory, I unpacked my trunk, there were many brand new items including something which Mum had told me I had to have for playing rugby, it was the jock strap. It didn't offer any useful protection but its main feature was a voluminous pocket in the front where my bits would go. I didn't know anything about puberty but wondered if I might undergo some magnificent changes.

All of the new boys to the school in that January term, about twenty of us, had been invited to a social gathering on day two of the term, another boy saw on the list that both he and I were named 'Timothy John'. He sought me out and reminded me recently that we'd clicked straight away, and from there on, everything was hilarious.

This was Bucknall who was in Fisher's Social and subsequently, when I wanted to visit him, I had to ask the duty prefect at the door and the person I hoped to meet was a friendly giant, the head of house and second school prefect, JK Mullard.

He rowed in the First Eight and would go on to row for Oxford. Later, he became the captain of Leander Club, the famous rowing club at Henley where he and I would row at 5 and 6 in a 'Grand Challenge Cup' crew at the Henley Royal Regatta.

The college bogs were frozen solid, the long trough latrine at ground level was full and frozen for weeks, sports were badly affected, and a notice on the sports noticeboard read: CLEARING SNOW. So that's what we did.

The Dry-Bobs couldn't play anything on the games pitches and the Wet-Bobs who hoped to go rowing, couldn't, but towards the end of term, we braved the trip on icy roads and started rowing in tub fours, clinker-built☐, short, wide and heavy with fixed seats.

They were well-built training craft, our Social Prefects and senior boys taught us the rudiments of crew rowing and we looked up to these boys who were knowledgeable and patient. Bonds of friendship across the year groups were made in this way within the Social, our common aim being to keep Crowson's at the top on the river.

*

I needed a haircut, the procedure was to obtain permission from the Social Tutor to cycle to Abingdon, three miles away, or to Oxford, four miles. I went to Abingdon and on arrival at the hairdresser's, had to sit and wait my turn.

There were three attractive young women cutting hair with their 1960s hair-dos, tight jumpers, short skirts and legs, but I'd only ever had my hair cut by a man before and while waiting, there was nothing to do but to watch the young women from behind. When they smiled in the mirror, I was embarrassed, viewing women was new to me but I knew it was wicked.

She ushers me over to sit in her chair
and feeling thoroughly inadequate
I sit, and looking up I see
she's facing me in the mirror
we're eye to eye. She's beautiful
"What do you want?" She's asking
my chest's so tight, I can hardly speak
"A trim and straight across the back"

I'm trying to be normal, she's relaxed and smiling
it's routine work for her
my heart's pounding as she works around me
she's taken my breath away
her body's so good and her hair spills down
her soft breasts brush my shoulders
she's just working, I'm thrilled but guilty
does she have any IDEA
is it OK to focus on women
really LOOK at them, I mean
the conflict totally numbs my brain
(blows my mind, in fact)
there wasn't much in it before
and now, it's gone away

My brother Steve and I were brought up together but we turned out quite differently in that Steve was comfortable in the company of girls whereas I was mixed up and inhibited. After puberty, the force of my feelings put girls on a pedestal fifty feet high, which wasn't helpful, and Victorian attitudes during our upbringing had affected me deeply.

Every week I had two music lessons, one on piano and another on trombone. Singing in the chapel choir was stimulating and the acoustics in chapel were great, and whether singing psalms, plainsong, anthems or hymns, it was superb.

I have vivid memories of sprinting to the Music School to play music regularly after lessons. They were dashes which made me feel good, but better than that, they injected adrenaline, endorphins, spirit and fun into my days, so they were the very best.

Towards the end of my first term I sang in the Social Choir in the music festival, Steve was singing a lower part but he also played the French horn in the Social Orchestra. It was a privilege to be involved and to see how everyone rose to their individual challenges in the social choirs and orchestras.

We knew that Mum and Dad had moved to a different parish and at the end of term, Mum drove us to Haslemere, a little further south in Surrey and we were excited to survey our new home. Steve was sixteen and was given a second-hand motorbike by parents and grandparents for his birthday, so he was off. Free on the roads.

The control-line model plane which I had at the time, with its noisy engine, had no wheels for taking off, I had no one to launch it into the air for me by hand and Steve never wanted to join in with my things. I had to be creative to get it into the air if I was to fly it on my own. The plane flew round me in circles on its two control wires, and normally I had to turn on the spot facing the plane and could control it up and down, as it went round, holding a handle with the 'up' and 'down' wires fixed to it. My plan was to design a device to go in the centre of the circle which the plane would fly round, I would be outside the flying circle and would launch the plane myself with one hand while controlling it with the other using a joystick.

I ended up with a simple device swivelling round on the top of a stubby Meccano tower in the middle of the circle. The plane pulled on its control lines as it flew and it was to pull my device round continuously as it went. My challenge was to have a connection between the device and the joystick on the outside of the circle. The answer was a single wire, down through the central swivel bolt of the device, and because it was in the very centre it didn't get tangled by the circling plane. This wire would have been twisted, but I used a fishing swivel half way down to the ground to allow it to turn. The wire went round a pulley and along in the grass to a simple Meccano gubbins anchored in the ground outside the circle with a joystick mounted on it. This allowed me to control the plane up and down as it circled, and it worked well with the plane stationary.

The hardest part had been using Dad's hand-drill (wheel-brace) to drill a hole vertically down through the centre of the central steel pivot bolt. I'd started drilling from each end and had met in the middle without knowing whether it was possible to drill steel without some sort of machine!

When all was ready I started the engine and, kneeling on the ground, launched the plane into the air with one hand while holding the joystick and controlling it with the other. It flew round, passing close by me at about 30mph about once every three seconds. That very loud, repeated rising and falling noise right by the house must have distracted Dad from writing his Sunday sermon, as well as annoying the neighbours, but Dad said it was ingenious, which it was!

My first outing on the river during the summer term of 1963 was to be in a sculling boat and I asked if I could go in a 'best boat' because Grandfather had already taught me to scull at Putney. *NO,* you'll go in a *FENNY* like everyone else, so there I was in a short, open, clinker-built* boat with a fixed seat but I shot off up the river leaving all the others behind.

Later in the term when I was in a tub four, my brother Steve was delegated to coach us up to the Junior Social Fours competition, I sat in the stroke* seat of Crowson's fourth tub four and it's recorded in the *Social Chronicle* in Steve's own handwriting that we were unskilled, some crew members were reluctant to row at higher rates, but that we won.

During the school summer holidays, I bought a motorbike from my old friend Prof for £10, a 125cc BSA Bantam with a rigid rear end and knobbly tyres, and all the heavy stuff stripped off it. Steve was 16 and had his bike on the road but I was 14 and had a track bike in the garden, which was superb as our long garden went down a steep bank at the end into a small wooded area.

I pottered around at the end and raced up and down the bank but I needed a proper circuit where I could do laps at speed to emulate the motocross riders. Dad's long handled 'Slasher' was used to clear a track through the bracken and brambles, and after a bit of practice, I was happy with fourteen seconds per lap on the BSA.

*see Glossary

Me and my BSA track bike.

I'd hoped to come out with the front wheel pawing the air.

I needed a set of spanners (£3) and wanted a crash helmet (£14) but as I had little money, I did jobs for Dad. Both he and Mum were surprised and amused at how quickly I dug the potato patch and did other jobs and very soon, I got my spanners and 'crash hat'.

I was obsessively busy messing with model planes and my motorbike and bought the *Motorcycle News* every week. My motor biking hero was Jeff Smith, one of the BSA motocross works riders, who would win the World 500cc World Motocross title in 1964 and again in 1965 on a BSA 440cc Victor.

September 1963 was the start of the academic year, I was to start learning to play the organ, it was time for me to join the Combined Cadet Forces (CCF) and I joined the RAF section. The sport for that term was rugby, which didn't please me.

During biology lessons, we learnt about reproduction in mammals but there was no mention of humans, so it was all irrelevant to my life, so when my hormones of puberty arrived, what was this overriding FORCE? Ah, it was a 'no-no' and not spoken about, so was there anger mixed in with my confusion? Oh yes, resentment about the secrets of this overriding change.

I became a rogue and a rebel, couldn't concentrate in class for many reasons, finding places for surprises and humour where I shouldn't, but at least I had plenty of fun and jokes to save my mood.

My poor academic results pushed my self-esteem ever lower and when lessons finished, my most common escape was my sprint to play music. Trombone first, till my lips were blown, then piano, back on trombone and so on. I'd escape to anywhere, in fact, to the school workshops, the bike sheds. I was obsessively active and most often ran between endeavours. In modern times this kind of activity might lead to a diagnosis of ADHD but, although the symptoms were first documented in 1798, ADHD wasn't widely recognised until the turn of this century.

The first thing I did on arriving home for the Christmas holidays was to go to the tiny brick built store room beside the back door where my BSA was stored, I turned the petrol on under the fuel tank, tickled the button on the carburettor to get the fuel through. A kick and a ROAR, a 125cc Bantam can't roar, but in that enclosed space, it did.

One day, I was on my haunches, playing with the tick-over adjustment on the carburettor, communing closely with my motorcycle, revving it up, revelling in the noise and vibrations in the enclosed space. Suddenly, I felt faint, stood up and was lucky to fall out through the unlatched door, collapsing onto the hard ground outside. I'd discovered carbon monoxide.

During March in 1964, I was invited to join the CCF band to play the trombone and through the summer term, we played on the march once per week. It was particularly good as there were no French horns in the band, no brother Steve, so I could misbehave.

The trombone glissandos in the 'Liberty Bell' were my favourite, we had superb harmonies and counter-melodies in the tunes and it was rousing and fun. The Drum Major led with the drum section next, followed by us trombones in the front row and all the other wind instruments behind. We were much admired, even though one day, I led all the wind instruments off into the bike sheds.

Chapter 8
Finding My Sport

School sports had often been disappointing. I was highly motivated to perform and as a younger boy, I'd found that my skills at football were limited, hockey was tricky as well as dangerous, rugby had the most promise for me but those games were all frustrating.

I played rugby as a forward in the scrum and when I got the ball, could run with it, but seldom managed to do anything of much use. Trying harder, and harder than that, could lead to unfortunate moments where I'd gone for the player rather than the ball and I was at times ashamed of myself. During the spring and summer terms, I loved the rowing and sculling.

Near the end of the summer term, a year before my O-level exams, we had the internal school exams, which hadn't gone well, but a few days later, I was sitting in the stroke seat of the Crowson's first tub four, the heavy clinker-built training machine. We'd progressed to sliding seats* earlier in the year and were about to race the final of the Junior Fours against the favourites, Goldsmith's.

A prefect on the bank shouts
"Are you ready? – Go."
and after ten strokes, they're ahead
they're leading before third gate
over half a length in front
the bend, it's in their favour
then nearly a length, we have to push
our coxswain,* Biggs: *"READY – GO"*
Biggs was short for bigamy
I go, and drive off hard

---

*see Glossary

it's a spirited burst, we've shifted a gear
my guys are with me, steaming
we're strong, I love it, we're coming back
powerful, sprinting, faster
we *are* coming back, together, yes
still fighting, gaining, catching
but it's over, we're down, we've lost the race
tired out, worn out and down
but the staggered finish gives it to us
and we've won, EPIC job

Winners of Junior Fours, well done, CROWSON'S, and later, well done, Crooks. How cool was that, and within days, many of us competed in the fixed seat fennies for the Junior Single Sculls and I won that too.

A clinker tub four is constructed like this. (Shown is a skiff with seats, etc. missing)

I'd found an outlet for my energy on the river where I could stand tall.

Sculling and rowing became my thing, and if there was frustration on the river, it was channelled into going faster. When I really wanted to row harder, on every stroke I would imagine my oar anchored behind my French teacher's head in the water, then drive legs, back and arms, Full power, more grip for my oar, and more speed for the boat. All very satisfactory. It's a secret. No one knew and no one was hurt.

Chapter 9
The Rugby Term

In September 1964, the sport was rugby but we weren't taught the game properly, or the skills we needed, and the standard of play was poor. I was all fired up when moving boats on the river but 'Wet-Bobs had to play rugby during the autumn term along with the Dry-Bobs' When playing sport, I wanted to be actually playing the ball, but for most of the time, I was running, trying to catch up, but watching others do the business. Totally frustrating.

My attempts at tackling others with the approved technique round the hips and legs were unsuccessful as well as being painful, so I tackled people by grabbing arms and shoulders. In wrestling people to the ground, I was often aggressive and then ashamed.

[SOMETHING'S WRONG, BUT WHAT? WHY AM I LIKE THIS?]

My frustrations and confused feelings were coming out as anger and I didn't like myself.

At about that time the school chaplain, alias 'Gibber', asked me if I would be an 'altar boy' at some of the communion services. This gave a connection between vicarage life at home and school life, I decided to take it up, had instruction from the chaplain and on some Sundays, performed this duty.

I didn't sleep in Long Dormitory any more, but slept in a small dormitory at the top of Croome's Tower. One night early in the term, an event:

I gotta pee *NOW,* not in a minute
one floor down, it's two flights
dressing gown on (compulsory)
I run down the steps in panic

six steps first, then nine, I think
I launch off hard after seven
and fall, slow-motion, crumple and piss
confusion, what's gone wrong
grab Willy through clothing, and jumping up
eleven, of course, stupid
holding the pressure, I run to the loo
what are my options now
the only way is let go and be quick
I can do this, or maybe not, it's not going very well at all.

I'd been playing the organ for a year and my efforts on the magnificent instrument in the school chapel were at times grand but I wasn't committed to it. I found that if I used the 'Tromba' pedal stop and the 2 bottom pedal notes, a semi-tone apart, the two frequencies produced a terrific beat three or four times per second as the slower frequency was overtaken by the other.

In the enclosed space of the chapel, it sounded as though the unsynchronised engines of a tethered twin-engine plane were trying to pull the pews out of the choir stalls. There was an unfortunate window by the organ loft, fighting to get out of its frame, what a racket, real power, a loud resonant shake, right through everything, and my chest. Epic.

I often defied the establishment, which was rebellion, and yes, I got my kicks, which I needed often, and there were many times when other boys looked up to me and my rebellions. All of that boosted my morale, but of course, much of the behaviour was bad, silly and stupid, which I knew really, but I did it with no understanding of what was driving me.

We studied Shakespeare in English lessons and on a day when my mood was low, we were taken to the theatre at Stratford-upon-Avon to see Shakespeare's *Much Ado about Nothing*. I knew that this day out was a privilege but I hated the whole trip, and I simply couldn't raise my interest. These moods were becoming a serious problem.

While playing rugby one day, I tackled a good friend of mine by grabbing him round the shoulders and throwing him down while running fast. At the time, it was my best attempt to play the game and it wasn't done in anger, but we fell awkwardly and when we hit the ground, his head was under my backside. He wasn't badly hurt, I was very sorry but was so shocked and ashamed, I couldn't speak.

Aggression is an unattractive trait and I had no desire to harm anyone but I was driven in almost everything. My fear of depression prompted action which *could be almost anything,* and again, *never mind the consequences*. I hated myself.

Anger is an emotion which can come out when you're upset and vulnerable, and for me, it was often when I was mentally exhausted, having been fighting the mental battle to avoid depression for hours or days. Anger is never a good thing but it puts you in charge.

That can be helpful when you're feeling tired and vulnerable, but if you're angry all the time, the upset is never addressed, so it continues. People around me must have been frightened, particularly when I 'lost it'. I regret it and am sorry for all of it.

I was shocked when my study-mate made arrangements to move into a different study because he was frightened of me, but I'd never been angry towards him. My anger, if it did come, could be caused by the smallest 'last straw' and it was always short-lived as well as much regretted, but harm was done quickly.

We had a lot of laughs too, good times and fun in the Social and around school but there were occasions for me, typically when on a bit of a high and telling an amusing story to friends that my mood collapsed suddenly in the middle. That was difficult as I had to act high to get through the story while feeling awful, then I'd make an excuse and go, running somewhere to try to recover my mood.

[OH GOD NO, WHAT'S HAPPENING? NOT AGAIN.]

When I'd started at Radley, I'd teamed up with Bucknall, that other 'Timothy John', but we didn't see much of each other because he was in Fisher's Social and we weren't timetabled together for any regular school activity, but when we did get together, life was an adventure and we rebelled.

We're better off here, away from the school
they won't wear us down, we're fine
no way, we're busy having a smoke

roll-ups are tricky but great
we're confirming our thoughts about restraints on our liberty
Sod 'em, no, fuck 'em, yeah

FUUUKK—'EM, FUUUUKKK—'EM

Ha-ha, why not?
It's hilarious.

    One Sunday in Covered Passage, I was picked on by two senior boys who made me a target of ridicule. I was feeling depressed already and they ripped my expensive Sunday suit which Grandfather had bought for me. I was upset, so they got their result, the bastards.
    I asked myself at times whether other people have the moods and feelings I suffered from, but as this sort of thing was never spoken about, I assumed that that difficulties were normal and that everyone coped in their own way.
    Organ lessons had become a trial as I wasn't practising enough. One day, I was worried when my teacher made an exaggerated expectation of a great performance. When I messed up my piece of music, my eyes welled up and he said, "Oh God, don't CRY." That led to me quitting the organ a few days later, feeling thoroughly done in.
    The procedures for the communion service were straightforward but my mental faculties were closing down and the simple duties as 'altar boy' had become a burden. I quit that too and felt that I'd failed the family, my world seemed to be shrinking around me. I found it difficult to talk to anyone and was feeling increasingly isolated.
    During that December, I felt mentally drained, was sleeping badly and had to push myself hard to keep going through each day. It was frightening and then it was the end of term, two years at Radley already with so much good in it but I was worn down, not well, and very relieved to be going home for Christmas.

Chapter 10
The Die Was Cast

It's clear to me now, all these years later, that a change took place that winter when I was fifteen years old. I had always assumed that I'd simply become more rebellious at about that time, but while writing this book, I've recognised that the depression leading up to Christmas in 1964 had placed fear of low mood more firmly into my subconscious.

From January 1965, that fear caused my mind to be more focused on maintaining my mood (it was instinct, I didn't even know about moods at the time), and the result was that I did even less of what depressed me, i.e. academic work. At the same time, I involved myself in more extra-curricular activities, which included misbehaviour. It was all a subconscious strategy to keep buoyant but I didn't recognise any of it, I was just doing my best to get by.

I was faced with two options in connection with behaviour:

1) Good behaviour, which led inevitably to depression.
2) Poor behaviour, which helped me to be on form.

The latter was the preferable option, *and, as usual, never mind the consequences.* I was managing my moods, and it would be seven years before I would visit a doctor to discuss my 'troubles', aged twenty-two, and a further twenty-two years until my diagnosis of bipolar disorder at the age forty-four.

My subconscious was often taking control of my actions, but I've always been aware of my poor behaviour and am grateful to those around me who have been so tolerant and understanding.

There was 'Boxing Day Scramble' (Motocross), advertised in *MotorCycle News* to be held at Pirbright between Woking and Farnborough. Dad drove our family of six to watch, it was sunny and chill with the distinctive racket of motorbikes racing and the evocative smell of 'Castrol R' vegetable oil in the air.

The riders set off with a roar in a cloud of mud and dirt at the start of each race, power-slides round the bends, jumps and wheelies, all action and thrills, this was definitely going to be my thing.

During January 1965, I was invited to join the school orchestra to play the second trombone, and I was proud to join the brass section behind Steve who was playing his French horn. To be able to contribute the third, the fifth or anything to a chord, with the progression of harmonies was so satisfying, and moving through the seventh was pleasure indeed.

To be exposed to all of that was a privilege and an education in itself, and when listening to certain orchestral music, even now, I sometimes find myself humming the trombone part. Oh, well.

Steve was a member of the school Brass Ensemble, which performed in school concerts and sometimes at other venues, and I was invited to join. There were 2 trumpets, 2 French horns and 2 trombones, all of us were quite exposed in that small group and it was an enjoyable challenge.

Music is one of the things that stimulates dopamine release, causes emotional arousal and the 'feel-good' effect, which spills over into other things, it was good for me and for all of us.

Brother Steve was getting on well in his studies and had earned his place in the stroke seat of the First Eight for the 1965 season, and I rowed at number four in the Colts First Eight, which was an important step up.

There was so much to do at school and I threw myself into activities including learning to operate the big old-fashioned cast-iron printing machine. It was powered by a foot treadle, one sheet of paper at a time had to be fed into it by hand, and in order to avoid hands trapped in the mechanism, a high level of concentration was needed, which helped make it quite therapeutic. The school woodwork shop was another creative destination of mine.

I fitted knobbly tyres on my old pedal bike and went out riding on rough ground with friends, I learnt to drive the CCF car and practised opposite-lock slides on the grass below the running track where I wouldn't be seen. Increasingly, I involved myself in schemes and japes around school, which were mostly harmless; it all seemed very worthwhile at the time, and most often, it was the Bucknall and Crooks team, TJB & TJC.

Bucknall always reckoned we hit it off because we both had the same defiant outlook towards the independent school regime and discipline, and both possessed a great sense of fun, and he said, "Tim always saw the funny side of any situation, and when there wasn't one, he invented it!"

During summer '65, Steve was to take his A-level exams and was in the First Eight, I would take my O-levels, and while rowing in our Colts Eight, I found out about pain in racing. The fear you feel before racing is because of the pain which you know will come if it's a close race.

It's the lactic acid formed in the muscles, and there's always the chance of making a mistake and letting the crew down. You can't admit to any of that, you have to be a man and keep your fears to yourself, you can't ever give up, people look up to you and admire you.

Before a race, you're pumped up and nervous but you're committed and you have to face it. We had humility in the knowledge that we would suffer together, each individual's effort helping to ease our collective pain, and the better a crew performs in training, the higher the confidence, the morale and the race performances.

Towards the end of term, I rowed in the Crowson's Social Eight in the four seat with Anthony Robinson at six and Steve at stroke, which was superb as they'd been in those positions in the school First Eight. They set a powerful and steady rhythm and it was easy to follow their length and stride. That was rowing as never before, and Steve lifted his blade out of the water boldly at the end of each stroke. I've tried to do that ever since.

We had a battle in the final and narrowly beat Goldsmith's for the Social Eights title with Steve driving us along from the stroke seat, what a buzz and a privilege that was.

My O-level exams went badly; at times, I sat, unable to answer anything, with my mind blank and black with depression. My Latin, History and Additional Maths results were bad but my English Literature was terrible.

I'd been playing the euphonium, a half-sized tuba, just for fun during my spare time in the Music School and when the band master heard me playing it, the question came, "Would you play the tuba in the Military Band starting in September?"

Yes, I would. The bass line had been played previously by another boy on a trombone, but the B-flat tuba sounds an octave lower and is much more resonant.

I practiced straight away and the school's instrument was a beautiful double B-flat tuba, huge, brass and shiny and the sound was *grand*.

[YES, THIS IS THE BUSINESS!]

Euphonium, trombone and cornet. A B-flat tuba is twice as big as the Euphonium.

My friend, Biggs, said to me one day, "Come with me, I've got something to show you."

I followed him to Clock Tower and he took me straight into the OUT OF BOUNDS doors and up the stairs. He showed me the clock mechanism, which was old-fashioned with a line of three big electric motors, one of which was running and driving gears.

Very soon a second motor jerked into life and a mechanism pulled wire cables, which rang bells up in the tower, DING-DONG! It was crude but very good! After four ding-dongs, the third motor started and made the hour bell chime, which was fantastic.

The mechanisms and electrical switching was vulnerable, partly covered by clear Perspex and later, I asked Biggs if he had plans to make any adjustments to the clock and he smiled. "No, you're welcome."

Oh What Bliss
what Transport of Delight,
I can definitely mess that up,
Wahey.

I went back up Clock Tower and studied the mechanism and there were options for cunning sabotage but the easiest jape was to physically cross the quarter hour chime cables, which I did. A minute or two later, I was gone and then, *DONG-DING. Rebellion*, broadcast widely every 15 minutes, 24/7, a big result for a small effort.

The clock chimes were still ringing 'Dong-Ding' when Mum picked us up at the end of term two days later and Steve, looking suspicious, asked if I had done it.

"Nothing to do with me."

Each of these japes and schemes gave me a boost, they were a punch in the face for my demons. I was devious and not a good person at times, but this was survival. I was involved in a personal battle without understanding any of the parameters.

Back home for the summer holidays, Steve had left Radley and would study at St Thomas' Hospital as a medical student. I was 16, Steve was given a second-hand Morris 1000 estate car and his motorbike was passed on to me. It was 125cc BSA Bantam, similar to my old track bike but newer and had the headlight and big mudguards, etc.

I was now free to ride on the roads and I raced around with my old friend, Guy Tod, from Cobham. His bike had a bigger engine than mine but I could catch up round the bends with my footrests scraping the ground. I sawed an inch off each but they still scraped.

125cc BSA Bantam.

Back to school in September 1965 it was my first term without Steve and it started with a surprise. Clock Tower was still ringing *DONG-DING*. Everyone living at Radley College had been subjected to that all summer, as well as Radley village, and anyone could have fixed it. The cables were crossed over in plain sight and after a couple of days, it was just too much, I went and put it right.

Playing the bass line on the tuba in the Military Band was superb, most of my notes were a simple OOM-PAH bass but there were plenty of interesting runs and a few counter-melodies. My contribution strengthened the marching rhythm, but in music, the bass line is the foundation for the harmonies and without a strong bass, harmonies are unsupported and adrift.

I gave it some stick and it was thoroughly satisfying to be giving the instruments playing the harmonies a solid base to stand on. We were told how much better the band sounded.

The autumn term marked the beginning of my two year A-level courses, I'd chosen the sciences and was in the same chemistry group as my friend, Bucknall. It was the first time we were to see each other regularly, we sat together at the front bench and were to enjoy chemistry.

Every time our teacher got fed up with us, he'd tell Bucknall to get to other end of the bench, but a couple of lessons later, Bucknall was always back.

This was another rugby term and the stupid ball bounced all over the place. Outwardly, I was a happy chappy, running here and there and doing stuff around school, but so often, I was covering up my moods and mental turmoil, my academic work certainly wasn't going well.

Obsessive commitment to rebellion and many activities were my lifeline, I had fun, but too often, I was being chased by demons, which spoiled things. And then, we went home for Christmas. Three years at Radley.

Chapter 11
The First Eight

At the beginning of term in January 1966, I was surprised to be invited to join the 'Trial Eights' group from which the first and second eights would be selected, and when Ronnie Howard coached us, I understood why Steve had spoken so highly of him. The standard of rowing was a step up, I had the 'rowing bug' already but these were superb days on the river. A few weeks later, I found that I was to sit at six in the First Eight, which was an even bigger surprise and a significant boost for me.

Radley College First Eight 1966. Very formal.
Left to Right: Galbraith, Padfield, Johnson, Crooks, Allott, Grove, Robinson, Dickinson, Hawksworth.

Radley crew on the far side.

My recurring dreams changed around that time; there were no longer any monsters, I could fly up at will to a height of twenty or thirty feet and it was always at school over the games pitches where there were others on the ground below. I alone could fly.

Rowing in the First Eight was thoroughly enjoyable and I was, in fact, establishing myself as a six man, which is where I've been most often in eights since. We had regular evening outings while most of the boys at school were working on their prep in their Socials and those quiet evenings on the river with the setting sun were just the best.

We won an eights event at the Walton Regatta and Ronnie rewarded us by taking us to supper at Leander Club at Henley as his guests. Some of us hadn't noticed that on that day at Walton, the Senior Eights event had been won by the exceptional Emanuel School crew who, as schoolboys, had beaten all of the grown men in the club eights.

Bucknall and I saw each other regularly during chemistry. I fiddled with a Bunsen burner one day and used the rubber tubing to connect the gas tap to the water tap. After both were turned on for a few seconds, water came out of the gas tap.

[WOW, THERE'S POTENTIAL THERE!]

The teaching staff and I had excellent relationships considering all things, I was always on time, cheerful, positive and polite, but they learnt that when things happened in class, I was usually at the bottom of it.

Radley College gave so many opportunities, I was thoroughly involved in different aspects of music but my musical skills never reached their full potential. I simply didn't have the aptitude or patience to practice properly. Steve had his French horn, which I didn't play, but also a trumpet, which I borrowed at times, so playing four brass instruments as well as the piano gave me broad musical experience.

I became a competent and confident player but didn't commit to the scales, arpeggios and sight reading studies. I practised the tunes needed for my lessons and ensembles and found written music for many familiar tunes, which I played just for the fun of it.

My gas and water discovery in the science labs was just too tempting and one evening, Bucknall and I climbed into our ground floor chemistry lab. Once inside, it only took a few moments to connect a rubber pipe between the gas and water taps and turn them both on.

I came back early the next morning to take the pipe off and found the room full of gas, and water on the benches and floor. Holding my breath, I took the rubber pipe off and got out fast.

When we approached the labs for our chemistry lesson, there were Midland Gas vans parked around and workers carrying pipes and pumps. We learnt that we'd cut off the gas not only to the school but also to Radley village, and later that morning it came out that Bucknall was under the threat of expulsion if he got involved in any more pranks.

On the next day, we heard that the police were coming, so I went and knocked on Warden Milligan's door. He let me in and I told him that I had 'done the gas', he paused, said that he'd talk to my housemaster about it, but I never heard another thing.

We, the children at home in the vicarage, were to learn years later just how many pranks our dad had been involved in at school and university. Bucknall told others later that I went to the headmaster on my own, without his knowledge, and owned up.

"Crooks was such a successful oarsman, six man in the First Eight at the time, he could not possibly have been expelled! He wasn't, and he saved my bacon. A debt of gratitude I shall hold forever."

I saw an advert for a single cylinder 500 cc AJS motorbike with a box sidecar to carry another motorbike. The AJS was for sale in Abingdon and was exactly what I needed to transport a track bike to motocross events.

The price of the AJS was £23, I went to look at it and was surprised to find that it was almost identical to the big old British bike I'd ridden in Prof's garden five years earlier in Cobham. I tried it down a farm track and it was a seriously *awful pig* to steer, needing great strength to keep it on the track. I had to have it though, left a deposit and would collect it at the end of term.

An AJS 500 identical to the one I bought, but without sidecar.

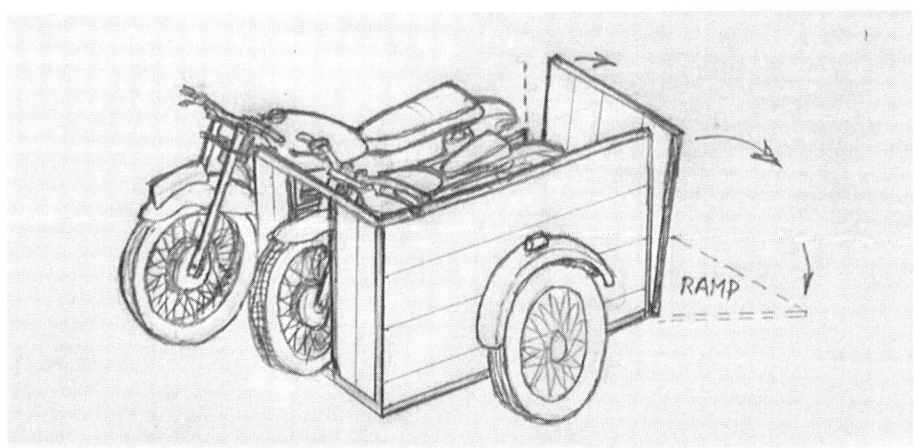

A sketch of the AJS 500 with a motocross bike in the box sidecar.

At the Henley Regatta, although we won some races, we were soundly beaten by the exceptional Emanuel School crew who went on to win the Princess Elizabeth Cup.

Afterwards, Ronnie asked me to be Captain of Boats for the following season and he trained us in small boats for the National Youth Championships. The coxless four I was in won our event and our coxed pair, Allott and Robinson, won also.

Anthony Robinson, who had enjoyed rowing in the First Eight with my brother Steve during the previous year, said of me, "My overriding memory of Tim is of a happy teenager with an impish sense of fun. He arrived at Radley two terms after me, and later, as a prefect, I had to be responsible for him, which was at times a challenge."

"He found ingenious ways with his co-conspirator, Tim Bucknall, to pull off a variety of pranks; there was nothing malicious in their actions, just youthful mischief."

Chapter 12
Motorbike Madness

At the end of the summer term in 1966, the AJS sidecar machine took me home from Abingdon to Haslemere. It had no tax, MOT or insurance but that didn't seem important at the time, and as soon as the outfit got moving, the steering was unstable and the handlebars wobbled forcibly from side to side.

When accelerating, the massive weight of the sidecar box dragged the outfit hard to the left, but when braking, the sidecar's momentum pushed to the right towards oncoming traffic and it wobbled left and right fairly uncontrollably all the time. The whole thing was dangerous. It was a trial of strength, the outfit and I were all over the road for the first few miles but the faster I went the straighter our track, as long as I didn't touch the brakes. I made it home with a serious pain in my back.

I joined the Haslemere Motor Cycle club and their club nights on Fridays were informal, just a drinking session at The Mill, Shottermill. They called me 'Vic' (vicar), and drinking with the local men seemed to me like real life.

I'd been brought up rather posh in vicarages and independent schools and had found much of the Radley stuff rather false and stressful. The motorbike men were good guys, they said it how it was, didn't beat about the bush, and I liked it, especially when we were all a bit pissed.

One of the guys who rode in motocross events said, "I like it when it's muddy and someone falls off in front of you, you can ride over them and get some grip." We all drove our bikes home after a few pints but luckily, no one was hurt, I had an advantage as my bike had the sidecar and couldn't fall over.

Granny had given each of us four children premium bonds worth £250. I did some research, spoke to my Dad and ordered a brand new motorbike in kit form.

It was a Mark 1 Sprite with a 250 cc Villiers engine and cost £154, which meant that I'd spent a big chunk of my premium bond money. Granny wasn't pleased.

The bike parts were delivered in a wooden crate and I set about assembling it, when I'd nearly finished, I phoned Bucknall and we agreed to finish the bike off at his farm in Devon. Once the AJS sidecar was loaded with the Sprite and everything else, the outfit was very heavily loaded and by any normal standards, was unroadworthy (impossible to steer). I said a goodbye to my rather incredulous folks and they knew I was on an adventure.

A handful of throttle
and a massive force on the handlebars.
Up the short slope to the road.
Hell that was hard.
Hard on the engine.
Hard on the clutch.
Hard on my arms.
Hard on my back.
Only 140 miles to go, no problem. It's a proper challenge!
This is *real living*.
I'm *invincible*. I'm in the *First Eight*. And I'm *Captain of Bluddy Boats!*

The loaded outfit was so heavy, it had a will of its own and I had to work very hard to keep it under control. After a while, the pain in my back was terrible and I had a break for a few minutes. When I got going I had to push myself beyond normal bounds of endurance, but I made it.

Bucknall and I unloaded everything, he jumped on the back and we went to the Ashen Faggot pub in Northleigh. After a few pints, the pain in my back was forgotten and all was well.

After a few days, we finished the Sprite, she was ready to go, we tested her in the fields and the engine went well but she steered badly. Oddly, the front end had the same steering instability as the AJS, waving from side to side, but only on bumpy ground. It turned out later that there was a fault in the design of the frame, the steering head was too steep.

PHOTO 12/1. A motocross bike similar to the Sprite.

I left the Sprite in Devon and went on to Cornwall to meet up with the family, it should have been a good time with parents and the young ones, swimming, boating, and relaxing in the sun, but my demons ruined it for me.

Nearly every holiday was ruined this way because during holidays, the pressure was off, I was supposed to be happy relaxing, but the lack of a challenge allowed my demons in.

There was a family who lived in Reigate in Surrey in our hotel with a teenaged daughter and on the way back from the beach one day, I kissed her. It was in a way a big deal but it did nothing to help my brain.

Back on the farm, Bucknall and I took the box off the sidecar chassis to improve the bike's performance, it was still a sidecar outfit but with no weight on the sidecar at all. The result was superb, she steered well with no wobbles or other steering troubles at all.

Left-hand bends were dangerous though with no weight on the sidecar, so we both climbed half off the bike onto the sidecar chassis for left-handers. That had to be done for fast cornering, but sometimes we rode along straight with the sidecar wheel in the air. That had to be done too.

Bucknall wrote, "We spent a lot of time together during holidays, I stayed with his family in Haslemere, and Tim with mine on our Devon farm. We had so much fun together, I could write a whole book of our exploits! He would talk to anyone and was everyone's friend."

When it was time for me to go back to Haslemere, we bolted the box back on, loaded everything in and I only just managed to get up his steep drive. The burden for that engine was brutal as there was no level ground to get up any speed. Full throttle and blaring engine, but then hardly any revs. I could almost feel the crankshaft bending.

Back in Haslemere, I had motorbikes, great Friday club nights, Mum cooked and was happy to wash my muddy clothes, Dad was interested in all things motorbikes, so it was a good time. Mum met a lady at church whose son also had a motorbike, I was introduced to Ian Greig, who had a 500cc TriBSA motocross bike, it was a BSA bike with a Triumph engine.

He let me ride it around his garden and when he came to the vicarage, the Sprite was too noisy, so we took turns on the replacement for my Bantam, an old 200cc track bike which I'd had for a while. He helped me fix all my bikes, we had like-minds, loved the ridiculous and saw humour in everything.

I'd been doing my own thing all year, which had helped me avoid any serious depressions but I was driving myself, taking risks, promoting the highs, living on the edge, simply doing what I could to get by.

If I felt impending doom, I could be unpredictable, outrageous, funny, mad, all of those things and more were in my 'toolkit' to raise my mood but the details of what was really happening in my mind were a mystery. I didn't know anything was wrong, I was just getting on with it all.

Chapter 13
Last Year at Radley

My parents didn't query it but in September 1966, I rode the AJS sidecar outfit to Radley. Motorbikes weren't allowed at school, so I had to find a place to keep it. I knocked on front doors near school and struck gold almost straight away. An old chap was interested in my AJS outfit, lived on his own and didn't use his living room where there was no carpet. There were French windows onto the front garden, it was ideal, he gave me a key and said that I was welcome to drive straight in anytime, saying that I didn't need to knock.

"Just come and go as you please."

Big smiles and thank yous. I rode my bike in, bumping over the threshold, it was just the job, and from there, I walked down Chestnut Avenue, the wide grassy avenue, to school.

My new housemaster, Mr Taylor, wanted to see me, he explained that because of my poor behaviour, I was not to be appointed as a prefect; however, as I was to be Captain of Boats, he had to make me a prefect after all. This seemed very fair.

I got on with all of my usual activities and the AJS took me out three or four times per week, I wore my old open-fronted crash helmet and hid my face with my First Eight scarf. I reckoned no one would ever think a member of the Radley First Eight would be riding that blatty, bangy old box sidecar machine.

[YEAAH, BOLLOCKS, ETC.]

Ronnie Howard had arranged for a few members of the boat club to go sculling instead of playing rugby during the autumn term, I was relieved to be in the sculling group and we were entered into two 'Head of the River' (HOR)* sculling events, which have many boats competing and are timed events.

In these races, the boats are started individually at about ten-second intervals and are timed between a start line and a finish on the river, and these times are posted in order as the final results.

The first one, the Weybridge Silver Sculls, is just over two miles long, I won the Junior Division, and in fact, recorded the fastest time of the day, beating all of the men in the senior event. Two weeks later, I won the 'Juniors' of the Marlow Long Distance Sculls, a much longer race, and came fifth overall.

My primary aim at school should have been to study for A-levels but I was living for everything else and occasionally I felt guilty that I was letting the family down, but to keep going from one day to the next was all I could do.

Bucknall and I were great in chemistry, not especially in the academic work, but we enjoyed each other's company, and there was an unspoken challenge between us to create fun and farce while pretending to be model students.

The recurring dreams had changed again, there were times when I could fly up and look down with confidence on those below but at other times, I struggled and was fearful of falling.

On the last day of term before Christmas, soon after 9 am, I walked boldly into Clock Tower and made a tiny adjustment to the complicated-looking hour chime mechanism. During the end of term chapel service not long after, the bell struck 10 but then continued ringing hundreds of times.

Afterwards, I walked up Chestnut Avenue, collected the AJS outfit, rode into school up the back drive, collected Bucknall plus our luggage and the clock tower bell was still ringing as we set off for Haslemere. It was an eventful journey with many (orchestrated) near misses, plus occasional screams from Bucknall and hilarity from both of us, which surprised people in built-up areas.

Bucknall had made arrangements to go for a pub crawl on the outfit with two other Radleians from Surrey, making four of us in all. Fireworks were brought without my knowledge and we had a crazy time with two of the guys sitting on the floor of the box, firing rockets into the trees as we blatted between country pubs on the old AJS outfit. There was more to that evening, but I can't tell them all.

Bucknall went home by train before Christmas and on Boxing Day, I set off early on the AJS outfit to Pirbright with the Sprite and gear loaded in the box for my first motocross competition. The Pirbright track was fast, over sandy ripples and the Sprite's steering proved a nightmare, it took all my strength to hold onto the handlebars, which were waving around all over the place.

I simply had to open the throttle and hang on tight. A couple of lads tried my bike and said they didn't know how I could ride it at all, but on my first day out, I'd done well as I beat quite a few others. When I finally got home, aching and tired, I enjoyed a long soak in the bath. It had been a good day.

When packing up to go to Radley in January 1967, I was concerned about leaving the Sprite in the damp and cold outhouse at home until Easter. I suggested to Dad that it would be better in my bedroom. "Let's do it quick before Mum gets back," he said. We were careful not to damage the vicarage walls and bannisters on the way up.

The AJS took me back to Radley and I noticed very soon that the hour chime on Clock Tower wasn't ringing at all. After a day or two when I could see no one around, I went to check it out and could hardly believe how someone had disabled the continuously chiming bell by tying part of the mechanism up with a piece of rope. The electric motor had been running continuously for over two weeks as it was hot, so I put everything back as it should be.

Ronnie Howard had his 'Trial Eights' group from which the first and second school eights would be chosen, and after a few weeks, I sat in the First Eight at six again.

Chris Baillieu was in the stroke seat and he would later go on to an illustrious rowing career at Cambridge before winning a string of World Championship medals and an Olympic silver medal in 1976 with Mike Hart in the double scull. Ronnie was coaching the Oxford University crew as well as ourselves, and during March each year, there is a race called the Tideway Head of the River Race on the tidal Thames in London. The race is for over four hundred eights and is timed, starting from Chiswick and finishing at Putney, it's four and a quarter miles and takes winning crews about eighteen minutes to complete. It's generally knows as the Tideway Head or Tideway H.O.R.*, short for head of the river, and is raced over the Oxford/Cambridge Boat Race course, but in the opposite direction.

The results that year were that the Tideway Scullers School took the first two places, the incredible Emanuel School crew came 7th in front of Oxford University who were 8th, and our finishing position of 10th place was encouraging.

*

During the evening 'prep' time, I should have worked for my A-level exams but I worked very little. I didn't understand my depression and difficulties with concentration, and as usual, I was simply doing whatever I could to get by. Included in those activities was filing out the inlet port of a spare AJS 500 cylinder head, and spending time in the music school, which wasn't allowed.

My aim after leaving Radley was to secure an engineering training through an apprenticeship, so I wrote letters to the British motorcycle manufacturers. BSA Motorcycles replied to my letter, suggesting an interview date just before Easter.

As soon as I arrived home for the Easter holiday, I ran to my bedroom and fired up my motocross bike, a loud *rev, rev, rev,* plenty of ripping two-stroke noise and smoke in the bedroom. Two days later, I had my second motocross event, which was near Petersfield on a steep hillside. The course was much smoother than the sandy ripples at Pirbright and the bike steered much better on the smooth ground.

During my first race, I lost control after a big jump and went into big wild slides to the left and right, the back wheel slid off the side of the hill, the bike flipped and I got launched off the hillside headfirst.

My dad took a photo, I flew a long way down, but rolled comparatively smoothly on sloping grass and ended up draped over the crowd-control rope with my chest on a post. My bike was toppling slowly end over end and landed saddle first on my back, I was unhurt, got going and rode along until I found a way back up to rejoin the race.

Launched off the hill. See my bottom and underside of bike.

Between races, I walked round and went back to see where I'd fallen, another rider fell and he slipped down the hill on his backside, a guy in front of me laughed and said to his mate, "Not like the nutter before." I walked away, amused.

My friend Ian had been helping me with my bikes and he came with me as my mechanic to another event at Ash near Aldershot. In my first race on that day, two riders fell in a narrow and steep uphill gully, and as I tried to get past, my bike and I toppled onto one of the other bikes and my fibreglass petrol tank was pierced by a footrest.

Petrol poured on his hot engine, fizzing and boiling instantly, and I got a cloud of petrol 'steam' in my face. I heaved my bike off with petrol slopping out and finished the lap, feeling lucky there hadn't been a fire.

There were only forty minutes till my next race but all I had with me for fibreglass repairs was filler paste, no glass matting or resin and nothing to mix anything in. It was an emergency and Ian offered his hand with a little laugh. He mixed filler paste with hardener in his hand and the job was quickly done. Thirty-five minutes for it to set and my second race went well but I didn't make the final.

My interview at the BSA factory for an apprenticeship had taken place earlier in the school holidays and an envelope arrived at home with the BSA logo on it. They offered me a four-year apprenticeship to start two weeks after the end of the Radley summer term.

I let them know that I would be there, and yes, could they arrange lodgings for me? That was a relief. I had a future, thank God, and was really looking forward to it.

Dad took me to a car showroom in Haslemere, there was a second-hand Standard 10 van in the window, ideal for my purposes and Granny was prepared to pay for it for my birthday. The front end of it was the Standard 10 car, the back end was wider and higher, very similar to the Morris 1000 van. With the back doors open, a motorbike could be strapped in with the front wheel and handlebars sticking out.

During the summer term of 1967, the First Eight training went well, we were a good crew but the Emanuel School boys beat us with ease at Marlow. At Henley in the Princess Elizabeth Cup event, we won some races but were beaten by Tabor Academy from America and Emanuel School almost won the Thames Cup, the event for the men in club crews.

My A-level exams, immediately afterwards, went very badly, but I got through them without too much heartache as I'd pretty much given up with the academic work and was looking forward to my apprenticeship in Birmingham.

Ronnie prepared us in two fours for the first World Junior Rowing Championships which were to be held after the end of term in Germany. I was rowing at two in the coxless four with Chris Baillieu at stroke and we qualified for the championships to be Ratzeburg.

On the water before the racing, a coxless pair stopped alongside us, they were our British pair, two slim sixteen-year-olds with long hair from the Thames Tradesmen's Rowing Club.

They were young, cheeky and fun with their London accents and were obviously enjoying themselves, whereas we were posh and serious, really very different. I'll never forget that meeting with Bill Mason and Lenny Robertson and had no idea that we would race together in the British Eight years later.

On finals day in our four, we had a bad start in rough tailwind conditions, were last at 500 metres, and despite being in a photo finish for third place, we came fifth. Before we left for home, Ronnie told me that there would be a meeting at Leander for new recruits for the Leander Cadet Scheme on September 16th. My brother Steve had rowed in a Leander Cadet crew. I would be at Henley for the Leander meeting.

I had a few days at home in Haslemere before the start of my apprenticeship. Mum told me that she and Dad were going on holiday, so I'd have some time on my own, and she asked me to clear all my childhood stuff out of my bedroom, which seemed a bit harsh at the time.

My Radley days had finished and it felt odd that all of that was behind me. I knew that I'd been privileged, and in many ways, I'd had the time of my life, but I was excited at the prospect of the engineering training at BSA Motorcycles, along with the chance of rowing at Leander.

Chapter 14
'The BSA'

On a Sunday afternoon, with my parents still away, I set off for Birmingham in the van with the letter from 'the BSA', informing me of the address of my lodgings. The road handling, acceleration and braking of the van were terrible by modern standards, the top speed was about 76 mph with the roof rack on, and I drove flat-out almost always.

She was top-heavy and rolled badly on corners and had a strong tendency to oversteer, losing grip on the back tyres. The 948cc Triumph Herald engine was smooth and reliable, high revs were her thing, and she sang so high that every day was race day.

It was terrifying for other road users and really, there was nothing good about it except that for me, it was great/wonderful. I was having the time of my life. Close shaves were common but fear didn't come into it, I was busy saving the day, and experienced 'time slowing down' many times.

Evolution has given humans the capability in moments of great danger to see movement in 'stretched time' and with that comes the ability to react within this slow-motion to save ourselves. Those times were the very best. I arrived safely at my landlady's home, a modest three-bed semi in King's Norton, Birmingham; she welcomed me, provided me with a good meal and all was well.

On the first day at the BSA, we learnt that we, the new apprentices from the thirteen companies of the BSA group of companies including Triumph Motorcycles, were to spend a year in the training centre learning basic engineering skills.

There were introductory lectures, then I was sent in a small group to the Lathe Section to learn 'turning' skills. At the end of four weeks, there was a test, we were each issued with a piece of metal and an engineering drawing, and my finished piece was almost perfect, which was most satisfying. On Monday, we were to start on milling machines.

This new engineering life with a crowd of good lads was rich. Most of the apprentices were local lads straight from school aged sixteen, and there was me—a very posh eighteen-year-old straight out of the vicarage and Radley. I was probably accepted because of my sense of fun and the ridiculous, but one of my apprentice mates said years later in his Birmingham accent that I spoke so funny, he thought I was a German.

These lads were not inhibited by having to be polite and say the right thing, they could be abrupt but they said what they meant, which was all good, no faffing around. If it was fuck-it, then that's what it was, or if it was fuckin' bollocks, even better.

Our weekly routine consisted of four days in the factory and a day plus an evening class at a technical college, this was 'Day-Release'. I was in my comfort zone, doing mostly practical work. I had no need to pretend to be OK as I was very much OK, living the dream.

The four weeks on milling machines went well and we went on to 'Bench Work', which included hack-sawing, filing, riveting and sheet metal work. These were superb skills to learn, we each made a set of small tools and a metal box to put them in.

One of my new friends noticed that I was filing a cylindrical shape using the wrong technique and he asked me if I'd done metalwork before, I told him that my school didn't have metalwork, he said, "*Every* school has metalwork, your school was *pretty crap.*"

We weren't allowed into the factory but the production work was all so *interesting*. I walked into the main factory block occasionally for a quick look but my purple first year apprentice overalls were a giveaway and I was told to go back. Later, I was given the tip that if we held a piece of paper (anything) and looked purposeful, we could go anywhere.

On one of my walkabouts, some men were watching a fork-lift truck lift a heavy lathe into position over other machines. The lathe, weighing over two tons slipped and fell onto the concrete floor with a terrible thud. I was horrified, especially as we were upstairs, but all the men laughed and I moved swiftly on.

By the time I'd worked at the factory for a while, my outlook had broadened considerably and my transition from life in the vicarage and Radley to the factory was seamless. My use of expletives had expanded exponentially, but the question in my head was, 'Why, when a motorbike wouldn't start, or a machine was broken, was it described as fucked?'

I knew roughly what that meant although I hadn't done it, and it was apparent that many things in the factory were fucked, but why that? The question hovered in the back of my mind for years but the answer which eventually came was that if a woman was abused, fucked and broken down, perhaps men imagined that anything which was broken down was fucked.

We spent a month on forge-work and welding and I loved all the heat processes. Steve Cooper from Yeoville was in my group and we agreed that blacksmithing was superb. There was plenty of hacking, bashing, welding and creating things, and I came back to it about fifteen years later when I needed a change in my working life.

I moved into a flat with two others in Acocks Green about three miles from the BSA factory. One of them was my friend, Steve Cooper, capable and steady, but who always joined in escapades and pranks with enthusiasm, and there was Jim McDonald from Nottingham.

He was a bit mad, living on coffee and fags in a dream world of motorbikes; at times, he spoke bits of gobbledygook language with style and panache. He was a good man and his invented words were his trademark. Jim lived at times in a parallel world.

Steve and I contributed to his inventive language by degrees and the three of us could be heard talking total bollocks at times. We got weird looks when out and about, but smiles and admiration too.

One morning, I heard a factory worker say, "Hello Nobby," to his mate, and that evening, I was giving my flat mates a lift to technical college in the van. We passed a lad sitting by the side of the road and I shouted, "**NOBBY,**" very loudly at him through my open window.

It went down well (for us) and was the first of many thousands of NOBBYs shouted, not just by me but by lots of people, as I've spread the word and taught it widely. It lifts the spirits, you should try it, anytime, anywhere, but it has to be shouted loudly with conviction, otherwise people think you're a bit potty.

Lunch in the factory cafeteria had staggered sittings for different groups of workers, we had to wait in a passage until a crowd of machine-operators came out at 12:30. I'm reminded by my flatmate Steve that one day, when faced with the crowd coming the other way, I charged them fast and hard. Bodies everywhere, Steve says.

We had to clock-on by 8:30 am at work and to be late was a disciplinary issue dealt with by the training school manager, 'Lumpy', who was large with a grey suit and grey hair and an unsightly growth on his cheek.

I used to give my flat mates a lift to work in the van and there was always a traffic jam on the A41 before it narrowed from four lanes into two at the bottom of the hill in Sparkbrook.

We were late one day and again on another, and anyone who was late was summonsed to Lumpy's office and spoken to individually. Some weeks later, Jim delayed us one morning, something to do with fags, coffee or trousers.

The normal two lanes of stationary traffic on the Warwick Road had backed up much further than usual and approaching the back of the queue at speed, I couldn't slow and steered to the right involuntarily into the two empty lanes on the other side of the road.

I was on the wrong side of the road and drove for about a quarter of a mile past all the stationary cars, down the hill, then a car came towards me and another. But they had a lane and so did I, so all was well. The road narrowed into two lanes and I had to force my way into the single left lane while waving a thank you.

Not far to the lights and our right turn but the lights turned to red, we were all shouting and round we went. Nearly there at 8:27. On that particular day, I clocked-in at 8:30, Steve 8:31 and Jim 8:32 (it was the fags). They had to see Lumpy again.

One day, Steve and I coasted to a standstill in the van with a fake breakdown at the top of the single lane Digbeth flyover in the rush-hour, Steve asked what we were doing.

"We've broken down."

"Oh, right," and with concerned looks on our faces, we opened the bonnet and took cover behind it. The drivers behind were very patient, but then we 'fixed it' and were off. Any excuse for a jape, anywhere.

Having finished our year in the training centre, we were each sent into the factory to learn production engineering and one of my factory moves took me to the development department.

I was given a variety of work and one day, was issued with a boiler-suit and told that I'd be emptying the inspection pit in the middle of the workshop floor, it was known that some old and interesting engines had been stored below.

After I'd lifted a dozen engines out, someone said, "There's a Bantam engine."

There was a pause and then a firm response, "No, it's the wrong way round, it must be the German one."

I lifted the engine out, a Bantam, but no, it was a mirror image with the gear change on the left, I turned it round and read out DKW, a German manufacturer. Someone confirmed that we (British) had taken the German design in 1945 as one of the spoils of war and BSA had marketed a mirror image of it as the BSA Bantam. I was shocked that the respected and loved *British* BSA Bantam was no such thing but rather a German design.

Another example of spoils of war were BMW car designs, which were given to the Bristol aeroplane company when their aeroplanes were no longer needed. The cars were built as Bristol cars. *We won, we'll have your stuff.*

The BSA competition department was next to the development department where I worked and I'd see Jeff Smith, who'd been my hero on motocross bikes for years, and the other professional works riders, going out to test their 440cc Victor works bikes. Jeff came to acknowledge me quite soon, having seen my interest in the bikes and my respect for him.

Jeff Smith leading a race on the BSA 440cc Victor.

Meanwhile, I'd been driving to Henley every Friday after work and had been spending my weekends at Leander Club. I'd joined in the sculling and rowing at Leander shortly after the beginning of my apprenticeship.

Chapter 15
Leander Club

During the early 1960s, Leander Club, originally for Oxford and Cambridge oarsmen only, was very run down. It had been successful for a long time, but after the 1948 Olympics, when the Leander eight won the Olympic silver medal, the club's standards had dropped. During the 1950s and 1960s, Leander and Great Britain fell behind, new methods and bigger commitments were needed.

Donald Legget had rowed for Cambridge in the Boat Race for two years and was the secretary of the Cambridge University Boat Club. Having won the race in 1964 he was invited to be the Leander Captain and to run a 'Leander Cadet Scheme'. The cadet scheme was to utilise talented eighteen-year-olds straight from independent schools and was a farsighted plan to revitalise Leander Club.

The first cadets came together in January 1965 and trained for six months as a crew, and although they were quite good, they didn't make any impact. The 1966 crew included my brother Steve, was a little stronger but again didn't shine, and there was talk of the scheme being wound up.

Donald Legget, the club captain, heard, however, that Derek Drury, the coach of all the outstanding Emanuel School crews, had moved from teaching at Emanuel School in Wandsworth to Shiplake College near Henley. He persuaded Derek to help him with the cadet squad, and between them, they generated a plan.

Donald rustled up more interest in the cadet scheme; this resulted in a bigger batch of new recruits starting in September 1967, which included myself.

I'd been living and working in Birmingham for about six weeks before the meeting of new recruits at Leander in September. About twenty-five of us attended, Derek Drury and Donald Legget introduced themselves and Derek said confidently that the following summer, we'd win the Thames Cup in an eight at the Henley Regatta.

I was surprised by this bold statement but wasn't aware at the time that Derek had been the coach all of those successful Emanuel School crews which had been beating all the rest of us schoolboys. He'd also brought three of his First Eight with him to row at Leander, so he knew we could do it, but it was two or three weeks before I found out those important details.

We were to arrive on the following Friday evening and were to go out sculling straight away. The club would provide weekend board and lodging for £2 per head, we would train on Saturdays twice and Sundays once. Land-training was to be done near our homes on two further weekday evenings and we were to be committed to all of it right through to Henley Regatta the following summer.

This plan seemed almost military in concept and Donald tells how an Etonian asked after the meeting whether it had to be *every* weekend as it would interfere with the hunt. We were given a land-training program and lunch before we went on our way.

I drove home to Haslemere to stay with the family and on Sunday morning, Dad took the communion service. I robed up with cassock and surplice to boost the regular church choir at St Bartholomew's church. The rest of the family were near the front of the congregation, this was to be the end of any regular church attendance by me for many years, and after a Sunday roast, I set off back to Birmingham.

On the first Friday evening at Leander, we went sculling in small groups as people arrived, and each group, after a short warm-up, began the interval training, six times one and a half minutes flat out, with the same resting time between each. During the resting times, we paddled the boat along gently 'paddling light'*; afterwards, dinner was served and we were allocated to bedrooms which were fairly shabby in those days.

Almost all of the training on the water was to be intensive interval training in single sculling boats, there would be regular sculling trials and the fastest eight scullers would be in the First Eight. From the beginning, the training and sculling was very competitive.

[THIS IS DEFINITELY MY THING. IT'S THE BEST.]*

---

*see Glossary

Friday evenings soon became routine and two lads who drove from Manchester arrived late but always went sculling. During the winter in bad weather, we'd see those two pushing out into the river under the flood-light, they were whipped away downstream into the white horses and darkness. We wondered if we'd ever see them again.

There were no lights on the boats, no safety launch, no anything. We competed in the fairly local Weybridge Silver Sculls and the Marlow Long Distance Sculls, which some of us knew from previous years, both of those timed HORs are annual events still.

We were short of stroke-side oarsmen[†] and the Shrewsbury lads remembered Graham Davidson from their school days, he was at Birmingham University and was happy to join us, he had a car but usually travelled with me in my van. He soon got used to my driving fast and to opposite-lock sideways slides in the wet, it was good to have his company and he proved himself strong on the river.

Every Friday evening was a reunion of enthusiastic friends and recently, one of the men told me that on arrival, I always had a smile and a tale to tell, and that something had happened during the week or on the way down. "You amused us all."

A new Donoratico eight, a beautiful polished wooden boat nearly sixty feet long, was delivered to Leander from Italy during the late autumn and one afternoon, we weren't taking things seriously on the water.

Donald delivered an angry speech from the coaching launch, saying that we were the most privileged oarsmen in the country, we should do our very best at all times, and he pointed out how much Leander Club, Derek and he personally, were putting into our squad.

While walking outside a cinema one Saturday evening behind a group of Leander mates, I suddenly ran a few feet and did a handspring. I'd never done one before, but I reckoned I could, so I did, and there were strangers around but I didn't care, it was done out of sheer exuberance.

My friends heard my leather shoes slap on the pavement on landing, they turned round and asked what had happened but I shrugged my shoulders (nothing!). I was feeling particularly good and my extrovert behaviour had burst out. Later that evening in the cinema after an ice cream advert, I shouted, "We're gonna have *ICE* cream," which raised a laugh.

[†] See Glossary

Donald organised the sculling interval training from the launch, he grouped us closely with the fastest at the front, gave us the starts and stops, kept an eye on steering but no motivational shouts were needed as everyone was fighting to the death to earn a seat in the eight.

Once per month, we had sculling trials, pairs of scullers would be started from stationary to race 1000 metres, we were timed and it was repeated in the opposite direction, all the times were recorded and as it happens, my name was always top of the results list.

We had started at Leander during September and one of the results of my training was that I was always hungry, our lunches at the BSA factory were subsidised and we only had to pay a (pre-decimal) sixpence for our meal (2½ p.). The options were fish and chips with peas, or a roast lunch with veg and gravy, I had one of each every day.

The pattern of our lives continued through the winter and two eights were selected from the cadet squad (there were no other crews training at Leander) for the Tideway Head of the River Race. Nearly all of the training in the eight consisted of rowing intensive one and a half minute intervals, usually sets of eight rows, and these were done at high intensity, absolute blasters.

On race day, we set off fast and after three or four minutes, my legs were blown but we had to race on for about another fifteen minutes, it hurt, I'd messed up and I learnt a lot about pacing myself on that day. We finished in sixth place out of about four hundred, which was slightly disappointing as we'd hoped to be in the top three or four.

The girl from Reigate, who I'd kissed in Cornwall, and I had kept in touch, and one Saturday evening after rowing, I took her out to a dinner dance. Afterwards, we had a kiss and a cuddle in the van and were beginning to go further, natural forces were pushing me on, but I was having a serious battle with my old inhibitions. It was getting late and I took her home. I'd suppressed the forces of nature.

The level of my commitment to Leander and BSA in Birmingham left no space for this atom bomb in my head, she lived 140 miles from me and my life was in danger of being de-railed. I broke off the relationship despite knowing that it was exactly what I wanted.

The Scullers Head (HOR*) came next on the Tideway and Graham beat me by 12 seconds over the distance of four and a quarter miles. He reminded me recently that he was two years older than me and generously said that it would have made a difference.

The day after that race, we had a fright when driving back to Birmingham, on the way down a hill at speed, I turned smoothly into a right-hand curve, the van leaned alarmingly to the left, the back swung out and I had to apply opposite lock to retain control. The back tyre howled in protest but we got round before coming out straight and level.

"I DON'T MIND DOING SKIDS AT 30, BUT NOT 80," complained Graham. I apologised, and stopped to check my tyre pressures, we'd had a lucky escape with one tyre at 14 psi.

The Leander 1968 crew after winning the Thames Cup. The captain, Donald Legget is second from the left, and Derek Drury and his wife Dagmar are at the extreme ends.

We competed at four summer regattas in the eight, losing the first one but we won everything else. At the beginning of Henley Regatta week, our squad moved out of the club to stay at Fawley Court, half way up the Henley Regatta course and included in the group was a pair of old Radleians, Steve Crooks and James Hayter, ex-Leander cadets rowing for St Thomas' Hospital in a pair.

I joined in with fun there but not the bad behaviour. That might seem out of character but I felt a weight of responsibility as a Leander member, and was shocked that damage was done to the fabric of Fawley Court.

A bill for £180 was presented to Leander for repairs (approx. £4,000 now) and the Leander Committee wanted to pull us out of the regatta but Donald persuaded them to let us race because we'd broken records in training. The bill was paid by a Leander Committee member out of his own pocket.

Crooks senior and Hayter could/would have gone to the Mexico Olympics that year in the London University eight, as they were faster than some of those who were in the eight, in their pair, but they couldn't because being medical students, they had to work prohibitive hours.

During the Henley Regatta, we won all our races including the final against Cornell University (USA) and when putting the boat on its rack at Leander, an excited Derek arrived, congratulating us, saying that he'd just been asked by one of the British rowing team selectors 'to form a crew for the 1972 Olympics in Munich'.

Derek laughed. "And you're all in it," smiles all round, but four years away, too far in the future to even be considered.

Harold Ricketts at Leander had promised that if we won the Thames Cup, he'd fill it with champagne but he hadn't realised how many bottles it would take, and at regatta prices, it cost him a fortune. Drinking champagne like beer out of the Thames Cup was pretty good though.

When Donald Legget was asked about the Leander Cadets and my place in it, he said that during the third season, when he could barely muster a four for Henley, he managed to persuade Derek Drury to help with the cadets' scheme.

Donald had cast the net far and wide and had gathered oarsmen from all over the country. "And from Radley, there was Tim Crooks, you could build a crew around him—he was a natural for the six seat, which he rarely relinquished in future years. Tim hardly needed any coaching, he was incredibly strong and always pulled his guts out in every race."

Off the start at Henley, clocked at 52 strokes per minute.

Having enjoyed our win at Henley, we went our own ways on the Monday morning but I felt an emptiness after our huge commitment. We'd climbed a pinnacle in winning the Thames Cup at the age of 19, any other pinnacle in rowing seemed out of sight to me and I couldn't go on rowing just for the sake of it.

Chapter 16
The New Challenge

Having put the rowing aside, I was free to join in the motor biking activities with my mates in Birmingham, but first, I drove to Cornwall in the van, via Bucknall's and the Ashen Faggot pub, of course. My parents were on holiday near the Helford River with young sister and brother, they had a good time but I didn't. I felt terrible, didn't know what was wrong in my head and had to pretend to be OK.

In Birmingham, I rented a garage near our flat to keep motorbikes, raced in motocross races, got involved in the Birmingham life with my mates and felt better for it. I'd taken the sidecar off the old AJS 500 and used the bike often around Birmingham.

One of my motocross events was over ripples of hard sand, the unstable Sprite was a real handful and on top of that, the last two laps were done with a rattling, clapped out engine. I'd tuned up the engine but had unwittingly caused a bearing to fail.

My old friend, Guy Tod, had come to watch with his girlfriend, he took photos, one of which showed a terrible grimace on my face. People suffering mental torments can display an awful facial expression as if they're carrying the world on their back. I didn't know why it happened, but usually knew when it was happening, and would hide it, but couldn't while I was racing with an open face helmet.

Some of my factory mates were competing in 'trials' events on motorbikes, and these trials events are much safer than motocross as they are tests of skill rather than being races.

One rider goes at a time quite slowly through very difficult 'sections', the idea being to try and get through each section balancing the bike without putting a foot down, stopping or falling off. As the competition day goes on, penalty points accrue when mistakes are made. I bought a Greeves 250 cc trials bike and started competing in trials events.

Practising skills on the 250cc Greeves for trials competitions.

On the same day, with my Standard 10 van in the background.

My first few events were enjoyable but my results were mediocre and it became obvious that if I was to be competitive in trials competitions, I needed much more practice in varied and difficult terrain. I could see that wasn't going to happen, and trials competitions weren't working for me, I needed a challenge with more of a buzz anyway.

My instinct had always driven me to escape bad feelings by challenging myself, whatever necessary, to get by. My subconscious was too often in charge, I wasn't making all the decisions and being on an out-of-control rollercoaster was at times scary.

Fear drove me to do things, *anything, and never mind the consequences.* The implication that I was not responsible for my actions is highly questionable, but this is a problem for society as evidenced by the high proportion of mentally ill in jail.

One weekday morning in Birmingham, I awoke feeling terrible, mentally disabled and weak. I got out of bed, desperate doom had control of my mind, I was frightened, and feeling awful dread about my day, I couldn't go to work. *I had to escape.* The AJS now had no sidecar.

Only one option, to ride my bike, direction south, I'm off
morning traffic, but mist and *FOG*. Accelerate, weave and charge
between and round the cars and trucks, and off into the countryside
the open road, but foggy still, I see just thirty yards
escape, push on, fuck the fog. I'm driven by dread and fear
just steer the road, I know it well, terrible risk but I've slipped
down into the monster pit. Don't stop me, I have to push on
the mental stress pushes me and fuels this dreaded dash
speed in fog should frighten me, but no, just keep going
it's all too fast, challenging fate. My joy's my engine's song
the vibrant rich and full-toned roar, the old five hundred single
the big brute blare, that sonorous sound vibrates my body and bones
love that blast, always have, it soothes my troubled mind
I lean back, listen, soak in the sound. Throttle off, ba-bang, and smile
the white line's mine, concentrate on getting through the gaps
cars loom past, on left and right, I'm sharp, on top of this
spaces open up for me, slow-motion, loads of time.
flying blind the well-known road, my route, my-get-away
past Leander, then fork right, my mind is on the road
I'm on the cusp, the tipping point, of flying high or doom
weaving, winding, red light, road works, can't stop, just steer through
Hindhead finally, engine-off, and coasting down the hill
done this before, nearly there. Thank God for blessed home.

Haslemere, foggy and calm, I used my front door key, went through into the kitchen and there were my folks sitting with a cup of tea. My head was down and I had no words to say, they looked at me and Mum said, "He needs us." Dad made tea for me and we sat quietly.

It was a Tuesday. In time, we did talk, just everyday stuff and we spent a few hours together. Later on, I was back in the real world and being sent off with love. Direction north, 150 miles, no hurry, but reflections, yes.

I'd been high-jacked by a mental event and was lucky to have survived, some would say it was a mad act; it was a mad act, but that's what happened. When people are threatened by torments which they know will engulf their mind, their behaviour can be seen as illogical.

The need to escape mental pain can prompt extreme actions which threaten physical survival, but many of the population suffer a breakdown of logical behaviour at some time and lives are threatened, and taken.

My experience of bipolar disorder, and living with fear, the dread of depression taking over, has made my mind sensitive to bad feelings and mental warnings of slipping mood.

My logic would often tell me what action to take to improve a situation, but so often, instinctive action was suddenly taken with little or no understanding of why I had acted unpredictably. My behaviour often surprised me as much as those around me and I would find myself laughing along with them.

Warnings provoke the brain to do almost *anything* to avoid plunging into the dreaded pit. The mind saves itself instinctively and this is clear to me because I've often registered my own actions before I've properly recognised a warning. I've learnt that, on the rare occasion I'm to interrupt involuntary action at all, I have to be both very quick and strong minded.

Premeditated action has, by definition, been thought about, but there's no *thinking* time when a warning of doom and depression has arrived and already been acted upon.

For many sufferers of mental illness, their instinctive methods of escape (their actions) include rushing, racing, gambling, alcohol, drugs, shopping, sex, violence, verbal abuse, stealing, violent crime and more. People can be driven to many things in torment, but with no understanding, and can anyone be blamed for actions driven by instinct? Society does, and must blame, unless an alternative can be found.

When people said that 'rowing held Tim together', they were right. Thank God for my sport, but I was trapped in my wonderful/awful world with my highs and lows, stresses and confusions as well as terrible 'mixed moods'.*

The fear of living with mental instability is about the terrible places your brain can take you. If you take drastic action and do stuff to keep depression away, whatever you're doing, *however dangerous, it's less frightening that the deep dark pit.*

Something had to be done to break out of my mood, action was needed, the BSA factory was busy with chat, I heard of a BSA 250 motocross bike for sale and I went to check it out straight away.

I bought the BSA and the Sprite had to go, sold to a guy in the factory, all he asked was whether she went OK and he was treated to a ripping two-stroke racket. No problem, and no comeback on that. The trials bike was sold not long after too.

My BSA 250 motocross special.

---

*See appendix

Myself and the same bike on another day.

Boxing Day saw me racing at Pirbright again, Ian Greig came to help and we were well set up with the BSA and the van, I raced well in two heats, didn't make either of the finals but my mood had recovered, I was on a high and enjoyed it. Next was Lydden Hill in Kent, sandy and dry with big jumps.

There was a muddy event in the Midlands, my front mudguard was fixed close to the front wheel and kept jamming with mud and long grass. Eventually, when the front wheel wasn't going round for the third time, I got fed up with it, aimed the bike down the muddy hill where there were no spectators, stood up on sliding feet and let the bike go on its own.

I sat down and slid along while watching the bike fall upside down under overhanging bushes. I left it there and joined the crowd to watch the racing.

[SODDIT.]

Something had to be done about finding a girlfriend. I had my weekends in Birmingham as I wasn't rowing and decided to go to the Opposite Lock nightclub in Gas Street, central Birmingham. I bought myself a pint at the bar, glanced round and there was an attractive girl apparently with her parents, which was surprising.

I spoke to them and danced with the girl, Diana, and then her parents wanted to leave early and she had to go too, but she gave me her phone number and they were gone. It was a little odd.

On the Saturday night, I met Diana at a disco near hers, we had a good time and she invited me back for coffee, her house couldn't have been any closer as it overlooked the disco tent in a small park.

She opened her front door and an anxious voice from upstairs asked, "Is that you, Mum?" She answered and whispered that this was her daughter. I was shocked that the daughter had been left alone and asked how old she was, nine. Her mum seemed too young, I was only 20 but she asked me if I wanted to come in, or did I think I'd better go. I was shocked at the situation and opted to go.

A week or two later outside my flat in Birmingham, the realisation came to me suddenly that girls and sex were NOT a problem. I looked at the houses all around, sex was happening all the time, everywhere. The penny had finally dropped, I'd been brainwashed, damaged actually, for so long.

So, there I was, standing by my van in the road, wishing I'd stayed on with the young mum after the disco. I'd liked her very much and realised that I'd been on a dead cert. I thought of ringing her but considered myself on a significant fork in the road of life and put that experience behind me.

Donald Legget contacted me during February and asked if I'd row in a Leander First Eight for the Reading and Tideway HOR races, I told him that I wasn't fit but it seemed that I was in the six seat, so I was back to training.

After two or three weeks, we won the Reading HOR before coming third on the Tideway behind the two Tideway Scullers Eights. Donald asked me afterwards if I'd continue rowing through the 1969 season, but no, I was busy with motocross.

While on my way to Surrey one Friday evening, I dropped into Leander with my BSA motocross bike in the van and was persuaded to show how it went. So, there I was, racing around the Leander car park, making a lot of noise, doing wheelies and power-slides on the wet stones and grass while trying hard not to drop the bike at speed and ruin my smart trousers.

During May 1969, Ian came with me as my mechanic at another event at Pirbright, it was sandy, dry and bumpy as hell but it was good to be lining up on the BSA and not the Sprite.

My parents and brother Steve had come to watch, I came fourth in my heat of the 250cc event and sixth in my heat of the 'four strokes' and I'd qualified for a final, which was a first. It was a good day, and during the middle of the afternoon, I lined up for my final.

My face hurt, my neck hurt, I had a headache and felt crap, I opened my eyes, I was in bed in a room on my own.

[OH, NO! HOSPITAL.]

I checked that I was complete, yes, all my bits and limbs, but my *face,* and my *neck*. I couldn't remember what had happened but eventually, a doctor arrived with a nurse and it turned out that they were doing Monday morning rounds.

I'd been in a motocross accident on the day before, they told me that I'd been concussed and had a dental injury, which my dentist could sort out, but that I should be fine.

Later in the day, I saw my face in the mirror, I had a black-eye and some cuts, my neck had a motocross tyre tread-mark across it and my upper jaw hurt on one side. Two of my top teeth were pushed upwards and I could feel the bumps under my top lip where the roots were pushed up through the bone. Two more days in hospital, then time at home in Epsom, I was back at work on the Monday.

I didn't have anything organised for the BSA annual two-week work shutdown and I rang Leander to see whether I could help coach up to the Henley Regatta. Hugh Twiss, the new captain who I knew well, answered, and I offered help as I was free, his answer was an enthusiastic yes.

I packed some sports kit in my bag in case I might go sculling, and on my arrival, two weeks before the Henley finals, I was warmly welcomed by Hugh Twiss and Jock Mullard, but there was a surprise. I was to race the Senior Sculls at Marlow as well as the Diamond Challenge Sculls at the Henley Regatta. They'd entered me into these events without my knowledge.

"But I'm not fit."

"You'll be alright."

"When's Marlow?"

"Tomorrow."

"What, you must be joking, I've just had a year off."

But no, they were quite amused, and at Marlow Regatta, on the old town stretch the following day in my race, I felt absolutely great.

[THIS IS MY THING.]

I shot into the lead but when the lactic acid arrived, my legs wouldn't go any more and I lost the race. The challenge had lifted my mood however and the prospect of training and competing on the river was so good.

Training for the 'Diamonds' began in earnest with intensive interval training on the following day, the Sunday morning. Five days later I won a qualifying race but a week later, was beaten in the main regatta. The new cadet eight won the Thames Cup again. Those two weeks were significant because I was reminded just how good it was at Leander, especially with all the young men looking up to me even though I was losing races.

I decided to get back to rowing in the autumn, partly for safety reasons, but I'd been more successful in boats. I'd made better friendships through rowing and couldn't wait to get back to physical training and my endorphin 'feel-good fixes' on the river.

Back to work in Birmingham and I raced in another motocross event, in Market Drayton this time, where I met a guy who had seen my crash after the start at Pirbright. He described how we were all bunched up tight, a rider in front of me lost control of his bike, which had flipped on all the bumps, sending him high in the air and he landed on my head.

I went over bumps with him on top of me before we crashed in a heap. We found dents in my handlebars (the steel was three mm thick), which matched the positions of my damaged teeth. I'd had my handlebars in my mouth with a bloke on my head while going over severe bumps. They have padding on handlebars these days.

The 250cc motocross bike wasn't needed any more and I part-exchanged it at Comerfords in Long Ditton for a second-hand 440cc Shooting Star, which was the road version of the bigger 440 BSA Victor motocross bike. The road bike was very light compared with my old AJS 500 but with more power, and careless use of the clutch when setting off resulted in wheelies, almost over backwards from the traffic lights.

The BSA Shooting Star.

Chapter 17
The Grand Challenge Cup

The Leander restart was good, I arrived early and there was another batch of new recruits looking for Donald Legget and Derek Drury. When we, the older ones met, it was a reunion of old friends and it was confirmed that our aim was to race for the 'Grand Challenge Cup', the top eights event at the Henley Regatta. The new recruits would row a second eight and go for a third win in the Thames Cup.

At the Weybridge Silver Sculls, Glyn Locke beat me, he'd been the top sculler in the winning Thames Cup squad during the previous year, but two weeks later in the Marlow Long Distance Sculls, I was regaining my fitness and was the fastest Leander sculler.

As I'd finished with motocross bikes, I sold the van and bought a red 1100cc Ford Escort Mk. 1, but as I wanted more power, I put a 1300 GT engine, which I bought cheaply into it and my power increased from 49 to 75 bhp. I was using my bike, the BSA 440, for transport while working on the car but was told on a Friday that I should start work at the BSA and Triumph research establishment eight miles to the south of Birmingham after the weekend.

The roads were icy on the Monday and at one point, the main road was closed due to an accident, I turned off into the country lanes and was glad of my motocross experience to stay upright on icy patches. At a T-junction, there was an old bloke (probably in his 40s or 50s) standing in the road next to his motorbike, which was on its side.

My bike suddenly skated out from under me and, rotating slowly on the ground on our side as we slid along, my rear light smashed into the kerb, no problem, there were plenty more rear lights in the factory. It was definitely a good crash and something to celebrate, so I jumped up and shouted, "SNAP," at the guy who was still faffing about. He wasn't amused.

I got going and turned carefully onto a main road but was a bit lost and it was getting late. The warm sun was beaming down on the straight road and I went flat-out and was loving the sound of the big single.

All of a sudden I'm floating, that's odd
no grip to be had, none
sheet ice, 'black ice', no connection at all
the steering is light and free
all senses alive, I close the throttle
the engine's roar dies
the back wheel's *stopping*. Oh God that's worse
clutch in, focusing hard
attention fixed in slow-motion time
my speed is dying, but *ages*
before my wheels are linked to the road
good one, no crash this time
Epic, I dunnit, wahey. No drama, it's business as usual. Ha.

Brother Steve had joined the navy and was stationed near Helston in Cornwall, he and his wife Terri were living nearby and at Christmas, I was with them along with all the family including Grandfather. The pressures of training were off me and my mood had crashed, I was trying hard to be OK but one evening, the *Towering Inferno* was on TV.

Suddenly, I was overcome with the misery of it all and had to get out. I stood up and with an outburst of, "HAPPY, HAPPY, HAPPY," I walked out. Shame on me, but that was the only time I let go in front of the family. I went outside and sat on a low wall, with padding in my brain, stress, confusion and self-loathing.

I stayed at Bucknall's on the way back, it was a boost to see him and to get to the Ashen Faggot for a drink, I always felt good with Bucknall. We'd gone on the tractor for a change and after a couple of beers, Bucknall suggested that I join him in his agricultural contracting business, which he ran.

Things were improving fast, the beer, another bunch of good lads, a possible job/career in front of me, and yes, there was a *lot* going for Bucknall's way of life. I was very interested.

Bucknall said it was my turn to drive the tractor back to the farm, only my second time driving it, bit pissed, dark, plenty of revs up the hill, a couple of screams, a shout of, "NOBBY," from me. We arrived at the farm. [SLOW, SLOWER. IT'S SERIOUSLY STEEP GOING DOWN.] But I did it, we were safe, to bed, and dreamless sleep.

While driving back to Haslemere, there was torrential rain, I drove fast, risk-taking, living on the edge. My tyres aquaplaned and the steering went light. I know now that I was daring fate to supply the loss of control and a mood-boosting, slow-motion challenge to save the day.

I would probably have survived a crash, but the risk was worth it to escape the hovering and terrible torments. It was irresponsible but I never did it with people around or with oncoming traffic.

The dipping mood and inner turmoil drove the risk-taking, and something usually drove the demons out, but failure meant trying another tactic or else giving in to the dreaded pit of low mood, and I sometimes had to do that. Occasionally, a risk led to a crash, but most crashes were great, slow-motion, every detail remembered. Epic, yes, even though sometimes, it hurt.

Bikes and cars don't REALLY matter
repair or replace them, that's what we do
It's the *risks* which *matter,* the spice of life
take them, enjoy them, it's *great* to feel *good.*

Now, thank the good Lord *again* that I never injured anyone on the roads.

Early in 1970, my commitments to Leander and the BSA were complete. Adrenaline, endorphins, dopamine, serotonin, all these hormones combined into a cocktail of 'feel good', which was my fuel for getting by. The rowing and sculling were superb, they were busy days, and for most of the time, I was genuinely happy, hyped up and giving off all sorts of good vibes.

If my behaviour was extrovert, it was perhaps a sign of exuberance and high mood, but if my mood was low or falling, then being outrageous/ridiculous in company could save the mood/moment. My behaviour was similar, whether I was high or low, and I think it unlikely that at any moment, people would have known whether I was having a great time and being exuberant or in fact, fighting off the low.

The brain is very sensitive to the pain of depression and to the early-warnings of low mood, and my experience is that when depression is coming in social situations, surprise or humour often saves the moment. A small mental warning called for a small surprise, the stronger early-warnings of doom called for bigger/better actions and when the mood plummeted, then being ridiculous or outrageous could still save the day.

Occasionally, nothing worked and my mood fell very flat, then there was the need to put on a brave face and pretend that everything was fine. I refer to that as acting, it can be so hard, it's exhausting, and along with experiencing fear, pain and upset, these contribute to being irritable, bad tempered and angry.

Of course, both the celebrations of good mood and especially the more desperate attempts to reclaim mood give the sufferer a reputation, whether it be admiration or 'he's just attention seeking'. Any of these actions could be inappropriate but two or three people have generously said quite recently, "It's just how you were."

[A BIT NUTS, YES, I KNOW.]

When moods fluctuate quickly, which they can, or when there are 'mixed moods'‡, actions can be particularly unpredictable. That's often when there is mental torment, stress and inability to cope. Difficulties can be experienced in many different ways, whether it's dealing with people, with a working life or simply with coping at home.

The First Eight which Derek and Donald put together had Jock Mullard at five, me at six, and the others had been in the latest Thames Cup winning crew. There'd been too many oarsmen named John in the 1969 squad, a nick-name had been needed and Donald had said to one, "Your name. Yallop. Stupid name. Wollop, WOL."

So that was that, and I would row with Wol almost all of the time till Montreal 1976. Our second eight were fiercely competitive and they pushed us hard. We were all pushing, and morale was high.

We came third in the eight in the Tideway HOR for the second year running behind both of the Tideway Scullers Eights, this was understandable considering our age against their experience and strength. Our coxswain was Jeff Easton who had been cox of the winning Thames Cup eight during the previous summer.

---

‡ See Glossary

He took control of us with authority and good sense and when he called an order, there was never any doubt about what was to be done, he coached us when necessary, all of his calls were useful and he steered us well, so we knew we were safe. These were some of the hallmarks of a good cox and if anyone thinks that the small person in the stern just steers the boat while shouting any old stuff, they are so wrong.

After training on a Sunday, I occasionally went home to see the family who had moved from Haslemere to Epsom. One Sunday, I was on the BSA 440 behind a car and while pulling out of a right-hand bend, accelerating to overtake, my back tyre slid away on the white line sideways towards the car.

Full lock to correct the slide, the back end then went to the right, then left again. Out of the corner of my eye, just feet away, I could see a face staring out of the back window of the car, my bike straightened up, an adrenaline rush for me and I accelerated away. That was a first on tarmac.

Our busy summer in the eight training for the Grand Challenge Cup at Henley included a trip abroad to two European regattas. At Henley in our semi-final in the Grand Challenge Cup, we led Aegir, the Dutch students for most of the way, but they were strong and they caught us before the end. The Dutch Olympic Eight for Munich two years later was based on that crew.

Off the start at Henley against Aegir, the Dutch students. Vic Pardhy our bow man, Phil Angier, Dickie Clarke, John Yallop (Wol), Jock Mullard, Me, Glyn Locke, Jon Pemberton at stroke. Jeff Easton coxing.

That 1970 season was sunny and fun, our crew morale was superb throughout, we'd aimed high but won almost nothing, and it was the most enjoyable rowing season I've ever had.

Our second eight won the Thames Cup, which made three Leander Thames Cup wins in a row. 1968, 1969, and 1970 and the name 'cadets' had been dropped by the Press as Leander crews had re-established themselves as a force to be reckoned with.

Donald Legget had carried the Leander Cadets for nine years up to that point and his huge personal effort helped so many people including myself. Six years later, the three oarsmen in the stern of the 1976 silver medal GB Olympic eight were from the 1968/69/70 Leander Cadet crews, one man from each of those eights.

Christopher Woodhouse, and later Professor Christopher Woodhouse FRCS, the cox from the first two Leander Cadet eights told me that from the beginning of the Cadet Scheme, Donald was in charge and that although others contributed, he considered Donald to have been the driving force which lifted Leander Club to the world-class position it holds today.

And I credit Donald, as the captain of Leander, to have contributed a huge amount to the resurgence of British rowing.

But Derek Drury, family man, schoolmaster at Shiplake College, and housemaster with many responsibilities, was the figure who injected charisma and the methods he'd used at Emanuel School into Leander. He insisted that a fleet of sculling boats was made available so that each person was individually challenged to raise their game on the water. Leander Club was run down at that time and there was no money, but somehow it was done, and Derek came when he could to help coach the eights.

Donald was working full-time, miles away, but he did the donkey-work and coaching every weekend at Leander, year after year. His personal effort was huge.

Chapter 18
'The Grand' Again

The Weybridge Silver Sculls came not long after we'd started at Leander again during September 1970. I was on form and racing well and won it by twenty-two seconds. A few weeks later at the Marlow Long Distance Sculls, I won by sixteen seconds over Pat Delafield who had just come back from the World Championships and had finished tenth in our GB double scull. I was unaware that my sculling was of that standard, I didn't even know he'd competed in the World Championships, as I was much too busy *doing stuff* to follow other competitions.

After the race, Pat Delafield and I met in the Marlow RC bar, he was confident and outgoing, offered me a drink and was much amused when I asked for two pints of bitter, he said that I was his kind of man! After a while, Pat suggested that we should get together in a double for the Olympics in Munich, two years away, I was honoured but brushed it off gently. I couldn't look that far ahead; for me, the future was a foreign country, everything was uncertain there.

One Sunday morning at Leander, we heard the terrible news that Jon Pemberton, the stroke man from our eight, had been knocked off his Triumph motorbike and had sustained serious injuries to his left leg.

Before Christmas, I had an accident in my Ford Escort on a busy junction in Birmingham and the car went to be fixed. I used my trusty old AJS which by then had no sidecar, but a few days later, the crankshaft broke after years of abuse.

I had to get to Leander for the weekend and borrowed my flat-mate Steve's BSA B31, an old touring 350 classic bike. Riding to Leander on the Sunday morning after staying at home in Haslemere, I slid off it on a damp road; I parted company with the bike and slid along the road backwards on my backside, leaning back on my rucksack which had an electric iron in it. No problem! Luckily, there was very little damage to the bike but when I returned it was embarrassed and sorry.

For the following weekend, I borrowed an old Triumph T21 motorbike, like the lovely Triumph twin my dad had owned, from one of my apprentice mates. On that particular bike the back brake was vicious and the front brake did nothing, and when riding into a bend on the BSA test track fast during Friday lunch-time, one of the workers from the factory walked in front of me. He'd come out of the factory over the Grand Union Canal bridge, and walked across from the steps without looking. I braked and went sideways with a howling rear tyre, there was a brick building ahead and I held onto the big slide on tarmac, the bike straightened up, wobbled badly, and I was shocked as I'd been lucky.

The BSA factory and the Grand Union Canal foot-bridge.

The photo shows rough country where motocross bikes could be tested, and behind the railing on the right was the BSA road test circuit and the canal. We used the canal bridge daily in and out of the factory and parked our vehicles nearby.

After work, having had a near-miss at lunchtime, but riding south to Leander, I was enjoying my ride, but almost lost control of the bike on a fast bend. The rear tyre had a puncture but when I took the back wheel out to fix it, one of the wheel nuts was not just loose, but undone by about two turns.

I'd been lucky again but at the time, didn't think about it, my mood was hyper and I was pushing the limits of everything. If ever I felt my mood slipping, I had my bag of old tricks and strategies to save the day, which helped me out often.

A four-wheeled vehicle was needed for the 1970 Christmas period, I borrowed my old van back and after a party in Cobham, I skidded on packed snow, slid sideways over a high granite kerb and crashed head-on into a tree.

There weren't any seat belts in those days, the van's engine was shunted back, the body shell was distorted, which jammed my driver's door, the high kerb had blown out one front tyre and had pulled the other front wheel and brake drum off. I never found that wheel, it had rolled of down the road to an unknown destination.

My knees dented the metal parcel shelf on each side, my chest broke one of the two sturdy spokes of the steering wheel but luckily, my head was cushioned by hitting the flexible steering wheel. I was bruised but had escaped serious injury and my friends heard in the pub next day, "Have you seen that van crashed in Mizen Way? Bloke must have been killed." My knees and chest hurt but I was rowing and sculling as usual four days later.

The line-up in the First Eight in March 1971 was a little different from the previous year and our result in the Tideway HOR was third place for the third year running behind both of the Tideway Scullers Eights. Our race time was only five seconds slower than the winners, however, in a race of over four and a quarter miles.

When things were good for me, I could be that extreme hyper-manic extrovert, this rubbed off on others, and two or three of the Leander men have indicated that I added another dimension to those days. They all knew that I could be irritable, and one day in the club room, I picked up one of those huge old-fashioned upholstered chairs with a castor wheel on each corner and threw it.

Nick Aitcheson fended the missile off with a laugh, we all laughed as it was ridiculous. I hear stories about myself occasionally, typically they start, "I like the one about," followed by something like "when you threw your oar away when rowing a pair," which I didn't, or something else which often had an element of truth in it, but exaggeration too.

I did stuff, yes, different things done in a variety of moods. Low moods and 'mixed moods' could cause frustration, anger or mental exhaustion, and hyper-mania could result in exuberance and high spirits. It really wasn't clear what caused my actions at times but of course, unpredictable behaviour gave me a reputation.

Around Easter time in 1971, we heard that the ARA (Amateur Rowing Association, the sport's administrative body) would be starting a National Rowing Squad*§ in the autumn to form a stronger team for international competition. It was about sixteen months until the 1972 Munich Olympics, but as usual I was living very much in the moment as I couldn't plan far ahead, and the idea of trying for the Olympics hadn't been on my radar at all. I was limited by trying to get by from day to day.

The results of the 1970 World Rowing Championships held in Canada were typical of those times, GB came tenth in the table of countries attending. Great Britain had given the sport of rowing to the world but we had become a weak participant and had a lot of catching up to do.

During the early 1970s, the strongest clubs in the country were the University of London, Tideway Sculling School at Putney, Leander Club at Henley, the Thames Tradesmens RC at Chiswick. Members from these and other clubs would join forces in the National Rowing Squad to produce British crews, which it was hoped would be stronger than any crew an individual club could produce and thus more competitive on the international scene.

*

In my spare time, I'd been rebuilding my AJS 500 in the cellar at our flat, each of us rebuilt our bikes and when a newly rebuilt engine was started for the first time, it was always good. The big single roar in a closed room was a resounding racket, and always smoky on the first start-up, and I gave mine some stick. Smoke, a very big noise and three blokes laughing, yes.

I couldn't complain, I had a good job with a good bunch of mates and had superb Leander weekends. I was living the dream while knowing subconsciously that I was on a knife edge, but was *loving it*. The awful truth came to me that I might fail my HNC exams (Higher National Certificate) in Mechanical Engineering, and therefore, might be delayed in going back to the London area. The plan to row in the National Squad working towards the Munich Olympics seemed by then a real possibility.

---

§ See Glossary

For the first time in my life, I was highly motivated to pass my exams and found myself able to commit to revision, but there were only seven weeks before the exams. I found twenty-three hours of free time during my busy weekly schedule and made copies of my Monday to Sunday free-time chart.

Topics to be revised were allocated to time slots on particular dates. I was totally focused while riding the wave of commitment to all my activities and rushing from one thing to another.

Life was good, wonderful, in fact. I was even enjoying revising while sitting on the side of a bed in Henley between training sessions, as well as early in the mornings before work in Birmingham. I passed my exams and applied to the University of Surrey to read mechanical engineering.

My autumn, later that year in 1971, was all worked out. I was to be a university student while rowing in the brand new National Squad. My Ford Escort was driven hard always and was a joy to drive, particularly after I'd fitted a brake servo in the engine compartment, which meant that it could now stop as well as go.

I found a differential from a 1300 GT Escort on a scrap yard for £4, and when fitted, I could drive down Bix Hill towards the Fairmile and Henley at well over 100mph without the rattle of valve bounce under the bonnet. My Escort looked like a standard 1100cc De Luxe model, and on one occasion, having blown off a noisy, souped up and lowered De Luxe Escort at some lights in Solihull, two boy racers looked puzzled when they, (four inches lower), eased up beside me at the next traffic lights.

We were training in the eight for the Grand Challenge Cup at Henley for the second year running. The Tideway Scullers eight had beaten us in ARA trials earlier in the season, so they would row for GB in the European Championships but a brand new wooden boat, a pair, arrived at Leander from Stampfli, the world renowned boat builders of Switzerland.

Glyn Locke and I from our eight were to row this boat but were to race in the eight as well at the Henley Regatta. Donald Legget and Glyn had rigged the boat so that I'd steer it from the stroke seat (without asking me of course), but it is best steered by stroke on straight courses as you don't have to look where you're going, you just point the stern straight down the course.

During our first race in the pair at Henley against Summers and Hart from Cambridge University, we dominated from the start, but after taking the rating down, we were hard-pressed. We won the race but it was seriously heavy-going.

Mike Hart went on later to scull with Chris Baillieu in the double to win a string of World Championship medals and the Olympic Silver in Montreal 1976. After our race at Henley Glyn had it all worked out that we should always keep our rating at 34 strokes per minute or above.

That worked, and from there on, we won races comfortably including the final of the pairs event. Later that day in the final of the 'Grand' in the eight, we led our arch rivals, the Tideway Scullers, to the mile post, but after a fine scrap, they won by half a length. They had always beaten us, but never by much. We were young and as keen as mustard, but they were older, stronger and more experienced.

PHOTO. Glyn and I in the pair winning the final at Henley Regatta 1971.

Surrey University offered me a place to study mechanical engineering, which I accepted, and around that time, I didn't see Bucknall at all as I was too involved in the rowing, but at some stage when I was particularly agitated, I wrote a letter to him.

A week or two later when speaking to him on the phone, he was upset that he hadn't been able to read my handwriting. I must have been in a bad state with very shaky hands, but the fact that I'd done that without realising it was a shock to me.

Five days, on Friday after Henley Regatta, Glyn and I arrived at Lucerne in Switzerland in bright sunshine to race the pair on the eight lane rowing course on a beautiful natural lake, the Rotsee. Cattle graze on the lower mountain slopes and the continuous clanking of their cowbells is the gentle soundscape.

The Rotsee near Lucerne.

On Saturday, we qualified for the semi-final, and on Sunday morning in the second race of the day at 7:03, with the sun just above the water and shining straight into my eyes, we qualified for the final. During the afternoon in the final Slusarski and Broniec the Poles, and Klatt and Gorny from East Germany finished first and second, they'd won silver and gold respectively in the previous year's World Championships.

We had a spirited row, came in a group not far behind and were pleased with our fifth position in that company. The ARA selected us to row the pair for Great Britain in the European Championships, which were open to the world, to be held in Copenhagen six weeks later. It felt good to have arrived rather suddenly on the international rowing scene.

Chapter 19
Mood Crash

On the following morning, Monday, at work at the BSA research establishment in the country, I felt awful, I'd never experienced such a sudden and extreme mood collapse. I wasn't ill physically but was exhausted and had to push my acting skills very hard to be Tim Crooks, that successful sportsman who had been named in the national newspapers that day as one of the British Rowing Team.

When Glyn and I met at Leander on Friday evening to start our last five weeks training before the European Championships, the club was dead, with no atmosphere at all.

Everyone else had finished for the season.

All the excitement was over.

We'd raced our hearts out in every race.

[THAT'S WHAT YOU DO, ISN'T IT? WHEN SOMEONE SAYS 'GO', YOU RACE YOUR HEART OUT.]

I could feel little motivation for the training and we struggled to find our form again, I was all used up and Glyn has said more recently that he 'was off' too, I had no understanding of how to peak for a championship event.

Although I was feeling weak, confused and terrible, the training always worked a short-term kind of magic, it picked me up enough when we went on the water, so that I could do the training. I didn't sparkle, I never felt unbeatable, but I did enjoy it.

It was absolutely the only thing that I did enjoy at that time, and my feelings of well-being after training would last typically for an hour or two before I felt bad again. I was devastated by the dreadful feelings in my head during that period and I hated pretending that I was OK. Little did I know how long those feelings were to continue.

The 1971 European Championships were held on Lake Bagsvaerd outside Copenhagen. Our team management told us to race every race flat out to make sure that we qualified for the next round, and to earn the best lane for our next race.

In our heat, we were neck and neck with Slusarski and Broniec up to 1,400 metres but they pulled ahead gradually to finish half a length up. We'd qualified for the semi-finals but had rowed very hard, and as we'd performed well, the press wrote us up as potential finalists if not medallists.

In our semi-final, we couldn't find our form and didn't qualify for the Grand Final (for places one to six) and on finals day, we finished second in tailwind conditions and rolling waves in the 'Petite Finale' (for places seven to twelve), which placed us eighth overall. The Thames Tradesmen four also came eighth in their event and our two boats were placed highest in the British team.

The end of the season is known by many to be the time of 'Post-Championship Blues'. The anti-climax is only natural but my form had dropped disastrously some weeks before the championships. My strategy to maintain mood had always been to do more, but the reality was that 'more' could not be done at that time. This awful mental event had been beyond my control.

Don't ever tell a seriously depressed person to 'get a grip' or 'snap out of it'. Just don't. During September 1971, my apprenticeship had finished, and I lived briefly in Epsom with the family before starting at Surrey University.

They hadn't seen much of me over the years, I'd been rushing, never keeping still for long. Mum wasn't well and was battling depression courageously in a huge effort to be the same loving Mum to the young ones.

No one spoke about mental illness but I could see the signs of her suffering, and increasingly, her drinking and smoking. She and I had a strong background of love but no in-depth communication, we each carried our secret and there was a divide between us which was to grow thicker with time.

I found myself years later saying that I lost my Mum ten years before she died. Cigarettes and alcohol denied her reaching her allotted time of three score years and ten.

My university degree course represented a significant challenge to me, I was to start only a few days before the National Rowing Squad was to begin. These unrealistic plans had been made during the summer season while I was hyper-manic, I'd imagined that I could conquer the world and had felt that I could do *anything*.

It was a busy scene at Surrey University just outside Guildford with so many happy boys and girls, all younger than me, moving into lodgings. I was seriously depressed and felt drugged, just pushing on with what had to be done. Within a few days, the National Rowing Squad began and just for that weekend, it was based at Leander at Henley for the whole squad. Glyn and I were at home at Henley and were the fastest pair.

Serious conflicts soon arose for me, the engineering work was too difficult because of the depression, and it demanded commitment, which I couldn't give. I was obsessive with the training but was isolated and lonely. There was chemistry between myself and one or two of the girls at university but my low self-esteem and busy life put paid to any of that.

I was very badly messed up and getting worse, but couldn't share my difficulties with anyone. Then, sleep evaded me. One night in my brick built student lodgings in complete desperation, I tried three times to knock myself out on the solid wall above my bed; it didn't work.

A visit to a doctor wasn't helpful in getting to the bottom of my troubles, but I came away with a prescription for Valium (Diazepam) and Mogadon sleeping pills. One of each to be taken before bed. I slept.

The ARA training weekends were held about once per month in different locations. There was one in London on the Tideway, another at the Nottingham course, and on the intervening weekends, we trained from our home clubs. From Christmas onwards, all of the monthly training weekends were held at Nottingham where crew assessments could be done properly on the six lane 2,000 metre course, although bad weather made it unpopular.

During the Nottingham weekends, all of the boats, whether single scullers, double scullers* or pairs, did the same workout during our outings on the water. We carried out low rating training, 3 x 2,000 metres, or 3 x 1,000 metres, turning between each, lining up and going straight off with no real rest, each piece of training became a race, but at the controlled rating of twenty-four strokes per minute.

*

My normal subconscious method to improve my state of mind was to challenge myself further. The possibility of single sculling within the National Rowing Squad presented itself, but the prospect of taking on any more pressure at that time should have been out of the question. I could continue rowing in the pair or take on the challenge of single sculling.

I told Glyn that I was going sculling and I could see his disappointment, he had to find a new pair partner. Since the psychology of my situation has been revealed to me, I can say that if I hadn't done the sculling, I would have almost certainly have been immobilised mentally in some way. Breaking down wasn't an option. I simply had to challenge myself more and push harder.

In the sculling boat, I found myself pitched against Kenny Dwan, our GB single sculler from previous years and Pat Delafield, the Cambridge man who I'd raced before. The weekends were intensive and all the times were recorded, I was holding my own in the single scull and more often than not, Pat or myself were a little ahead of Kenny.

Glyn Locke, my pair partner, lived for rowing and sculling, he and I were good friends, we never had a cross word and generously, he's written, 'Anybody who has had the privilege of rowing with Tim will know that there was no one more committed to winning and you could rest assured he would give it his all—and more. He was the truest and most cheerful man to accompany you into battle and for me, it remains a huge honour to have raced with Tim'.

Christmas came and went and it was difficult for me and for Mum, but for the family's sake, we had a good go at it, but the two of us were lonely with our thoughts. At university, I was falling steadily behind in my studies, I'd found a girl but the relationship never went anywhere as I was up against everything.

Suddenly, I knew I couldn't go on, I was too far behind with my studies, I'd been living in denial and having spoken briefly with my parents, I discontinued the engineering course and lived at home while concentrating on the training.

On midweek evenings, I did the weights and circuit training at Guildford and at the weekends, stayed over at Leander but had minimal contact with the younger Leander oarsmen. In theory, I could have increased my training as I wasn't working, but it was all I could do to keep to the regime that I knew.

I was hanging on, went to see a doctor and came away with antidepressants 'for depression', but with no real understanding of what I was up against. My world shrank and during my midweek days at the vicarage in Epsom, I wasn't well occupied.

I walked around the shops in Epsom regularly, Mum had opened an account for me with a butcher and I went to buy food for my suppers after training. In Epsom, I shared footpaths and spaces with others but felt isolated in some sort of parallel world.

Aside from living in Epsom and training, there was nothing, and to see all my old friends in Cobham only eight miles away was too difficult as I had to avoid social contact. I'd have found it impossible to convince my old friends that I was alright.

My training routine varied little and my low mood during the days at home were always picked up by the magic of training where I could perform. Having driven fast to Leander for training, I was OK, people looked up to me, that helped, and after training, the depression sometimes stayed away till bedtime.

Every morning, I woke up feeling awful, and with huge uncertainties about my future, my mind had too much time to explore dark caves and caverns. Long-term plans didn't exist. Competing at the Olympics seemed uncertain, but it was the only thing I had.

I wasn't really excited by it, it seemed to be an end point with nothing beyond, and as far as earning a living was concerned, there was no plan at all. Tragedy and fear had their place in my mind.

During January, we were briefed by the national coach, Bohumil (Bob) Janousek, that the team to be selected for the Munich Games would consist of 'small boats', so there was no intention of forming an Olympic eight. The weather was cold and with the prevailing wind on the course at Nottingham being against us, we did our thing as usual on those weekends.

You have to give it to Bob and his team of ARA selectors, with stop-watches and clip-boards, they weren't keeping warm like we were. We raced on the water at controlled low ratings on each of the nine timed pieces over the weekend and those training pieces/races were closely fought, timed and logged.

As a single sculler, I could have teamed up with others to travel to Nottingham but couldn't face the social contact. Driving fast on my own had its uses in that I arrived at the rowing course very much stimulated, buzzing, on-form and ready to go.

'Bob' Janousek, Chief National Coach.

During the January weekend at Nottingham, Pat was narrowly the fastest sculler overall, but in February, I was. At the beginning of March, Kenny came out narrowly on top and before we went home, we were told by the ARA team selectors that Kenny would be the Olympic single sculler and Pat and I would be in the double scull.

We were released by the ARA for three weeks to train and compete in our club eights in the Tideway HOR. In the race, we, the Leander crew, came third *again* for the fourth year running behind the two Tideway Scullers Eights.

Leander, third for the fourth consecutive year in 1972

Chapter 20
Towards Munich 1972

Pat and I made arrangements to train in the double from Kingston RC, which is on one of the best stretches of the Thames, and was about half way between our two homes. The ARA provided us with a new Stampfli boat and Ayling's sculls and at the beginning, Pat sat in the stroke seat, but I suggested we swap round and it went a little better that way. He always called me Timothy, so from that time onwards, he was Patrick.

The training on the river was very good and my demons were banished by the hormone rush on the water, daily, but only temporarily on each occasion.

At Nottingham one weekend, the headwind on the course was blowing at about 25 mph, which made the training on the course impossible, we carried the boats by hand across to the river Trent and wasted time in rough water there. After the blowy morning and a bite to eat, Patrick said that the planned three times 2000m on the course during the afternoon was simply not going to happen, he was going to a pub.

Willy Almand from the Tideway Scullers four and I joined him and we found the Reindeer Pub at East Bridgford. Patrick bought three beers and when he turned round to say 'cheers' to me, he was amused to see that my glass was empty, he got me a refill, which only lasted about four seconds. Willy downed his pint and he got another round in.

A little while later, it was my round, so by the time we got back to the course, I'd had four, but on arrival, we were dismayed to see the others getting their boats out. We learnt that 'the work' was three times 1000m, all of them to be on the course and with the strong wind. Oh, alright then, bit pissed but here we go. Those pieces went surprisingly well in the rough water. Never gone so fast.

Our first regatta at Mannheim was in a dock off the Rhine with vertical concrete sides and warehouses down one side, but on our side were cranes, gantries and railway lines as well as the boathouses.

We were billeted at the Bundeswehr Army Camp and Kenny Dwan come out of lunch on the first day, saying, "You wanna watch the cabbage. It's not what yer reckon." He'd been surprised by sauerkraut. The cutlery had the German Eagle stamped on it and I kept a few pieces for myself, which was justified because of the war.

The weekend regatta was run as two separate one day regattas, Patrick and I dominated the double sculls events on both days and the German official who gave us our medals on the second day said, "You mark my vords, you guys vill go a long vay."

Patrick and I in the double.

Two weeks later at Ratzeburg, we broke the course record in both of our races on day one and finished three lengths clear of the West Germans. On day two, we led early on but were caught by the Norwegians, Hansen and Thorgersen, the silver medallists from the previous year's European Championships, the Russians were two lengths behind us.

At Amsterdam regatta, we were caught again on both days by the Norwegian double, but had by then established ourselves as a force to be reckoned with. Typically, I was feeling depressed and weak, but just before training or racing, my hormones picked me up and allowed me to perform.

Life in Epsom was hard but at least I came away from each evening training session feeling good, I ate well and was drugged to sleep. During the days, I fixed up an old valve amplifier into a small oak cabinet and was in a small world of copying pop music from the radio onto cassette tapes as well as playing the piano.

There was padding in my head and I was fighting a defensive battle against all that. On the face of it, for those in the rowing world, I was having a wonderful time boating in the sunshine and winning races, we won the double sculls event at Henley and went on to win the doubles event at Lucerne. The Norwegians, who had beaten us previously, weren't there and we were challenged late in the race by Korshikov and Balenkov, another Russian double. My legs were seizing up and the only way I could hold them off was to shorten up and go for it. We won, but afterwards, Patrick complained about my rating of forty at the finish, which had done the trick!

The East Germans came in sixth place, almost three lengths down, and we were told that we had been selected to represent GB at the Olympic Games, to be held in Munich seven weeks later. I didn't feel joy or satisfaction, my feelings were dead, long gone. Joy didn't exist in my world.

The high intensity training continued at Kingston with Donald Legget coaching us but it didn't seem long before we in the rowing team went to St Moritz in Switzerland for altitude training prior to travelling to Munich. Bob Janousek took over coaching us from Donald, he was a man of few words, quietly efficient but socially easy-going, not that he opened up with us at that time.

Short of oxygen at St Moritz. Altitude training.

The first high pressure training row started well but after about a minute, the lack of oxygen hit us but we pushed hard in the rarefied air, and trained for two and a half weeks in those beautiful surroundings. Having pretended to be OK for a year, this was more of the same, and I tried again to do without the Diazepam and Mogodon pills before bed, but gave up on that.

We travelled to Munich by coach and were shown to apartments in the Olympic Village, which were all brand new. I was to sleep in the same room as the Thames Tradesmen coxless four, two of whom I'd met five years previously when we were all Juniors, they were good value, and amusing, often. Little did I know that I'd row with all four of them two years later in the GB eight.

The Tradesmen four after winning their National Championship event at Nottingham.

Enjoying a moment at Munich before racing. Lenny, Jim, Fred and Bill

There was speculation in the Press that we, the rowing team, had been overtrained; however, at a team meeting, our coaches were given support by team members. Another issue was that we were told again to race all of our races flat-out to avoid being knocked out and to earn a better lane for the next race.

My Dad came to Munich as a spectator, he was brought, without a pass, into the Olympic Village by Donald Legget in the Land Rover and was fuelled with strong gin and tonics. Dad must have been concerned about my well-being overall, he was good at meeting up with young women and he introduced me to some German girls who were working at the rowing course as 'Olympic Hostesses'. I met up with two of them later.

'Olympic Hostesses'.

Dad and myself

When it came to the racing, Patrick and I won our heat comfortably, beating the East Germans and qualifying directly for the semi-finals and the Press wrote us up as medal prospects. We raced flat out again in our semi-final but were beaten into second place by the East Germans although we could have qualified comfortably by keeping ahead of the fourth boat.

On the day of the final, there was a cross headwind, which favoured the crews on the other side of the course but on the start, Patrick and I shared a few words of encouragement before setting off fast. Too fast.

We led for 750 metres but our pace was hot into the headwind and we'd given our all in every other race. We gradually slowed, allowing the Russians past, then the East Germans, followed by the Norwegians, we were even pressed by the Danes towards the end of the race. We were unable to hold them off and finished in fifth position.

It was all over, I was crushed and broken as we paddled light to the landing stage. We turned the boat and a photo shows my happy smile, pretending again. The long build-up had taken me through a most difficult year and had dumped me in a particularly crappy place.

After the final. Feeling terrible, but...

Chapter 21
Germany

The mental crash after the final was frightening, I felt humiliated, guilty and ashamed. These things were not spoken about because Olympic athletes were considered to have supreme strength, any confessions of mental difficulty were a failing.

We had the second week of the Olympics in the Village free to do as we liked. Our meals and accommodation were provided, as well as entry into all sports venues, what more could we ask. All I wanted was relief from the dreadful forces in my brain.

The challenges of training and racing had only just kept me afloat mentally but with the challenge removed, my demons moved in, I couldn't engage with others and I laid on my bed in the Olympic Village. The weather was good, it was an idyllic scene with young and beautiful people but I hardly saw anything. When I did force myself outside, I bought cups of tea, there were plenty of benches to sit on but they were all the same.

On the day after the rowing finals, Monday evening, I went to watch a film in the village cinema and within hours, very early on Tuesday morning, eight masked members of the Black September Organisation entered the Olympic Village. These terrorists were dedicated to the Palestinian cause to the overthrow of King Hussein of Jordan, they killed two of the Israeli team who resisted and took nine hostages.

The day's events are well documented elsewhere but suffice it to say that their demand for the release of two hundred and thirty-four Palestinians and non-Arabs was not met. In the end, the nine hostages were killed, making a total of eleven of the Israeli team, as well as one German policeman and five of the terrorists.

I walked to the cafeteria for breakfast and there were soldiers and police on the corners. I saw the beautiful Israeli athlete I'd talked to a few days earlier, sitting in tears, being comforted by her friends and one of my team-mates said, "Isn't it awful?"

"What?" I asked.

"Don't you KNOW?"

This day tore the heart out of the games, I'd seen the Germans giving of themselves in an effort to make everything a success, I was shocked and outraged by the events, as everyone was.

There was plenty of sport to watch but couldn't cope with the emotions of it all. I kept to myself but I'd read that there were activities organised for athletes who were no longer competing. I needed distractions.

The girl at the enquiries desk booked me to go to a party on a farm and on another evening to go to a free dinner party at a hotel. At the farm, by chance, I met up with one of the Olympic hostesses I knew from the rowing course, and at the end of the evening we shared a kiss and she gave me her address in Germany.

I took another Olympic hostess I'd met, to a free dinner party, we enjoyed our evening with a fit young crowd, I didn't try anything amorous but came away with her home address.

I went to see the enquiries girl in the Olympic Village again, and asked her whether there were any other activities I could go to. We talked for a while, I told her what had happened in our final, she arranged for me to go sailing and a family took me out on their beautiful yacht.

The father was one of the directors of BMW and he sailed his boat well in the sun and a stiff breeze. It was a real effort to pretend to be OK, there was serious chemistry between the older daughter and myself, but nothing could rescue my mood.

None of us talked much, certainly not about my sport, there was the language difficulty but I decided they'd been told I was depressed. The mother had looked into my eyes and seemed anxious for me.

On Sunday evening, the closing ceremony in the stadium was packed with happy athletes, I was there but couldn't enjoy the fun. I wanted to escape, needed to get away from there. At the end on the big screen were the words: SEE YOU IN MONTREAL. For a brief moment, I saw a chink of light, amusement really, but my reality was a black void.

Back home in Epsom, my parents must have seen how I was, I had no plans and no social life because I couldn't face anyone. I was told many times how good fifth place was, but I felt a failure and my world was the most dreadful and darkest place.

Three weeks later, I knew what I had to do. I had addresses in Germany and I decided to see one of the girls, my plan was to work there, to learn the language and to be with her. There was nothing else, so I packed up my car, caught an overnight ferry and arrived on her doorstep at 8 in the morning near Frankfurt.

She was surprised to see me, apologising that she was already late for her teaching job, she showed me her fridge and told me to help myself, I wanted to throw my arms around her, I was so desolate and lost.

At the end of her day, we walked and talked about my plans. She said she'd try to help me get a job through her rowing contacts, and straight away, she made arrangements for me to stay at the Mainzer Ruder-verein, a rowing club in Mainz, not far away.

The club was by the Rhine and I was met by one of the members of the German Olympic eight who showed me to a small room where he and others had stayed rent-free previously. He apologised, saying that it was very damp, which it was.

The bedding was dirty and damp, I slept there but got laundry sorted out on the next day and after a few days a job had been found for me, I was to be a mechanic at Lustenberger Motoraad, a motorbike shop. I went back to England to await my written job offer and when it arrived I went to London to apply for a work permit.

Feeling unwell and weak on a tube train, underground, and then outside the German embassy, I wondered how I could achieve anything and then get home. I did do it, although I was asked twice if I was alright.

During the three-week wait for my visa, I borrowed a 'German Language Course', which consisted of a book and an audio tape, and I spent time learning German for an hour or two each day, which was a helpful therapy.

Finally, I set off for my room at the rowing club at Mainz, and on a Monday, having started my job it seemed promising, however there were two problems, the technical language, and I'd stupidly brought very few tools with me. I kept having to borrow from the other mechanics and after a few days, my brief was to take good engines out of crashed motorbikes.

The blood on some of the bikes wasn't great but I soon got the sack anyway. My Olympic story was useful at the labour exchange when I went in search of another job, and a position was found for me in the quality control department of Jena Glas.

The veteran oarsmen at the club were very sociable and many evenings were spent drinking beer at the Augustinerkeller in Mainz. The conversations in German were mostly beyond me, but some of the guys spoke a little English and they included me. On the other evenings, I went running beside the Rhine, which is huge compared with our little Thames.

One weekend, I was invited to a party by my Olympic hostess; afterwards I was sitting on a sofa with her, she took her clothes off, lay back across my lap and I caressed the length of her beautiful body. She became increasingly excited but I knew not to touch her forbidden territory. Suddenly, she got up and put her clothes on. That was the end of that. We didn't live in the same town and I didn't meet her again.

I stayed in Germany for three months, working for the glass company, and for a few weeks after work, I trained on a running track doing interval training with other oarsmen at Mainz University. Later on, I borrowed a sculling boat and trained in a harbour off the Rhine.

Before Christmas, I received a letter from Imperial College in London. Jon Pemberton, my Leander friend, our stroke man with the leg injury, was now back in training and he'd acted on my behalf and had helped get me a post as a research student in the Lubrication Laboratory in the mechanical engineering department.

I was to be a research student to run engine tests to study the lubrication of piston rings in diesel engines, which would suit me well. My knowledge of engines plus my HNC in Mechanical Engineering qualified me for the job, not to mention that Professor Cameron, in charge, was gathering oarsmen. I was glad that again, I had a promising future. This time in London when I got home.

My parents had put me in touch with a German family. The mother was one of the 'German girls' who'd looked after me when I was a little boy and she now had a family with her own teenage children. I spent Christmas Day with them, it should have been a good day but my brain wasn't good and despite trying hard I didn't enjoy it.

On New Year's Eve at the end of 1972, I went with the Mainzer Ruderverein rowing club veterans to a party at a log cabin in a forest owned by one of the guys. The lighting indoors was by candlelight, we spent most of the time outside round a bonfire and everyone had a lot to drink. At midnight, when we'd let the fireworks off and kissed all the girls, the place burned down.

Two American soldiers had joined us and when one of them went round the back for a pee, his mate thought he was inside the blazing cabin. The only way I could stop him from going into the flames 'to rescue Jack' was to restrain him and then to punch him hard. He had a sleep on the ground.

Back in Mainz one of the veterans from the rowing club asked me if I would like to stay rent-free in his flat. His girlfriend lived with him, it was an offer I couldn't refuse and it worked out well. It was apparent to them that I was lonely and they found a German girl, a sculling champion who had seen me performing during the Munich Games.

She came to visit us at the flat, it was a blind date for me but I hadn't been told in advance. When she came, I couldn't suddenly raise my game to enjoy meeting her. She stayed for a few minutes but my head was down. This was just one example of how friendly and helpful people were.

Chapter 22
The Lubrication Laboratory

During February 1973, it was time to catch the cross-channel ferry. I thought I'd be pleased to see the white cliffs as we approached Dover, and I was, but I felt no emotional lift. In Epsom, we were all pleased that I was safely home.

On my first day at Imperial College, my friend Jon showed me around. He introduced me to Professor Cameron who had gathered about thirty students, many of whom rowed, to study different aspects of lubrication. The professor had plans to get an eight together and to train alongside (challenge) both Oxford and Cambridge at different times during their training for the Boat Race.

Ours was to be the Lubrication Lab Eight and I was asked to register the 'Lubrication Laboratory Boat Club' through the ARA with the professor as the president and me as captain.

My project for the first few months was to modify a diesel engine, which was already set up in the engines lab to run tests on piston rings with different lubricants.

There was a girl who I met and wanted to be with, but she chose someone else because she said years later, "You seemed to have more problems than I could cope with at the time."

I wrote a letter to the other Olympic hostess who's address I had, we'd got on so well, I hoped that she'd be pleased to hear from me. I invited her to join our whole family on holiday for a week in Cornwall during August, thinking it unlikely to produce a result.

Some of my fellow students in the Lubrication Lab were in the National Squad and they were released for three weeks to row in the Tideway HOR. I wasn't in any squad but I was fit and ended up rowing in the six seat in the Leander eight.

Our start position was number three, having finished in third place for *four consecutive years*, behind the two Tideway Scullers Eights, but finally, we won the race. The photograph of an eight at the end of the first chapter is that crew.

Afterwards, I was invited by the ARA to join the National Squad but my primary aim at the time was to try and live a 'normal life', so I stayed out of it.

I moved into a house in Barnes near the river with two girls and Andy Bayles, who was a friend from the Lubrication Lab, but was also in the National Squad. I bought a second-hand Suzuki motorbike, a 550 cc three cylinder two-stroke, which I hoped might boost my mood, but it didn't. It was powerful and one day when I'd missed a gear I looked down at the rev counter to see the needle passing back down through 13,000revs.

It was possible to spin the back wheel when accelerating on wet roads at quite high speeds, which added to life's rich hype. Why, why, why? Some things just had to be done. Anything for a hype, I suppose.

There was me, trying to find a way to exist while leading a normal life and I wanted a girlfriend, 'wanted' so strongly, but I was still feeling crushed after my failures at university and in Munich. Girls were unobtainable.

I said something to one of my friends about wanting to meet somebody and he told me that there were girls around who liked me, but I knew it was me who had the problem. I couldn't relax with girls, there was a protective wall around my emotions and if I'd loosened up at all, there might have a breach and a flood, so the wall had to stay up.

One Friday evening, after a particularly long drinking session with my student friends, the last of us took our leave, having agreed that we'd all be OK getting home. My car was parked round the back of college but I couldn't possibly drive.

I set off for Barnes, walking/weaving my way back and while on Hammersmith bridge, steadying myself on the handrail, I was looking down at my dear friend, my most faithful friend, the river. While marvelling at her swirls and reflections, I was enjoying her company where I'd raced so many times and I became aware that she was inviting me in.

A massive force was encouraging me to fly to her, and realising with shock what was happening, I strode out across the bridge as best I could to get away. I walked the last mile to my bed in Barnes.

On another Friday night after rather too many drinks, I drove back to Barnes, but while driving, the nightmare in my head was so bad, I had to do something to escape the turmoil.

[WHAT'S WRONG, WHAT'S WRONG? ESCAPE, BUT HOW?]

I had to do something, it was all unbearable. Yes, visit Bucknall in Devon. Flat-out all the way, and where the A303 turns off the M3 to go west, there was a place where there was a space between the carriageways and no barrier.[SPIN THE STEERING WHEEL, FULL LOCK AT 80 MPH]

The urge came suddenly and powerfully. I fought it.

[DO IT, GO ON, EVERYTHING'S FUCKED ANYWAY, NOTHING MATTERS, JUST DO IT. ANYTHING TO ESCAPE THIS TERRIBLE TORTURE.]

The moment passed. I arrived at Bucknall's farm near Honiton. There were no cars, and no one answered the door. Having found an outhouse, I laid down on the concrete floor, didn't sleep much and drove back, dehydrated, early in the morning.

There were good days in the Lubrication Lab, there was plenty going on and at times, my mood lifted, but always temporarily. There was time for good social contact and fun as well as satisfying work, but a few times, I had repeats of an earlier experience where my mood collapsed suddenly when telling a story to a few people.

On those occasions I had to finish off, make an excuse and leave, the alternative was to stay and my friends would have asked what was wrong. It was too awful to try to explain, I couldn't explain, it was too upsetting, but with the knowledge I have now, if I'd broken down at that time, perhaps I could have been helped.

Chapter 23
Not All Bad

The only training I was doing was running and some regular hard swims in the Imperial College pool. One day, when I'd done my forty lengths, I looked up, there was a girl standing at the side of the pool, dressed in a bikini, she was beautiful with long hair and 'California curves'.
[OH MY WORD, OH MY.]

I went and spoke to her, she was quite little but lovely, we introduced ourselves and spoke for a minute or two. She told me her husband was doing a PhD at the university, they lived in a student flat and she swam quite often. I was bowled over, we saw each other at the pool again a couple of weeks later and she asked me what I was training for, I told her about my rowing and she invited me to supper with her husband.

We had a good evening but my feelings for her were too much, I was trying so hard to 'act normal'. The evening ended on a good note between us all but I never saw her again, didn't search her out. That episode had to be blocked or I was in danger of, danger of, *what*?

The force was strong and it was wrong on every level, the guilt about coming between a man and his wife, the guilt of the want and the yearning, but mixed with it was the ignorance about relationships with women.

Months later, I met the husband and his Ford Escort bonnet was up, he ran the engine and the bottom end bearings were shot and knocking, I took his engine out and rebuilt it for him for nothing, because I could. He was a good man and I liked him, he paid for the parts, was very grateful and wanted to pay more, but I asked him if his lady was alright.

"Yes, she's fine, thanks."

A Lubrication Lab, coxless four was planned to enter the British Universities Championships (BUSF) at Nottingham during May, the crew members were to be me plus three National Squad members. Peter Summers in the bow seat, me at two, then Andy Bayles and Jon Pemberton at stroke. On the water, it was most promising.

When our race day came, the other three weren't allowed the morning off squad training in Henley, but at about midday, we jumped into my Ford Escort along with Jon's girlfriend, Gail, and I drove us fast to Nottingham. The others were a bit worn by their morning squad training, we were rather late, and on the way we laughed when we saw a foot stretcher (out of a boat) lying in the road, but it was one of ours. We were lucky at the regatta as a boatman had been employed there, and he fixed up a temporary steering stretcher for Peter who had trouble with the steering on the way to the start. We were rather late, and Peter told us to shout which way he should steer if we went off.

We didn't row well, someone shouted *LEFT* a few times, we hit a buoy, *LEFT*, and at 1500 metres, we were in the lead but only just, *LEFT. LEFT*. We got there first, but it was pretty poor.

After a couple of pints and a sandwich, Jon said, "What shall we do now?"

Peter, being a Cambridge man, replied, "Let's go punting at Cambridge." It was sunny and fun on the river Cam, a good day overall.

We set off for London at about five and while changing gear on the A1, there was a bang, my clutch cable had broken, and from there on, gears had to be changed without the clutch, which was OK as long as I didn't have to stop.

The traffic lights in Royston were red, we were all shouting, "Change," but they didn't, so I drove in circles in the four lane road till they did. The journey, which was eventful, was a good finish to my first properly enjoyable day for a couple of years.

I rang Leander and offered to coach up to the Henley Regatta, Hugh Twiss, the club captain, answered and was delighted by my offer. Yes, I could 'muck-in' with the crews.

Upon my arrival at Leander, I was warmly welcomed by all my old friends, Twiss had entered me for the Diamond Sculls at Henley and for the single sculls at Lucerne Regatta without my knowledge simply because I'd said I was free. The fact that this came as a surprise to me, having been caught in the same way four years previously indicates just how impaired my brain was at the time.

My Sims boat had been sitting on its rack, unused for well over a year, my first race at Henley wasn't hard, but in the quarterfinal, I was beaten by an American sculler.

Back in London, a letter had arrived from Germany from the German girl who had been too far away to meet up with when I'd stayed in Germany. I'd invited her earlier in the year to join our August family holiday, she knew my Dad from Munich and her answer was 'yes'. I could hardly believe it, she would be staying with her aunt in Bristol and I could pick her up on my way through.

On Friday after the Henley Regatta and in wonderful weather at Lucerne, I saw the list of top international scullers. I felt seriously inadequate. I was to race on the Saturday morning in a heat of eight scullers, some of whom were well-known, the semi-final was later in the day but the final was on Sunday. I reckoned I'd probably have just one race on Saturday morning and the rest of the time off.

On the start, I'm ready, we're off
halfway my legs are gone
shorten, keep tapping, and finally, it's over
that'll be it for the weekend
surprise, I've qualified for the semi-final
my legs had blown badly, what next

Line up on the start, it's about survival
go short on the slide with my legs
and not too hard, pace myself
it's the only way I can do it
at fifteen hundred, my legs are gone
I've finished fifth I think.

It's good, I have enjoyed my races
been a top weekend
I definitely need much more training
but that's no matter now
arriving back, I'm congratulated
fourth, I'm in the final

On the start, this is the deep end
rate high and use half slide
short and crisp. I'm in the race
tapping, not too hard
twenty more, I'm doing well
fifth in the big time, great

The finish order was: Kolbe (West Germany), Guldenpfennig (East Germany). Third was Sean Drea (Ireland), then Berger (West Germany). I came fifth in front of Alberto Demiddi (Argentina), the silver medallist from the Munich Olympics who I'd admired, particularly on the day when he'd won the Diamonds Sculls after Glyn and I won in the pair at Henley two years previously.

Twiss at Leander had done me a favour. I'd had a good time and came away from Lucerne, knowing that I could be competitive at top level in the single scull. Jon and Peter were selected to row in the coxed pair for the World Championships in Moscow.

They asked me if I would go as their coach but I said no, partly because I knew I wouldn't be able to maintain my mood, but mainly because I was on a promise, I hoped, with a German girl.

Having driven to Bristol and picked up the excited girl from her aunt's house, we went to Bucknall's farm in Devon for the weekend. He showed us upstairs at his farm house but I hadn't explained to him that we weren't a couple, as such.

We followed him into a room with a double bed, I paused with my mouth open and was elbowed in the ribs. It was a good start to a top notch weekend, which included the Hunt Ball at the Gothic Wiscombe Park house.

We went on to Cornwall to stay with my parents and young siblings for a very successful week, it was such a relief from the two years of illness. I was developing a very close and relaxed relationship, a totally new experience for me.

There was no hyper-mania or elevated mood above the 'normal' mood range, I was relaxed and happy although the feelings of background depression were still in my head. Each of those days were very good, but there could be no instant fix for me, there was no way that I could suddenly be made well.

We had a second, boozy week with a crowd of my old Cobham friends who were staying nearby, Pete Wallace was organising the water skiing; he towed many of us behind SODDIT, the tiny nine-foot speedboat powered by thirty horsepower which almost stood on end when starting with full power.

Much time was spent in the 'Shipwright's Arms' at Helford where we drank copious amounts, and some of us have a copy of the photo of a line of us men out in the open, peeing on the beach. It was unusual as we were peeing towards the camera.

After the Cornwall holiday, my new girlfriend came back to Barnes with me for a few days before leaving for Germany, we were very close and I was dreading her leaving. After she'd gone, I felt terrible, really very depressed and wrote her a letter with a personal poem of love, but finishing with:

but men before now
have used cars and machines
as a means
to an end.

That was unfortunate as it must have upset her and I didn't hear back. Years later, she was pleased to hear from me when I re-established contact, she is married with children and has kept in touch with our family since.

Back at college, the engineering work was to keep me occupied but anyone who's experienced clinical depression knows that it sits on you, with you, in your head, and it took me a lot of high-jinks, risk-taking and playing the fool to dispel it. Any reprieve was only temporary of course. Outwardly, I was fine as I kept busy, and was using my strategies to keep going but it was exhausting, and there were times when I had to accept that I'd lost the battle.

Two weeks later a letter for me arrived from the ARA, it was written by Bohumil (Bob) Janousek, the National Coach, with an invitation to join a squad to form an eight for the 1976 Olympics in Montreal.

Chapter 24
Aiming for Montreal

All of us receiving this invitation had a decision to make; as amateurs, we were working full-time or were trainees/students, but this was a once in a lifetime invitation. Could we commit ourselves to take on this challenge, as our lives, careers, friendships, and even marriages could be affected?

My biggest issue was what would happen to me and my demons, the thought of the Olympics in an eight coached by Bob Janousek was superb but I simply didn't know whether I could do it.

[I'M NOT WELL. SHOULD I COMMIT TO THIS?]

I replied by letter to say that I would join Bob's squad. The factors which led to Bob taking control of a small squad were that he had been National Rowing Coach for four years and had spent his time running coaching courses for the coaches of rowing clubs.

The coaches hadn't implemented his expertise, and during summer 1973, Bob had put it to the ARA that he could achieve results if he was given control of a small group which he would coach himself to the 1976 Olympics. The ARA gave Bob their backing but he knew only too well that he was taking on a huge challenge.

The ARA's resources were minimal, there were very few top oarsmen available and it was going to be difficult to blend this group with differing rowing styles into a successful eight.

Bob arranged to meet his squad during October 1973 at ARA boathouse at Hammersmith and we gathered in a drab and gloomy room with a 60 Watt light bulb hanging from the ceiling. I was delighted to see that there were seven of us from the 1972 Munich Olympic team.

The following oarsmen who were present would be central to Bob's squad over the subsequent three years:

Bill Mason, **Lenny Robertson**, **Jim Clark** and **Fred Smallbone** from the Thames Tradesmen four who had rowed three international seasons for GB previously, as well as three of them as Juniors in a previous season and Lenny and Bill before that.

David Maxwell, who rowed at Eton and then for Cambridge in the Boat Race.

Hugh Matheson who also rowed at Eton but then for Oxford in the Boat Race. These six plus myself were the seven from the Munich Olympic team.

Wol (John Yallop) had rowed with me for years at Leander, was tall and talented but hadn't made it to Munich.

There were seven or eight others at the meeting including **Pat Sweeney,** the cox from Thames Tradesmen who had been the cox of their four when they were Juniors, and he was the very best.

Most of those invited to join Bob's amateur squad took up the invitation, however, Carl Purchase from Wallingford RC turned down the invitation as he was a little older than the rest of us and had to concentrate on his business and young family. I had rowed with him at Leander, he was in the 5 seat behind me in the photo on page 21, and he was one of the top performers in the early squad days. In the long term, he was somebody we needed in the eight as Bob had so few top men.

Everyone knew Bob well and he welcomed us, saying that his priority was to produce a top class international eight. Hugh Matheson remembers, He made this completely simple speech with no hyperbole, no extravagance about it, promising nothing but incredibly hard work. He was completely engagingly, Janousekly clear.

"He said, I can't offer medals, I can't offer any big prizes. He never bribed us with any sense of achievement or glory. He just said, I can offer you the sense that you've done something absolutely fantastic." Chris Dodd. "Pieces of Eight".

Bob had a quiet style of leadership and there was no doubting that he was now in total control. He knew us all well and Lenny Robertson remembers Bob saying, "You English are like fat pigs. You're soft, the rest of the world laugh at you. You've got this great tradition of rowing but you haven't produced anything since Second World War".

"The world's moved on. Anybody who sees a GB crew in their heat just ticks them off as one they could beat. This squad is not going to be jolly boating weather. It's going to be hard." C. Dodd. Pieces of Eight.

Bob went on to explain that the group of fourteen oarsmen was the smallest possible number to achieve his aim, he described the proposed training and on the water, there would be three fours and a pair training through the winter. He would produce an eight and a four for Montreal. Bob spoke with conviction and exuded confidence.

The equipment available was limited and not the best, and Bob said later after looking at the Thames at Hammersmith, "When I saw Tideway for the first time, I couldn't believe you could coach a crew in this sort of water, running like hell one way or the other, boating in deep mud, it was crazy. I was used to clean water, still water, floating (landing) stage." (C. Dodd)

Bob had two Olympic bronze medals to his name from rowing in the Czech Eight and had gained his coaching qualifications behind the Iron Curtain with all the benefits of the East German sports system. He had three years to work on us before Montreal 1976 but our first year would take us to the World Championships to be held in Lucerne in 1974.

The land-training during the autumn was at a school in Chiswick, we played football in the gym until everyone had arrived and ran three miles on the road before a heavy weight-lifting session. One evening when finishing squats, I couldn't get the bar to rest in the two wobbly freestanding supports but finally when it did rest, it was tipping over, I was at my wits end with everything and let it go with a good crash. Fuck it.

Actually 'fuck it' was nowhere near enough, no one could imagine the torment, frustration, confusion and anger which I carried around much of the time. One small thing could be the last straw.

Yes, I'm ashamed of my temper and bad language, it's wrong, of course, but when your brain's that near to exploding, 'Piss-Bollocks', 'Arse'oles', 'Fuck it', *shout it*, that's better. Just let go, enjoy it, it took the tension away and my emotional crap and stresses had to come out, f—

At the weekends, we rowed in two coxless fours, a coxed four and a pair, two outings on Saturdays, and one on Sundays. Bob changed the combinations in the crews regularly and we rowed in uncomfortable combinations at times, Bob was trying to find out what might work, everyone was kept on their toes and Lenny Robertson from the Tradesmen four said, "When I rowed with guys from

Leander, it was awful. They had power but they had no feeling. There was a Cambridge group, Leander group, Tradesmen group. We thought maybe we should go back into our four and ask Bob to coach us. But he never put our four together." (C. Dodd)

One outing, I rowed in the stroke seat in a coxless four with three Tradesmen behind me, we set off paddling light* and suddenly, after about twenty strokes, the rhythm changed. They weren't used to paddling light my way, which was long and very steady with a fair bit of work, so that the boat covered a good distance between strokes.

They were supposed to be following me but they'd suddenly changed to what they'd always done in their four, short strokes with very little power and a higher rating. When they changed to their tapping rhythm, I reacted immediately and strongly because I was supposed to be in charge.

[YOU CAN'T HAVE THAT. IT'S DINKY-DOO, IT'S *AWFUL*.]

I exaggerated my length, held my finishes long and forced the rating back down again. There was a battle of rhythm for three or four strokes, but I killed it, I'd never felt anything so alien in a boat before.

To be fair to the Tradesmen, they were a light crew and their style of paddling suited them, and in the high pressure rowing, when we moved the boat fast, they rowed long and strong, although we still had to blend our styles.

*

Jim Clark, who'd been rowing behind me in that four, said later, "Winter training was quite difficult because the others rowed quite differently from us, also the fact that Crooksy was so strong that he could break down any rhythm that we could set up.".

"They felt they had no time, and we felt we had all the time in the world. It was quite fractious that first year, and it took quite a lot of getting together." (C. Dodd)

It was good for me to be training hard in Bob's well-organised squad, I had a structure and an aim which was helping, but years later, Wol (John Yallop) said, "You weren't the Tim we'd known in the Leander days."

Bob followed the fours on the water in his inflatable coaching launch, the work consisted of long pieces of 'Steady State' rowing at low ratings but maximum power. The competition between the fours was hot from the beginning whatever crews Bob put together and the wooden blades sometimes took a bashing on the sloping Tideway shores when going near the bank against the stream.

Bob did almost everything himself including repairs to the oars as he had so little backup from the ARA. He met us daily, organised and coached us and I assumed he was living somewhere close by but was to find out later that he wasn't.

On a rainy day, I was riding my powerful Suzuki three cylinder bike on the North Circular road near Wembley, some idiot turned across me on a dual carriageway and I couldn't avoid riding into the side of his car, I flew over the top and came down fifteen or twenty yards down the road on my head and shoulders, one of my shoes had slipped off and my heels came down with a bash.

A trip to hospital in an ambulance followed but nothing was broken and rowing happened as usual later on. The bike was bent and when it was fixed, I decided that my riding was dangerous anyway, so I sold it.

After a few weeks in fours, Bob put us out in the eight in our brand new Karlisch wooden boat from Germany just for one outing. Four of us from Leander were put in the middle, Lenny Robertson and Bill Mason, the two Thames Tradesmen who I'd met six years before in the Junior Team were in the bows, and Jim Clark and Fred Smallbone, the other two from the Tradesmen's four, were at seven and stroke.

I was at six and we set off, paddling light, Bob caught up with us in his inflatable launch and I was frustrated because I was having to follow the short Tradesmen's paddling light, which I couldn't stand. I simply couldn't do it, enough was enough.

[SOD THIS, I WON'T FOLLOW THAT. I *CAN'T* FOLLOW THAT.]

Quite suddenly, I rebelled, and stretching out for long strokes, I held my finishes in, so my blade came out of the water very late indeed, I had to rush forwards stupidly fast to catch up with Fred for the next stroke. This was an obvious rebellion on my part but neither Bob nor Pat Sweeney (cox) said anything.

Bob continued watching from his launch but said nothing, so I exaggerated it but very soon, I couldn't stand that any more either. I suddenly put the rating down from about twenty-five strokes per minute to under twenty, but bear in mind that I wasn't in charge, I was sitting at number six in the eight.

The three Leander guys behind me went along with me, and I suppose in order to avoid clashing or confrontation, the four Tradesmen went along with the lower rating too. I think everyone knew how angry I was and there was uncertainty as to what might happen.

When we rowed high pressure pieces, the whole eight synchronised pretty well together, rowing long and strong, but in the paddling light between those faster rows, I was totally stubborn and did it my way. I forced my will on the whole crew from the six seat, which I knew was all wrong.

I was angrily setting an example of exaggerated, long paddling light because I believed in it so strongly, but I didn't want to be in charge. I hoped that Bob or Pat would intervene to coach us to paddle long and steady, but they didn't relieve me of my load.

My frustration and anger was very much about me not understanding my emotions and there had to be an outlet. Nothing was said, it was weird actually. We continued our long distance winter training in the fours with different seating positions, the training was hard, the competition between the boats was high and we were all thoroughly tested.

Before Christmas, I was persuaded to join a group of students from college who were going skiing and I knew Bob wouldn't want me to go. I didn't ask permission, but asked Lenny Robertson if he'd let Bob know where I'd gone when I didn't appear for training a few days later.

I was the only one who'd never been on skis before but one day, we took turns to jump off a snow ramp and most of us had major crashes while the others took photos. Somehow, we all survived, but on my return, I assumed I'd get a lecture from Bob. It didn't happen.

During February, Bob put us in the eight more often, the evening training sessions in the gym had changed from heavy weights to circuit training, and the seating order in the eight started to take shape.

Our short-term aim was to make our mark in the Tideway HOR, we had two of the Tradesmen in the bows and the other two in the stern but Bob had rigged the boat differently and I was at three on stroke-side.

The rhythm in the light paddling was still a problem to me, but as I was at three, there was nothing I could do about it. My basic mood was still low but as always, the rowing work-outs picked me up, just for a while.

Most of the guys rowed all business-like, hard and quietly. Fred, at stroke, could chatter quite a bit, and Hugh Matheson, at five, occasionally got a bee under his bonnet and could reply to a criticism from Bob at length, sometimes effusively. I didn't say much at all, everything came out as frustration and pulling harder. It was dissipated in the Thames.

The Tradesmen guys were good value, there was a fair bit of cockney rhyming slang mostly from Fred, who seemed to need to make his voice heard. Very occasionally, careless talk caused friction because of different backgrounds, but the Tradesmen were cheeky and fun, we Leander boys enjoyed the banter but on the whole gave less than we were given. Our common aim was the essential ingredient which held us together.

We rowed many combinations in pairs, just two men in each boat, and Bob would avoid putting two weaker guys together or two of the strongest because he wanted to watch how people adapted to each other and how they competed in pairs of similar standards.

Hugh Matheson said, "I changed sides and ended up rowing with everyone except Tim. But eventually, he couldn't avoid putting us together. I discovered that rowing with Tim was magic. All I had to do was drop in a quarter of a blade early to keep him straight. We were doing Putney to the boat race finish at Chiswick, and under Hammersmith bridge, we were 40 seconds ahead. It was just embarrassing." (Chris Dodd).

Bob told Matheson years later that he wouldn't and didn't ever put us in the pair again because he was terrified we'd drop out in case we thought we could win the Olympic pairs, and the eight would have sunk.

My engine test rig was working well, I was getting repeatable test results, which was encouraging, but the video recorder in my setup failed and had to go away for repair. Two weeks they said, fair enough, I got on with other things, but it wasn't ready after two weeks, three weeks, or four weeks and I made telephone calls to chase it from the payphone in the lab.

There was only one payphone for all of us students and no mobiles in those days. I was frustrated because I couldn't get on with my research and there were often others waiting to use the phone, which resulted in bad feelings.

As the Tideway Head (HOR) approached, the Saturday and Sunday morning training programmes would typically consist of three rows of between seven and nine minutes each, they were rowed at race pace rating thirty-six strokes per minute. The emphasis was on quality and although the outings weren't long, we'd all pushed ourselves hard and came off the water exhausted.

The intensity of the competition both in the gym and on the water in the fours was teaching us how to go further into lactic acid and the unknown, Bob was fair and friendly but said little and was very sparing with praise.

The Tideway HOR was upon us. We were to start in the 'New Entries' as a Leander/Thames Tradesmen composite crew towards the back of the field; during the race, our cox, Pat, did a great job overtaking fifteen crews and we finished in second place 16 seconds behind the Tideway Scullers. Pat pinned his cloth number 284 up on the changing room wall at Hammersmith. It was there for years.

On Saturdays after rowing I got home to Maidenhead at about midday, but we had to be back in Hammersmith by two. Lunch varied, but was often based around eggs, and occasionally a tin of beans, followed by Ambrosia creamed rice, and sometimes sliced peaches, just like during my apprentice days. All eaten cold and fast with the same (serving) spoon of course. Just occasionally I dived into the Weetabix instead, being hungry and thirsty, but once I'd started it was difficult not to go on. There are twelve Weetabix in the normal big pack and I ate a whole pack at least twice, and on one occasion had sixteen. At least I had time to lie down afterwards.

Immediately before Easter after six weeks without my video recorder, I was on the telephone for half an hour, chasing it, and a group of my student colleagues were waiting to use the phone and were saying how selfish I was.

A voice told me finally that my video recorder 'hadn't been looked at'. My temper was then lost, but gripping that precious phone tightly and putting it down carefully, I turned and punched the top drawer of a filing cabinet, which went right through and out the back, hitting the brick wall behind.

I had to go to A & E with a broken bone in my hand, they fixed me up with a splint, which held my little finger out straight, I'd broken the fifth metatarsal behind my little finger, the classic break resulting from a punch. Idiot, fool, what was I thinking? Thinking? I was well past thinking, this was the emotional reaction of an angry primate and there was nothing good about that episode.

We were to be in Nottingham just over a week later, after Easter, to continue training for the summer races and the hospital splint was too clumsy for rowing. I'd fashioned a skinny splint from a strip of aluminium held in place with electrician's tape, my damaged hand had to feather the oar, so my little finger went up and down through ninety degrees every stroke.

It worked well but in the rough conditions when the boat rocked, the splint sometimes rammed the side of the boat, which was painful, but no fuss, I was managing just fine.

The splint was discarded a week or two later but before it was, while in a hurry in London and travelling by tube, I ran down to find the tube train doors closing but I managed to get my good fist between the doors as they shut.

After a few moments, the doors did their quick open/close thing, presumably to release clothing, bags or people, but I got my forearm in. The doors moved again, I pushed to my elbow. Then again, to my shoulder. The driver gave up and opened the doors, thank you.

Bob set off to Germany with a trailer on a Sunday to collect two new fours and on Monday evening, we found Bob with a beautiful new coxless four and a coxed four in two pieces. He'd had an accident involving a gatepost on the very last turning before the boathouse, having driven from Germany, but was positive about getting the boat repaired. The show went on.

The personal effort of our coach was only then becoming apparent to me as I heard that he, his wife and two young daughters had been housed near Nottingham by the ARA some years earlier to be near the 2,000 metre course, Bob had been driving from there to all our training sessions in London. I could hardly believe it, four hours of driving every day on six days of the week, with young family at home.

During the spring, I met a girl in Putney and we started going out together; one night, we had a protracted amorous encounter in one of the very narrow two-foot six-inch (75 cm) beds in her rented flat. Afterwards, I thought I can't just leave her and go to the other bed after doing *THAT* to her, but the bed was so narrow, I had to support myself with one hand on the floor all night to stop falling out.

In the morning, I said, "I feel a bit fucked."

She laughed and said, "Well, I'm *completely* fucked," and as we walked down the road, she clung so tightly to me that more of my confusion about sex was diffused.

April and May was the 'pre-race' period, Bob had twice won bronze Olympic medals in the Czechoslovakian eight and had studied Sports Science at Charles University in Prague. His own training and his sports education had steeped him in the Eastern Bloc training methods, which favoured long distance rowing for many hours in order to build up stamina.

There simply wasn't time for that in British amateur sport, we had done some of it through the winter, but Bob had devised his own program of training, which could take place after work during the week and at weekends which involved shorter training sessions at high intensity.

The East Germans stretched for each stroke, which they took with bent backs that could cope with the strain because they were trained for it. Bob taught us to sit upright and to use full length on our sliding seats, this was hard on the legs but we achieved full length without straining our backs.

One of Bob's calls was "…'smash it in'. His technique was the epitome of the Kernschlag (solid stroke with hard beginning) style as opposed to the *schubschlag* (thrust stroke) style around which all the East German boats, training, diet and medicine were designed." More Power. Hugh Matheson and Christopher Dodd.

While Bob coached, he worked on the two ends of the stroke, fast efficient catches at the beginning of the stroke, and to lift our blades out cleanly and fast at the end of the stroke with a swift hands away from the body. As the racing season approached, we rowed many two and three minute pieces intensely at high ratings, pushing repeatedly into lactic acid.

There was a short heat wave during May 1974 and one of our training rows was exceptional, it was the first time I'd experienced the feeling of speed with ease. We'd rowed hard all weekend and were tired, it was the last two-minute row and only later did I realise that this was 'flow'. We must have all been on form, all doing it right, all moving as one, every movement contributing to propulsion.

'Flow', what is it? The relaxed muscle memory to produce speed with ease, where time and pain are banished, the unified focus and the feel-good factor can give euphoria.

They say it's dopamine which causes it, as well as endorphins, which trigger feelings similar to those of morphia. Our sliding seats had runners half a mile long and I'd hit front-stops, and in the boathouse afterwards, Bob said it was good, but we knew it.

"A boat is a sensitive thing, an eight-oared shell, and if it isn't let go free, it doesn't work for you."

[*George Pocock, boat-builder and coach, from The Boys in the Boat by Daniel Brown. P173. (The story of the American gold-winning eight in 1936 in front of Hitler)*]

Chapter 25
Out of the Pit

Having been in Bob's Montreal squad from October 1973 for a little over six months, my long episode of depression was coming to an end, two particular recent life events had helped my recovery, these were the girlfriend and the good rowing.

My demons had been in control since the day after Lucerne Regatta in 1971, but I'd managed to get through the 1972 season to Munich, the 1973 season had been an odd one, mostly depressed, and during May 1974, almost three years after the dreadful mood collapse, I was recovering, thank God.

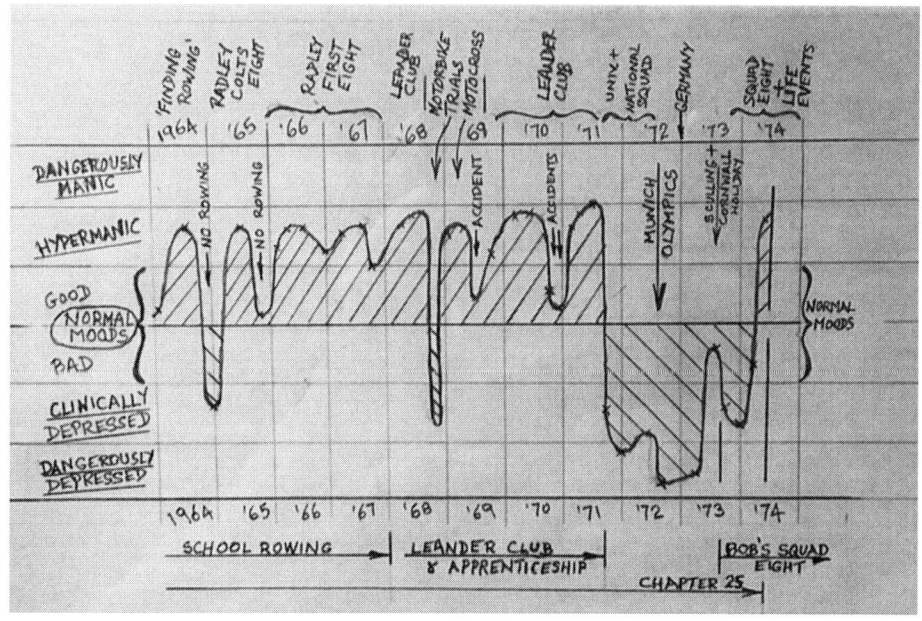

My moods, 1964 to 1974. Remembered in wonderful/awful detail while writing this story and re-living those years.

My life may have looked good from the outside but throughout that extended period, my mood had fluctuated from desperately deep clinical depression to feeling OK in the 'normal' range of moods, but much of my time was spent alone and feeling very unwell mentally.

The overriding factor of those times was that when my mood had risen, the pit was always still there, waiting to envelop me and *it was inevitable that I would be dragged back there, there was nothing which could stop it,* just as the darkness of night is inevitable, the black pit swallowed me up every time.

I had some great times during my extended bad patch but there was too much 'pretending to be OK', which was exhausting. I was so desperately lonely and when my mood got as high as the low side of 'normal', I was relieved and even happy *but mood swings out of depression were generally very short.*

My point here is that despite all of the undisputed good times and the rowing, I had been unwell for nearly three years, living with the background of clinical depression.

When the episode of depression finally lifted, I found myself hyperactive and performing well, it was so good to be feeling well after all that time.

[I'M BACK, I FEEL GOOD, REALLY GREAT!]

What was going on in my head was not recognised or understood at the time, but I felt the same as I had been up to July 1971 where for the majority of the time, my mood was in the hyper-manic range; however, as before, there were times when I was on the edge of slipping, so I was back to keeping my demons at bay through training, risk-taking, rushing, being cheeky and all the old tactics. *I was loving it.* Living again.

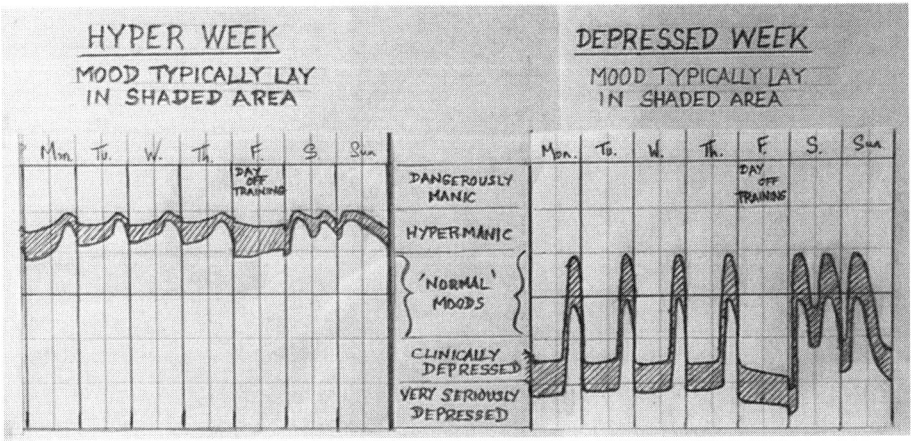

Hyper-manic (high) and depressed (low) moods.

These graphs show a basis for how my moods were during the good times in the left hand graph, and how they were during the bad times on the right. There were many other outside factors which affected mood from day to day, so there was never a week like either of these in reality.

Also these graphs show that we had Fridays off, but this wasn't our only routine, and there were some fairly short periods when we trained twice per day.

Chapter 26
Summer 1974

Our first regatta was at Mannheim in the dock off the Rhine where most of us had competed before, we were Bob's new squad, venturing abroad for the first time. We were amateurs, under pressure, we'd taken a day off work, had travelled on a Friday morning and were not at all relaxed.

We were billeted in army accommodation and the weekend was arranged as two separate regattas, one on Friday/Saturday and another on Sunday. This was to enable crews to compete in different boats in the separate regattas.

Between the boathouse and the landing stage, there were four sets of railway lines, one of which was in use, bringing spectators along the course in cattle trucks.

Hugh Matheson said that spectators and coaches could watch the races from old railway trucks along one side of the dock and he remembers Janousek sitting in a freight car 'like it was going to Auschwitz, peering out of little holes with his stopwatch'. Chris Dodd. Pieces of Eight.

This was to be a weekend of mixed fortunes.

Moving grandstand. Mannheim style.

We raced in fours on Friday and Saturday. I was the stroke of a coxless four, which had only rowed together for a few days. I had Wol behind me and Bill Mason and Lenny Robertson in the bows and we didn't go well in the preliminary heat, finishing third, but we would have another chance to reach the final in a repechage* race in the evening.

The coxed four had the two tall Eton (Oxford/Cambridge) boys in the bows and the other two Thames Tradesmen in the stern. They won their heat, beating the East Germans and qualified directly for the final.

In the coxless four repechage race, we didn't go well but qualified for Saturday's final. I was pissed off. Lenny Robertson, "As we were getting out of the boat, Crooks started having a go at Bill, saying the steering was bloody useless. I said it wasn't his fault. 'Oh yes, it was,' Tim said, and he threw a punch at Bill as we were carrying the boat to the rack, and Bill said, 'Crooksy hit me,' so I walloped Crooks and he dived on me like a wild bear and we came tumbling out of this boathouse at Mannheim surrounded by all these athletes from round the world. Bob came along and pulled us away like two cats having a scrap." Chris Dodd Pieces of Eight.

*

The coxed four went for a practice outing between races, Jim said later that the stroke man, Fred, was yattering on about stuff and David, the quiet Etonian at bow, shouted at Fred. Jim got involved in their argument and Pat, the coxswain, had to give them all a long and loud dressing down in front of all their opponents to shut them all up.

We got in the minibus and Bob said, "It's very important we don't start to argue with each other. Keep calm, guys, nobody expects you to win—you're bloody English. The English, they never win anything." Chris Dodd. Pieces of Eight.

On Saturday, our final in the coxless four was early on, we got dumped off the start and were fourth before half way. Bill Mason said, "Crooks jacked the stroking rate right up. We just went straight through the whole field and won by over a length." Chris Pieces of Eight.

That race was memorable for me as it was the first race where I'd performed with real sparkle for a nearly three years. The coxed four had seen us go by in fourth place but we didn't come back with the other crews and they were surprised to hear an American calling to their coach that the 'Crazy Brits' had gone ballistic and rowed through everyone. We were collecting medals.

In the coxed four's final, they had East Germany on one side of them and West Germany on the other. Hugh Matheson's description was that they were fourth to half way, then one of the East Germans came off his slide and they were out of it, they overtook the Americans and then the West Germans and won by a length. "It was easy." Chris Dodd. Pieces of Eight.

The regatta had been eventful so far. A punch-up for half the eight and an argument for the others. Both fours had come from behind and rowed convincingly to a win, which was a demonstration of capability from Great Britain and Lenny Robertson reckoned we'd gone up in Bob's estimation. "We weren't fat pigs. We're English, and we rowed 'em down." Chris Dodd. Pieces of Eight.

Back to the barracks and an evening meal and another place setting of cutlery and a large serving spoon went into my pocket, I couldn't resist freebies, especially when stamped with the German Eagle.

The crew order in the eight for Sunday's race was as it had been in the Tideway HOR, with two Tradesmen in the bows, two in the stern and four Leander guys in the middle. I was at three on stroke-side and we came third, which was disappointing.

Back on the Tideway, Bob swapped myself and David around, so I was at six, which I preferred except I had to follow Fred's rhythm in the paddling light. Unfortunately my anger was focussed on Fred, poor bloke, who was actually doing what he was used to doing perfectly well. I simply didn't agree with the Tradesmen's style but saw it as Fred's fault.

When we set off at the beginning of an outing, I'd follow stroke, which, as you know, is what you should do in crew rowing, but very soon, I couldn't stand it, bloody rebellion by me every time.

I'd put the rating down, row longer and harder strokes with a distinct 'send-the-boat-flying-away' finish on every stroke, and the crew went with me. I was highlighting a problem and trying to provoke a reaction from Pat or Bob *but I never got one.*

I didn't want to be in charge from the six seat, so I did it more extreme. How could one crew member screw around to that extent and not provoke comment or rebuke? I was taking control of the crew.

[FUCK YOU. DO IT PROPERLY, LIKE THIS.]

Oh right, for God's sake, I only just twigged it, all these years later. Bob saw everything, he probably wasn't sure how he was going to get us together because of the different styles of rowing in the boat, but he watched my anger. He saw it was useful and he let it burn.

Fucking hell, Bob, I was used. Yes, it was for the benefit of all of us, but I was suffering with the situation, my frustration and anger went everywhere with me and there were costs to me.

We knew that Bob had been well-trained in psychology during his training to coach in the Eastern Bloc, and he most probably recognised my mood swings and that I was suffering from bipolar disorder, but of course I had no knowledge or understanding of that at the time.

I think that he and everyone else knew me well enough to know that my behaviour could be extreme and were wondering what might happen next. But there was me trying hard to provoke a reaction, rowing differently to the stern pair, but no one spoke, I never heard *anything* said about it by anyone. As far as I was concerned, I was being ignored, which made me angrier and I exaggerated everything even more.

I don't know exactly what was happening in everyone's minds, but Bob used a difficult situation to make something fantastic, which was brilliant.

The others were very tolerant of my behaviour, nearly everyone had been to the Olympics before, we could all row different types of boats and had wide experience, but we were an odd mixture thrown together. We knew we were the best men available, our talents were varied but as Billy Mason said to me, we all brought something to the boat.

The others knew that whatever talents they had themselves, my particular brand of talent could be useful, but I've always been grateful that they put up with me.

At Ratzeburg regatta in the eights final, we were beaten by a quarter of a length by a West German crew and that evening, Wol, being a good chap, stayed up drinking with the winning German crew, he bought rounds of beers, joined in the fun and encouraged smoking as well as drinking on Saturday night.

On day two the Germans were rowing fours, but in our eight we were half a length behind the American eight at 1500 metres but our last 500 metres was superb, we found the 'speed with ease', which we'd had once in training and we won the race by two or three feet.

"When you get the rhythm in an eight, it's a pleasure to be in it. It's not hard work when the rhythm comes—that 'swing' as they call it. It's a thing they'll never forget as long as they live." (Quote George Pocock, from 'The Boys in the Boat' by Dan Brown.)

After our win on the second day at Ratzburg.
From left to right: Matheson, me, Jim, Pat, Wol, Fred, David, Bill, Lenny.

Back on the Tideway with two weeks till the Nottingham International Regatta, Bob made more changes to the seating order in the crew and I was put in the stroke seat, so I was facing Pat, our cox. In that seat I had control, but I was still troubled with frustration and torment and it all came out as exaggerated rhythm and power through the oar. My anger was focused into the water.

We did OK at the Nottingham International Regatta and afterwards, Lenny gave some of us a lift back to London in his high powered Ford Capri. I was in the front passenger seat and three others were in the back. We drove for an hour at 85 mph and had a blowout in the front nearside tyre just by my feet, the blown tyre was shredded, thrashing round in the wheel arch, causing body damage and it made a hell of a machine-gun noise.

We veered to the left, Lenny steered right to avoid another car, there was a howl from the good front tyre and after that, there was nothing to hit and I started laughing. What a relief. When we got back, someone told the others, "We had a blowout at eighty-five and Crooksy started laughing."

We had all four members of the Thames Tradesmen's four in the eight, along with us four Leander guys and our styles of rowing were still different at times. The Tradesmen were a light crew, had competed at international level for three years against heavier crews and had produced their boat speed by rowing at high ratings with athleticism and skill. They brought these things to the eight.

I was forcing my will on the crew in the paddling light, taking longer and stronger strokes because I believed in it, but over a period of time in the race pace rowing, we were blending together at a higher racing rate.

Two weeks later at Henley, I was still in the stroke seat, there were four entries for the Grand Challenge Cup and in our semi-final, we beat the Tideway Scullers comfortably and it felt good to stamp hard on one of the top British club crews.

In the final, we met the Russians who were half a stone heavier per man than us. We pulled three quarters of a length up but at the mile post were level and the Russians won a frantic duel by half a length.

At Henley with me at stroke, about to race the Russians.

The Russians leading just before the finish.

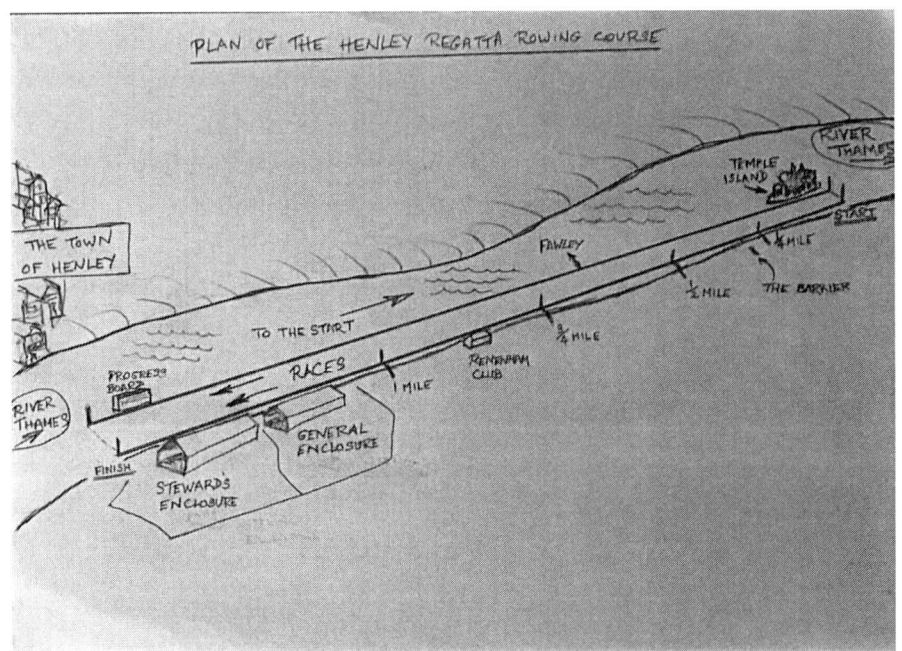

The Henley Regatta course.

After Henley, Bob made the final change to the seating order. He changed the bow four riggers back, so that the boat was conventionally rigged (alternate sides all the way down). Fred Smallbone was back in the stroke seat and the remaining three Tradesmen, Lenny Robertson, Bill Mason and Jim Clark were in the bows.

Us four Leander guys were in seats four to seven, David Maxwell, Hugh Matheson, me and Wol, and that seating order was retained for the rest of the season for the World Championships.

In the flat-out rowing, we were coming together but in the light paddling, Fred tended to do what he was used to, but there was me in the six seat hating it. I held the rate down, rowing long and steady, controlling and rhythm of the crew, which was totally abnormal.

[THIS IS WRONG. FOR GOD'S SAKE, PAT OR BOB, TAKE CONTROL OF THIS. I DO NOT WANT TO BE IN CHARGE.]

At Nottingham in the British National Championships, we won both of the fours events and in the eight, we beat Leander, the other top club crew by twelve seconds, which demonstrated finally that we were in a superior class to the British club crews.

We had two weeks until the West German National Championships which were open to outside crews. At that stage we carried out large numbers of high intensity training rows, at the end of each, we collapsed a bit and paddled light and short, which is normal for a short while. But after each row, we carried on paddling pathetic tapping strokes for too long, Pat never said anything, and I made the sudden and distinct change on my own every time.

[PADDLE……. LONG] and the boat runs on while we relax.
[LIKE…………..THIS]
[SEND US….FLYING]
[JUST…………DO IT] and the boat ran on.

The crew always put the rate down with me. I asked Pat recently why he never bollocked me for doing my own thing at six. He paused and couldn't/wouldn't say, but when I pressed him, he said, "Well, I thought you were doing the right thing."

I think both Fred and I were so stressed about the paddling that we couldn't talk about it, the rest of the crew wouldn't mention it in case they started a punch-up and Bob and Pat could see that somehow, it was working, so they didn't say anything at all. I was left doing what I believed-in to extreme while wishing Bob would remove the load off my back.

We arrived at Duisburg for the West German Championships and Bob talked tactics, introducing an extra burst for us at 750m and delaying our halfway push till 1100 metres. We won the straight final comfortably on Sunday. It was an outstanding win for us and was our last competition before the World Championships, to be held in Lucerne.

We trained full-time for two weeks before the World Championships, one week at Nottingham, followed by a week at Henley, and the World Championships would mark the end of our first year in the three-year effort to the Montreal Olympics.

During the week at Nottingham, we had the prevailing headwind and rough water, it wasn't much fun, everyone was pushed to their limit and during one of the afternoons, we rowed a series of two-minute pieces at flat-out race pace with light paddling between each. On the last one, we were to go for it and sprint the last twenty strokes.

Towards the end of the last row, Fred at stroke suddenly rowed short strokes and his head was down, which was a sure sign he'd got no strength left, or as we put it 'he'd blown'. We were about to go and Pat shouted, "Last 20, take it from 7 and 6. Go."

We went, and Fred's blade was dipping in and out short with no power, we finished the row, paddled in and as we carried the boat into the boathouse, somebody said, "That was a hard one."

Fred said brightly, "At least I kept on puttin' 'em down." Which was a trigger for me, he'd just been cocky after he'd blown. All of us had our moments in the boat, when working past our limits, finding ways to hang on, to row well to the finish post somehow. We'd all been there and would go there again, but our reliability was tantamount, lose one man completely in a crew and the machine is broken.

We saw it, he broke our machine, and I felt he'd denied it.
My awful anger was always around.
I'd been triggered.

I lost it.

I walked round and punched him, he let go of the boat punched me back, and the whole of the weight of stroke-side went onto David's shoulder at four. Pat jumped between Fred and me and the moment was defused. We put the boat on the rack and after Bob had been told about the incident, he had a word with the three other Tradesmen.

Jim Clark reported, "Fred had a bit of a whack. Psychologically, it was difficult for him because he felt isolated in the stroke seat, and we're up in the bows, with mad man Crooksy behind him, and he was mad. I mean, I love him and he is what you needed in a boat, but my God, he was a problem for the coaches."

"It's the only time I saw Bob concerned. He came up to me, Billy and Len, took us aside very quietly, and said, 'Go and look after Fred. I think Fred could go down after this, so look after him, make sure he feels part of the group'. The only time he showed a lot of concern for us in that way." Chris Dodd. Pieces of Eight.

The second training camp week at Henley was totally different, we stayed at the White Hart by the bridge and boated from Leander, nice place, good weather, no comparison. On day one, Bob produced the set of slim wooden oars reinforced with carbon fibre strips, which had been given to the ARA by GKN two and a half years previously, they were back with the slim looms wrapped in a sheath of carbon fibre material to improve the torsional stiffness.

The crew came together in every way that week, it was a relief after the previous tensions. Lenny Robertson, "It was so relaxed, one of the best weeks I've ever spent." Chris Dodd. Pieces of Eight.

Chapter 27
World Championships 1974

The World Championships were held at Lucerne, not on Lake Lucerne but on the Rotsee, between the mountains. The cows with their cowbells were grazing on the grassy slopes, and the period of ten days spent there was eventful. In one of our first outings, I became aware that my hands were crashing into my body at the finish of the stroke.

I decided that my hands should go smoothly round the finish of the stroke without an impact against the body. A cyclist doesn't hit his heels on the frame of his bike, pedalling is done smoothly. I tried a smooth semi-circle at the finish, just brushing my vest and got an instant improvement at all speeds, no crash, no discontinuity, just a smooth release, blade up and out.

And yes, I'd lost a centimetre or so of length of my stroke but by reaching out longer forwards, I could make up for that and it's been better for me ever since.

We were a diverse group but had become close and there were discussions of all sorts. David Maxwell said that something was nothing of consequence, a mere bagatelle, and Lenny Robertson: "Bag 'o what?"

Politics came up too and Hugh Matheson had strong views. Mike Hart said later that Robertson and Smallbone would react against anything Matheson said, and it would all go over my head. Also, it was reported that I composed and recited poems.

Lenny said, "We all tried to appear vaguely interested, but we couldn't upset him 'cos he'd throw a wobbly... He was like a guy packed full of Semtex, on a very short fuse that could go at any time. You wouldn't want to race against Tim, because he was absolutely fantastic in the boat." Chris Dodd. Pieces of Eight.

Discussions about politics were frustrating to me as there never seemed to be progress, and in order to keep my brain positively occupied, I sometimes composed poems and came to the start line relaxed, physically and mentally. Well, kind of.

Hugh wrote about me later 'We thought Tim felt no pain, but he was using his physical pain to cancel out the pain in his head.' When we talked more recently we agreed that pain through sport can be a form of self-harm. A method, in effect, of escaping mental torment. Self-harm is a big topic in connection with mental illness.

In our heat, we finished third behind East Germany and the Americans, which took us directly to the semi-finals to be raced four days later; however, we had two equipment breakages before we raced again. During a twenty-stroke burst in training, my foot stretcher bar collapsed away from me in the centre, my feet were twisted in towards each other and Bob replaced the part with a spare.

Then during the outing before our semi-final, a bang and a jerk. David Maxwell's steel pin on the end of the rigger had broken off, Bob, as our support team, replaced the pin. On semi-finals day, we gathered around Bob for our pre-race pep talk, he prepared us meticulously for our races, so that we knew exactly what we were doing, and we knew what tactics the others might use. There were two semi-finals of six boats and we had to finish in the first three in our semi to qualify for the final. Bob sent us off to get the boat.

Pat was then in charge, he was our ninth man who steered the boat and was the voice on the water, he martialled our routines with precision and authority, gave information and orders and had earned our absolute trust. Without his expertise in all things, we were nothing, eight rowers, one cox and one coach. A team of ten.

In the moments before a race, you control your nerves and you breathe well, and having checked that your equipment in the boat is all done up tight, you have the knowledge that everything has been rehearsed and you are ready.

This is a blast-off sprint, and this sprint is under six minutes in an eight. The pace is hot, so much energy and muscle power—it's partly anaerobic, which means the muscles are using oxygen faster than the heart and lungs can replace it.

There'll be 'oxygen debt', so lactic acid forms in the muscles and that causes pain. If you get it wrong, pace it badly and go too hard too early, you suffer, your performance suffers, and it affects the whole crew.

We're on the start,
this is not the time for doubts,
I'm on top, I can do it, I'm ready,
good to go, and breathing deeply.
"Come forward," says Pat
the starter begins his roll call, he's speaking in French,
it's always stressful on the start, time seems to stand still.
The cow bells are clanking and I'm strangely detached, in another world,
the starter (in French): "Are you ready?"
[SHIT, OH …OK]
That is *not* a question, "Partez."
and we're off, three strokes power but steady,
now blitz it, 4, 5, 6, 7 accelerating, driving to 10
"LENGTH"—it's Pat. Full length now, but we need more speed,
power and length, accelerate the boat to 20
and Pat calls, "STRIDE"
and it's good, we're driving, steady and long
as steady as a sprint can ever be.
He's pushing us to work hard, to race it
to be sharp and to get the rhythm.

It's essential to sprint and push on harder than you want, otherwise you get dropped and you're not in the race, it's a psychological barrier, your brain says don't do this, it's too much, it's going to hurt, but you've trained for it, and you can do it.

Wol used to say, "The first bit's like rowing in a vacuum." He never explained, but it's nothing to do with a lack of air, it's a space in time where there's something missing. It begins at the start and finishes about 60 or 70 seconds into the race.

It's the drive off the blocks, the reckless use of power, your senses are tuned, using peripheral vision and 'feel' for timing and balance, there's total commitment, it's your mind-set. You're one with the crew, pushing on harder than is wise, it's a matter of trust between you and your crew mates, you all have to do it.

So, where's the vacuum? *What* is it? The vacuum is that reckless time, your body is willing, and it does what you ask, but there's no feedback from your muscles, lactic acid takes time to form. You'll *know* when the feedback comes in, your muscles will tell you, it's your legs you can kill first, you go in faith and hope you'll be OK. If you've overdone it, you're partially done in, it's pain and you carry it, sometimes all the way.

The vacuum is that reckless time before the feedback comes in, I think that's what Wol meant, but we were well into the stride and pushing on, the rhythm was good and we were in third place, it was alright.

Keep it tidy,
pushing on, cox is encouraging us now,
it's good, we're on top, we're a well-oiled machine
500 metres. A quarter of the race, then
Five, six and seven—that's Hugh, me and Wol—hear a sound
alarm bells are ringing.

Our boat was the Karlisch eight from Germany, less than a year old but with metal fatigue problems in its fittings, there were four places on the aluminium riggers where we were finding fatigue cracks, but we'd had two steel rigger pins fail too. We needed just two more races.

Wol and I were looking at his rigger, there was nothing to see, so we pressed on. But Hugh behind me saw the trouble and he wrote about it later:

"A locknut was gone from Tim's seat, I heard it drop and a wheel was loose. The wheels on the sliding seats were threaded onto the axles with a locknut tightened outside each wheel to hold them in place. The wheel was screwing in and out, to the left and to the right as it went back and forth, the wheels were getting wider apart and I could foresee the outcome. The wheel would fall off."

"For some time, I hadn't heard Pat, our coxswain, had no idea where the other crews were, had no idea where we were on the course as I stared in horror at the accident waiting to happen under Tim's broad backside. The wheel was scraping one side of the slide runner and then, like a sled on the Cresta run, was riding up the curved side of the groove and threatening to pop out."

Fully committed, we're feeling good, concentrate,
nothing's broken our length and stride.
Fred's setting a good rhythm and we keep pushing on
I'm stretched to full reach and I drive my legs down,

my seat jams and I fly off onto the runners
can't stop, just keep going
but one short useless stroke later
I pull my oar in across the boat.
"Stop, stop, Tim's seat's gone," but the crew don't stop,
Hugh can't row, I'm in his way and my seat won't move
it's at a crazy angle under my legs,
so I thump it straight with the heel of my hand
it moves, but it won't run free, I sit on it, get my oar out and go.
That didn't take long, but we're fifth or last,
my seat's stiff and scraping like hell.

    Bob said afterwards that we were looking good early on but he'd looked again and we'd dropped right back and he couldn't imagine what had happened. Hugh was watching my wheel, it wasn't in the groove, but up higher, running on the flat metal beside it. Bill, rowing at two, told me later, "It went really well after that." It may have done, but I didn't notice, I was in a world of hell.

Oh God. Oh no, the scraping and friction, it's noisy and stiff,
I'm using my legs to pull me forwards
and my shorts are sliding around on the varnished seat,
and my seat's tipped up at an odd angle,
the scraping changes from time to time, I have no idea what's wrong
"We're gonna GO," Pat shouts

[NO, DON'T DO ANYTHING, I'M HANGING ON HERE.]

"We're gonna GO."
"Go NOW."
I don't want to go. We go. The noise and the friction,
I'm slipping around, both forwards and back on my seat
I'm in a world of hell, pulling myself forwards is hurting now.
The burst goes well but the stress of it all,
we stride out, thank God and the noise changes,
the seat runs easier, but not for long. Stiffer again, and even worse now
it sounds like an old railway truck.

Hugh was transfixed, watching my wheel running over a line of small screw heads. He wrote, "The wheel was screwing in and out randomly. It was just a matter of time."

My legs are burning, lactic acid, pain both ways, push and pull
but the race goes on, disaster any second
I'm hanging on here, it's the worst
"We're going for Home."

[OH GOD, NO]

"Go. For Home."
"Go — NOW."
It's the last 500 metres, we go
I have no idea how we're doing, my vision is narrow
my legs are screaming, push and pull
my disaster is right on top of me
I'm lost in my Cage of *Physical Pain*
and *God-awful mental stress*
Then: "Last TWENTY."
"Take it up—NOW."
It lifts, we're going for it, I'm with it but desperate, then
[I MIGHT DO IT]
hanging on somehow
"LAST FIVE."
and it's over. [AARRGGHH]

"WELL DONE, LADS. THIRD PLACE, WE'VE DONE IT."

It should be elation, but [MY LEGS. MY LEGS. OH GOD, MY LEGS]
One of my wheels had been running along beside its groove up on a higher level, which lifted that one back corner of my seat up, so one of the alloy hooks which kept the seat in place when the boat was carried upside down was lifted up with the seat. It was scraping the underside of the runner but somehow, we'd qualified for the final.

Finals day, we gathered for our crew briefing and all Bob said was that we'd already done what we were here to do, and, "If you're in final, you're somebody, if you're not in final you're nobody, you're in final, enjoy it." We paused, looked around at each other, and smiled with relief.

Ok, and off we went. Bob and Pat had checked the boat and the seats thoroughly but the metal fatigue was a worry, there were no guarantees, just this last race to do. We were in Lane 1, next to us in Lane 2 were the West Germans, then East Germany, USA, Russia and New Zealand in Lane 6. The conditions were good.

We're on the start, all the other crews are on our left,
this is it and of course, there's pressure, we're up against them all here
and concentrating on the job to be done, checking adjustments are tight,
breathing deeply the roll call starts, "Come forward," says Pat.
Time seems to stand still, the cow bells are clanking,
suddenly in French, "Are you ready?"
"Partez."
the start's good and goes as planned
we lengthen at ten, accelerate to twenty
At 500 metres, we're last.

Our burst at 750 metres took us through the West Germans like a hot knife through butter, Pat was giving us the calls, and then:
"Well done," lads.
"You're coming back.
You're coming back on the whole field.
You're coming back on the whole field."

This was feeling easy but of course, we were all pushing on, we were in a state of 'flow' where it all comes together, where muscle memory, strength, fitness, concentration, and confidence in each other all combine to produce a terrific rhythm and an effortless stride. Wol said to me recently, "It was easy."

But that's what I've said all along, when it goes really well, it's no longer a struggle, it's economical, the boat runs further between strokes, taking great big steps down the course. It's that particular form of magic, we were flying, we'd gone through the door in the sky, time was suspended and we were living in the joy of the ease of it.

The first operational jet fighter, the Messerschmitt 262 was developed during WW2, and a German pilot, an 'Ace', Franz Stigler was astonished by the thrust from the two jet engines, which accelerated him well beyond anything he'd known before, he said, "It felt like the angels were pushing", and if you have anything like that that in a crew, you have something very special.

We're 5th at halfway, but flying,
Pat calls, "Rating 38, WE'VE GOT THE EAST."
at 1100 metres, our second burst,
"We're gonna GO."
"We're gonna GO."
        "Go—NOW."
Fred takes it up, real spirit, and we're with him,
we jump on it together, it's not hard on the legs
because we did it as one, faster now
rating 41, but long and sharp
we're going so quick, no struggle today
jump off the foot stretcher, and power it through.
The rhythm. We have it at the higher rate
we're soaring at 41, massive steps
Pat tells us to "Stride" and we settle it
then he mouths to Fred that it's 39
Fred shakes his head (Don't tell 'em)
Pat tells us it's good, we're totally absorbed
it's smooth and it's great, so good
"We're going for Home."

[IT'S VERY EARLY, ABOUT 1350 METRES, OH GOD, OK.]
    "Going for Home."
        "Go—NOW."
Fred jumps on it, we all jump on it, we're flying, and flowing
steady as a rock on our knife edge of speed
rating 42, the rhythm is good, total commitment, all eight together
"WE'VE GOT THE RUSSIANS."

we're third, but I don't know, I'm in my world of flow and
much too busy to be counting crews. Lactic acid, it's coming
"LAST 500."
"We're gonna GO."
   "Go—NOW."
Fred goes, I'm there, we're a machine, we're sharp, it's long, rating 43
the pain in my legs, it's taking hold, I'm counting strokes, thinking perfection
got to be rowed out completely by one stroke before the end
I'm on top, I can do this

"Last TWENTY."
"READY."
   "GO."
and we go again, rating 44, but still long, and sharp
totally absorbed in the process of flying, flowing
on our knife edge with no possibility of outside thoughts
BEEP, BEEP-BEEP, BEEP-BEEP,   BEEP
five eights within a boat length,
and we're second, SILVER. WOW!

The results:
Gold: USA
Silver: GB
Bronze: NZ
4th: East Germany
5th: Russia
6th: West Germany

    We overhauled NZ in the last two or three strokes, but three crews from the 'West', in eights, had triumphed over the Eastern Bloc, we pushed East Germany and Russia out of the medals, very good. 'Russia' was the Trud eight from Moscow who'd beaten us by half a length at Henley in the final of the 'Grand Challenge Cup' two months earlier.

    When we returned to the landing stage, Bob was waiting with a smile on his face. He just said, "Well done, buggers," and he went down the boat, shook our hand, man by man, you didn't normally get individual praise from Bob.

After a good training outing, when you'd worked your bollocks off, worked to exhaustion, Bob would say, "Crew was OK." Onlookers at that World Championship final had no idea how much that handshake from Bob meant to each of us, our bond was deep in our ten-man crew.

The Finish. World Championships 1974.

GB: Silver nearest camera. East Germany: 4th. America: Gold. Russia: 5th. New Zealand: Bronze. West Germany last and out of shot.

- Bow: Lenny Robertson
- 2: Bill Mason
- 3: Jim Clark
- 4: David Maxwell
- 5: Hugh Matheson
- 6: Tim Crooks
- 7: Wol, (John Yallop)
- Stroke: Fred Smallbone
- Pat Sweeney (Cox)

Bob Janousek (Coach)

This result surprised us and was my favourite race of all time. We didn't expect the silver medal, the 1974 summer had been a good one for the rowing team and for myself, it was packed for all of us amateurs. It had been hard, but in aiming high as the 'underdogs', we had been in a good position, it seemed that as amateurs, our spirit had burned so bright that in the end, we produced something above ourselves.

Earlier on this day, Chris Baillieu and Mike Hart in the double scull earned their second World Championship bronze medal, and on this day, Bob Janousek, having smoked loads of fags before our race, was slapped on the back many times and was hailed as the man who had done, in just one year, what many had thought was impossible.

OK, I've got that chapter done, I know it was all about rowing, I'm sorry to you non-rowers, but I had to get it out of my system, it was that good. And for it to be *that* good was a privilege, I've been there, *loved it, want more*, but it doesn't come easy. Sometimes, it won't come at all. But I'm lucky, I have been there, the highs are superb, it's just a shame about the dreadful lows.

Chapter 28
The Second Season

A sailing holiday came next, September 1974 and Jon and Gail Pemberton had booked a holiday in the Mediterranean on a four-berth Halcyon 27 starting from the island of Elba off the west coast of Italy. This was a superb holiday, but of course, I brought my demons with me.

They'd invited Jon's friend, Roger and myself to make up the crew of four, we met at Gatwick and after travelling, sailed round Corsica, which included being caught in a storm and two waterspouts towering close one evening. Later that night, we were crashing through the short swell towards land, looking for the green and red lights of our destination.

There was, however, nothing to be seen because the harbour on the map, was long since dead and deserted. Jon was navigating on dead reckoning in the dark and he told us we should be there, and closing on certain disaster, all of us together, "Let's get the f—out of here."

We sailed out to sea and down the coast, taking the watch in pairs, two hours on and two hours off in the continuing storm. When sleeping, I lay against the hull with the sea racing past just an inch away. The sea at dawn was calm and beautiful.

My high mood continued that week but my demons hovered close. My rather wild behaviour and ridiculous sense of humour always kept me from tipping into the abyss, my madness saving the day for me and amusing the others. That holiday was the very best. Nobody would have known I had demons. Instinct and action kept them at bay.

Bob wrote a letter to invite us back into his squad, we got back to the routine of rowing fours at the weekends and land-training midweek, and there were a few new people. David had gone to India and Bill had left to get married but we still had six of the eight, Bob had his plan and he got on with it.

Jim Clark said, "We ended up rowing with a real hotchpotch, nowhere near as good as the year before, it was a difficult season." Chris Dodd. Pieces of Eight.

There was going to be a performance of Handel's Messiah in the Albert Hall, it was to be the first 'Messiah from scratch' with amateur choirs singing and amateur musicians in the orchestra. I signed up to play the trombone, which I hadn't played for seven years, on arrival, I found that I was to play the first trombone part, and luckily, it was straightforward.

We had a short rehearsal, practising about half of the music and we performed the great work successfully to a packed hall. My friend, Phil Gregory, the Leander oarsman, came with his Anne and afterwards, he said, "That was great, you looked like a real orchestra player." Thanks, mate.

Bob had to balance our training carefully and said much later, "In the early 1970s, we already knew that the East Germans were doing long distance aerobic training, three hours in the morning and three hours in the afternoon with massage in between, and all that stuff, we couldn't think about it." Chris Dodd Pieces of Eight.

We concentrated on anaerobic, very high intensity work and ran into lactic acid regularly both on land and the water as there simply wasn't time for high mileage aerobic training.

We started each land-training session with hill-sprints, racing up the hill in pairs, Pat starting us and Bob was at the top calling out the seconds as we passed. After each sprint, we jogged back down and in this way, the whole squad would be on this treadmill of speed, lactic acid and catching our breath.

It was a particular brand of repeated masochistic pleasure to go for the burn in that tightly choreographed competition with Bob watching us all fighting for a seat in the eight. The circuits which followed were intensive to the extreme and at the end of it all, we did no stretches but I didn't miss them as we'd never done any. All I wanted by then was food and sleep.

We had support from Leisuresport Ltd who were developing the Thorpe Water Park near Chertsey in the gravel pits close to the M3, they paid for new boats, training kit, a minibus, and contributed by allowing us to train on their water at Thorpe.

After meeting at Hammersmith, Bob drove us in the minibus to Thorpe where we pulled the trailer out of the Leisuresport warehouse, hitched up and drove on the gravel tracks to our 'boating place', which was simply a muddy bank. We slipped around in the mud in wellies to get boated, our piece of water was only 500 metres long, so we became good at turning the boat round efficiently, but very soon we had the use a piece of water 1100m long with a stony bank. This was to be our water for over eighteen months up to Montreal.

Muddy at Thorpe.

Winter weather.

Jim broke his ankle playing basketball while at work, teaching PE at Latymer Upper School, and was out for a month. There were other injuries but the show went on. My Christmas was spent at home with the family and on Boxing Day, I went off for a skiing holiday with my student friends again.

The mountains were a playground with unlimited challenges, somewhere that my demons had difficulty catching me, I was really not good at skiing, but that didn't matter, it was all falling and fun and we had another mad, beer-fuelled week.

Within days back in London, I was slipping into the dreaded pit, the days at college were generally OK but the training in the squad with two of our eight missing was disappointing. We were going to be pushed to make a top class eight for Montreal as there were so few really talented and experienced oarsmen.

Montreal seemed a long way off, my mood had slipped badly and I felt compelled during January in 1975 to take action. I went to Bob and told him that I was going to scull in my single. He reacted with understanding but pointed out that if my sculling didn't go according to plan that there might well be no eight to come back to. I respected him and his ambitious aims, and his response caught my slide into the unknown. I recommitted to our common goal.

With eighteen months to Montreal, we rowed many more combinations in the fours and occasionally rowed the eight, Matheson strained his back and was out for a few weeks but as the Tideway 'Head' approached, Bob put an eight together, which had me in the stroke seat and it included four people who hadn't raced in the eight.

Our training took on a particular form for about four weeks before the 'Head'. We were to start number two in the race, ten seconds behind the Tideway Scullers and in each training outing, we rowed three long rows at race pace rating thirty-six, typically nine minutes, seven minutes and nine minutes.

There was a one-minute burst in the middle of each training row, which was to be the push to get past the Tideway Scullers. Bob followed closely behind in his inflatable dinghy but never said much, Pat was in control, he gave us good calls, clearly and at the right times, he coached, encouraged and pushed us along, and he got the best out of us.

On race day, we set off, settled to our race rate and were driving hard to catch the Tideway Scullers crew. Going round the long Hammersmith bend, Pat wanted to start our burst and twice I said, "Not yet."

When Pat did give us the call, Alan Inns, the Tideway Scullers cox, called for them to go for ten. [NOT ENOUGH.] They did ten strokes and Alan called for another ten. [STILL NOT ENOUGH.] We pulled past and steadily rowed away.

It was a good feeling, our time was over half a minute faster than theirs and our time broke the record for the event, which was very good with four new men on board after a difficult winter. The result on that day lifted us and it gave us hope for Montreal.

Winning the 'Tideway Head' in 1975.

One morning, cycling hard to college, I'd gone up Kensington High Street and turning right into Queens Gate not far from the Albert Hall, there were many pedestrians. I chose my path just behind a bloke, but when he saw me coming, he stopped dead and I had to swing wide to avoid him.

My front wheel collapsed against the high kerb, I went down and rolled on the pavement, on the back of my hand, elbow, shoulder, before flying into the air and landing on my feet as I grabbed the metal railing. I was face to face with a shocked but attractive woman who asked if I was alright.

"I don't know, I've only just arrived."

Being on a high before the crash, and surviving the event, pushed me even higher. It was all very exciting but I'd been lucky not to hit my head. Hardly anyone wore helmets in those days and rowing training happened as usual at the end of the day.

As the regatta season approached, Bob formed two fours, coxed and coxless but we didn't know whether we were to race fours or the eight in the World Championships at the end of the season.

The regatta in the harbour at Mannheim went badly, we were slow in the fours and I was in the stroke seat in the eight, Matheson had recovered from injury and was back, as was Bill who wasn't too fit after his long break. We were beaten by the West German eight by six seconds and Ratzeburg regatta went no better.

Back at Hammersmith, we were confronted with an ergometer test, Fred Smallbone suddenly dropped out and Dick Lester, who I'd rowed with at Leander, went for it on the heavy old Gjessing rowing machine we had, he rated forty for 2,000 metres and he earned himself the stroke seat in the eight.

I was moved back to six, Richard Ayling, a tall, strong young man was put in the five seat behind me and Wol, who was talented, strong, intelligent and equally good rowing on either side of the boat, moved back to the four seat. At Nottingham International Regatta, we won on the second day and Bob told us we'd race the eight in the 'Grand' at Henley.

My diesel engine work, testing lubricants for 'Piston Ring Scuffing' had been going for over two years and it was time to write up the report. When it was typed up for me, with the addition of diagrams and photographs, it was bound into a most satisfactory report for the US Army who had paid for the research. It served also as my thesis to submit to college for a 'Diploma of Membership of Imperial College'.

There were just four entries for the Grand Challenge Cup in 1975. On finals day, we took the lead over Harvard, kept pulling away, and it felt good to win the Grand. There was, however, still the question whether we would row in fours or the eight for the World Championship.

We raced in fours at Lucerne Regatta. The stern four of the eight rowed in a coxed four, with me at two, we pushed the Russians hard all the way and came second. The coxless boat, the bow four of the eight also came second and that clinched it for Bob. It was to be the fours at the World Championships, which were to be held at Nottingham.

The World Championship venue was dubbed 'Nothingham' by many of the visiting crews because there was nothing of interest around the rowing course, and we didn't feel any of the buzz that we always had abroad. We finished in fourth place in both the coxed and coxless fours, which was disappointing, and we came away rather too familiar with the East German national anthem, which didn't sit well with us amateurs.

Blasting off the start in the final of the coxed fours.

The crews in lanes 1 to 5 were East Germany, ourselves, Russia, West Germany, and America. 'False starts' were common before the modern system using lights for the start, West Germany were blatant with theirs, got away with it and won the bronze medal from us by about half a length, which was galling.

Chapter 29
Montreal in Sight

It was September 1975 and another sailing holiday came next. Off the coast of Yugoslavia, Jon and Gail were in charge aboard Thyiatera, a broad and solid forty-four-foot wooden ketch built for comfort, not speed. Myself and others made up the crew of eight and a large amount of booze was consumed.

Starting at Dubrovnik, we sailed along the coast, round islands, anchored to swim off the boat, dragged anchor one night in a storm, I helped Jon hoist his teenaged sister Tessa to the top of the main mast one day and she wailed a bit when we made the line fast and left her there. All good fun.

The 'Post-Championship Blues' got me that year. The sailing holiday had all the ingredients for a good time and parts of it were superb, I was having a great adventure, but my mood kept dipping.

I sat quietly away from the others on two occasions wondering how I could rejoin the group. The only way I could do it was to walk back with my head up, pretending that everything was OK and join in with drinks and laughs.

Back to GB and the Lubrication Lab, my thesis had earned me a Diploma of Membership of Imperial College and I was lucky to secure a post in research and development engineering at Vandervell Products at Maidenhead. This was to start in November and wasn't too far down the M4 from Hammersmith and squad training.

At Bob's first squad meeting at Hammersmith, he outlined his eleven-month plan leading to the 1976 Olympics in Montreal. We had nineteen men including David Maxwell, Bill Mason and Fred Smallbone who had all had time away from the squad for one reason or other. We had the whole eight from 1974 plus others.

Bob confirmed his plan to produce an eight and a four for Montreal from this squad and that the winter training on the water would be mostly in fours at Thorpe near Chertsey.

From the beginning, morale was high, Montreal was in sight and everyone was fighting for a seat in the eight. The land-training was at Elliott School at Putney and when running hill-sprints as a warm-up, I was always alongside the Thames Tradesman Bill Mason who was tall and lean.

He was the fastest runner in the squad and he beat me on every sprint by a few feet. Recently, Bill said, "You always pushed me, you never gave up." Also, about my rowing, "I had the utmost respect for you. You were the engine." Bill was tall and a very skilled oarsman and always gave his all but was so slight that he was always going to struggle to keep a seat in a top international eight.

When I started my research and development engineering job near Maidenhead, I bought a maisonette nearby. At work, I was told that I would have a mentor, but we never met, partly because I had to rush off after work for training, but I was frightened to open the can of worms in my head.

I had decided when I moved house to Maidenhead that my girlfriend of eighteen months and I weren't right for each other in the long term, largely because I couldn't talk to her about anything personal. It was too much to ask of her really, she certainly couldn't cope with all my troubles, but although I did love her, I felt that I shouldn't string her along through the Olympic year and then end the relationship.

I tried to end it but she was so broken that I couldn't see it through. We drifted on but our relationship was never the same. She was a very close and special friend but she couldn't fix me, she was my first long-term girlfriend but I was crashing through life and wasn't ready to commit. I knew my actions had hurt her badly but I had to do what I thought was best for us both.

Before Christmas, Bob sat us down in the changing room and told us which of us had already earned a seat in the eight. There were six, Hugh Matheson, David Maxwell, Wol (John Yallop), Fred Smallbone, Jim Clark and myself.

The remaining bow-side seat would be between Richard Ayling and Lenny Robertson, and the stroke-side seat would be between Bill Mason and Dick Lester. Afterwards, Fred commented, "Fucking hell, at least we can enjoy Christmas." Chris Dodd. Pieces of Eight.

My student friends and I went skiing again immediately after Christmas, we went to northern Italy and had a superb time. Thank goodness for the 'quick release bindings'. I think Bob allowed me the ski holiday space, I never told him that I was going in advance but he never forbade it or ripped into me afterwards.

David slipped on the gymnasium floor during January one evening and fell, he was injured, small pieces of bone had broken off his spine and it was a serious blow as we needed him in the boat. He was tall and strong but had already taken a year off to go to India and needed to train. He was put in a plaster jacket for a month and was told to train gently to promote faster healing.

As a prelude to land-training, we used to play football in the gym until everyone had arrived. It's a fast game as the ball bounces off the walls. Jim described a football incident, "Hugh's an Etonian, so he's fucking useless. He tackles Tim, and Tim gets the arse because it's hurting, and lays into Hugh."

"Hugh stands there and doesn't hit back or anything, which is, you know, very self-controlled, and I'm the nearest one thinking, *oh fuck, I've got to step in between them, I'm going to die.* So, I leapt in between, and Tim's veins in his neck are out here somewhere and his eyes are out here and I thought, *'fuck, he's going to kill me if he hits me.'* And he stepped back, thank goodness." Chris Dodd. Pieces of Eight.

My own memory of it doesn't exist because I'd lost it badly and was in a red mist. I thought I'd squared up to Hugh but hadn't hit him. Hugh was hurt from my punch, he told Bob who sent him to Charing Cross hospital the next day where they found a cracked sternum and two broken ribs. Hugh was told that although it might be painful, there was no specific treatment for it, so he might as well continue rowing.

Bob told Pat because he needed to know, but Jim at three saw that Hugh, who was at five, wasn't rowing right and asked him what he was doing. Hugh told him about the incident but, "Don't say anything because Tim doesn't know. I don't want him feeling guilty." Chris Dodd. Pieces of Eight.

Over forty years later, I emailed Hugh to ask whether there was any truth in the story that I'd hit him and damaged him. Hugh's reply started, "Erm yes." I rang him immediately, feeling shocked. My apology was accepted with some humour.

One day Bob told us about a dinner he was going to have with his Czechoslovakian Olympic rowing mates in London. They'd won the bronze medal, some of them twice, in previous Olympics. They'd all succeeded in getting out from behind the 'Iron Curtain', and this was their annual reunion. Bob normally kept his own life very private.

Bob wanted to have early morning outings during the week as an extra during March, up to the Tideway HOR. The ARA considered the idea impossible because we were all working but Bob, with the ARA's permission, wrote to all of our employers and they all confirmed that we could.

The seating order in the eight was changing too regularly. We'd already had injuries, then Bill went out with flu, and Dick was back in. Fred stopped rowing alongside Oxford in a training row and was out, Dick moved to the stroke seat and Bill came back in at two but wasn't on form after his flu for the Tideway HOR.

We started at number 1 in the Tideway Head and beat the Tideway Scullers crew by about twenty seconds, it was a strong row and another good step towards Montreal. A few days later, our brand new Empacher eight arrived. It was a one-piece composite boat and at 90 kg was considerably lighter than our wooden two-piece Karlisch.

The clocks had gone forward, we were training on the water at Thorpe during the light midweek evenings but it often got rather late. After training, Bob drove us back to Hammersmith in the minibus, we jumped in our cars and drove home to cook, eat, sleep and work. The cycle—cook, eat, sleep, work, row went on.

Chapter 30
1976 Olympic Season

We had a weekend at Nottingham after Easter and the Olympic crew wasn't fully selected. David had been out of his plaster jacket for a few weeks and had been land-training. Bob put him in the eight for an outing at Nottingham and it went well. David had been one of the original six selected before Christmas, but had been injured, was out of it and Dick Lester had been put in.

After the outing where Bob had tried David out, Bob brought the six crew members who had already been selected plus Pat into a room at the Nottingham Watersports Centre and asked us to help him decide the last two places.

Bob asked us to choose between Bill Mason and David Maxwell for stroke-side. Bill had not been well with a bad chest and wasn't yet on top, but David had missed so much training. There was hesitation because we knew David would get fit again but that would push Bill out.

We said we wanted David in and then we had to choose between Lenny Robertson and Steve Irving on bow side. We chose Lenny. The crew of eight had been chosen but Richard Ayling had pneumonia and didn't get a look in, he'd been behind me the previous year in the coxed four and was at five in the eight when we won the 'Grand', he did recover for the summer and rowed in the four at Montreal.

These Olympic selection decisions are hard and have affected people's lives. Bob tried out a crew at Nottingham, which ended up being the Olympic line-up. Len at bow, then Fred, Jim, David, Hugh, myself, Wol and Dick. This line-up was almost identical to the 1974 crew, except that Dick had come into the stroke seat, Fred had moved to two and Bill was out.

The weather was heating up, it was the 1976 heatwave, the evenings at Thorpe were warm but at the weekends, it was baking hot, the intensity of training was high and the ground became baked. We came off the water thirsty but no one took water in the boat, it was never considered in those days and we only got away with it because our training outings, though intensive, were short.

We shared the mental pressures together, which helped us to bond as a group but Bob distanced himself enough so that his authority and our respect for him was supreme.

Bob and our cox, Pat Sweeney setting up our equipment.

Our training at Thorpe had become a pressured routine, we were a tight-knit group, I was working well but my frustrations were often close to the surface, but until something happened the guys may not have seen it in me.

[I LOVE THIS PERFECTION, DON'T DO ANYTHING STUPID, I'M WALKING THE TIGHT-ROPE. GOD, THIS IS LIVING, AND BOB, WE'RE YOUR MEN, WE CAN PERFORM, WE DO PERFORM, WE'RE SO LUCKY, DON'T ANYONE BREAK THIS PERFECTION.]

An outsider carrying a bag was waiting for us at Thorpe one evening, he wasn't introduced, I was already tormented and I resented the presence of an unknown stranger with an unknown purpose within our group. Our training sessions were private and personal. We were in privileged company.

[WHO IS HE? WHAT'S HE DOING HERE?]

On the water, he pointed a camera at us, my anger boiled and raged, I'd lost it internally but said nothing. I could have asked Bob for an introduction, but having lost it, I was beyond reason and couldn't speak, every time the camera was pointed at us, I pursed my lips to the extreme, which was ridiculous.

Bob may have thought that if I wanted to look that way in photographs then so be it but I had a problem and frankly, needed help with it. There wasn't a logical thought in my head but a few words could have defused it. The guys in the eight wouldn't have seen it.

The ARA had engaged the photographer to take publicity pictures of us but I ruined them all. There were other things I did over the years, not all within the rowing sphere, and I'm ashamed about the things I've done. This isn't much in the way of an apology but I'm sorry to all those I hurt, upset or wronged.

Our first race was at Mannheim where we raced only in the eight and on the first day, we were led by the Russian eight, which was packed with five World Champions from the previous year. They pulled well ahead early in the race but our stroke man, Dick, led our charge and we pressed them hard, finishing half a second behind, just ten or twelve feet.

Pat let us take an extra stroke as we crossed the finish line but the concrete end of the dock was so close, we did an emergency stop and held it much harder on stroke-side as always.

[COME ON, YOU WANKERS ON BOW SIDE.]

The bow swung across, we narrowly missed a large vertical obstruction in our lane just before the solid wall. The shout, "WAAARH," from the crowd reminded us of a near goal in football. Afterwards, they said it was *CLOSE*.

There was bad feeling afterwards within our crew about letting the Russians get ahead early on, the Tradesmen saying we should have raced it from the off. That evening, and again before Sunday's race, our stroke man, Dick Lester, who was totally capable and reliable, was told many times to 'blast off Dick'.

On the start on Sunday, there was chatter in the bows and then someone called down the boat something like, 'I don't know about you lot but we're gonna go', which I saw as a direct challenge to us in the stern from the Tradesmen. This was the kind of thing we *never* normally had, I wanted to defuse it and replied, "Ok, we can do some of that."

Off the start we went, it was a duel, rating forty plus, side-by-side with the Russians and Fred said later, "We went side-by-side three feet up and three feet down through 500, 1000, 1200, 1500 and then in two strokes, we had a length they'd blown up completely, and two or three strokes later, we blew up and wobbled to the line." Chris Dodd. Pieces of Eight.

It was a good win and we were applauded by the rest of the British team when we walked into the restaurant, Jim said, "It was an amazing feeling to get that recognition from the rest of the team. That was a real big one." Chris Dodd. Pieces of Eight.

Two weeks later at Ratzeburg, we beat all the opposition comfortably and the next regatta was the 'open' West German National Championships at Duisburg where both ourselves and our lightweight eight came in ahead of all rivals. We were to miss Henley Regatta, which didn't fit well into our Olympic preparation.

When I told my dear old grandfather that we weren't going, he said, "What. Not going to Henley? But that's what it's all about!"

The following week in Lucerne, we found ourselves in a straight final against the West Germans, the Australians and three other crews. Dick blasted off and we led, at 1500 metres, we were nearly three lengths ahead of the West Germans and Pat called for a big push as usual.

From the moment Pat called the push, it was falling apart, we fought it and scrambled, the Germans were coming up fast. We won by four one hundredths of a second or less than a foot and everyone in our boat was hurting.

Pat described what happened next, "We're standing on the medal rostrum with medals round the neck and people shaking hands and Tim's saying he's really pissed off because he hates losing a race. I was apologising for screwing up the call and Tim was ready to punch somebody. He didn't realise he'd won it." Chris Dodd. Pieces of Eight.

Janousek saved the day. The dialogue went something like:
Bob: "What's wrong, Tim?"
"We should have fucking won that."
Bob: "Have you looked at medal, Tim?"
"Bloody second place, I don't want to look at it."
Bob took hold of Tim's medal and said, "Tim, you won!"

"Oh, we won it, that's good." Chris Dodd. Pieces of eight.

On the second day, we had the same field to race again, Pat didn't call the burst at 1500 m and we finished comfortably a length in front. Afterwards, when we arrived back at the landing stage, I looked round towards Lenny in the bow seat as I often did after a good race, to see him looking down the boat to me. He was acknowledging his six man in the same way that I was saluting his skills. A nod was the order of the day, that's all.

Lifting the boat at Lucerne.

Winning comfortably on the second day.

Two revolutionary and very light boats were built by ex-Olympic oarsman, John Vigurs, from composite materials. Baillieu and Hart had been using their double scull, the 'Carbon Cub' for some months.

The eight, called the 'Carbon Tiger', was delivered to Thorpe for us to test during July and we could hardly believe how light it was, reportedly fifty-nine kg. When we tried to put it into the water, it stayed out at arm's length, wouldn't go down and we had to push it down.

The internal fittings were skinny, some of them were weak and the boat had to go back, but even with modifications, it was still very light. Jim recalled the next outing in the Tiger, "It went like the clappers, miles faster, we did 1000 metres in it and it was about five seconds faster than anything we'd done previously." Chris Dodd. Pieces of Eight.

Bob stopped the launch lit a cigarette, and said, "Fucking hell, we can stop training, we win Olympics in this boat!" Chris Dodd. Pieces of Eight. There was always some doubt however as to whether the boat would be used in Montreal.

I was given permission to take time off work at Vandervell Products to go to the Olympics but was given 'homework' to do while away. The company made plain bearings for petrol and diesel engines and I was given a pile of maritime technical magazines. My brief was to compile a list of all the large (and huge) diesel engines in boats and ships, along with relevant technical information.

We had a training camp for two weeks in Canada, staying at Brock University in Ontario where we trained on the Welland ship canal, we had both of our boats with us and the decision which boat to use would come later. I went to the reception desk at the university and asked whether there was a piano practice room I could use, the following day I was told that the keys weren't available.

After a pause, I had good eye contact with the lady. I said quietly, "But I really need to play the piano." The next day, she greeted me with a smile and a key. The Scott Joplin book of ragtime tunes I'd brought along was a life-saver because when I wasn't resting on my bed or compiling technical information for Vandervell Products, I spent many hours at the piano.

The training went well on the canal, Bob had his inflatable coaching launch and outboard motor, and as usual a minimum of words. Hugh Matheson quoting Bob, "500 metres, go six times."

We used the Empacher for most outings, but the Carbon Tiger was used enough for us to know that it was fast and that we could race it. There was a rumour that the boat was getting heavier, taking on water presumably, but I wasn't convinced.

At the end of the training camp, all the paperwork for my 'homework' project went into a box. A fair proportion of the work had been done but it was a large paperwork project, it all stayed in the box from there on as I had something more important.

We travelled to Montreal, the accommodation for the Olympics was pristine and with our competitor's passes, we had the freedom of the 'Village'. On the rowing course, Bob chatted to some of his old Czech rowing mates, and our first outing went like a dream. The other coaches were watching Bob on his folding bike with his shorts and check shirt on, they knew he'd produced something special. One of the Tradesmen said: "I see you've got your Czech shirt on Bob."

That was just one of various Czech quips.

The winners of the heats in the eights would go through direct to the final and the rest would race in a repechage, the East Germans led us in the heat and went direct to the final and in our repechage* two days later, we led throughout, which took us to the final.

Bob made the decision not to use the carbon fibre boat, saying, "The advantage we will gain would not be worth the risk we would be taking." Chris Dodd. Pieces of Eight.

He'd kept everyone guessing till the last moment and Jim said, "If I win a gold medal, I don't want some bastard telling me it was because of the boat. I want to win it off my own bat. It was a little bit arrogant maybe, but I think it was the right decision. I think it was the mind in the boat." Chris Dodd. Pieces of Eight.

The momentum of our group with outings, rest periods and my other activities kept me well focused, and my demons, though they played with my mind, never took over. I kept my top form and didn't suffer mentally as I had four years previously.

*

Pat knew us all well.

"They all loved to race and were great boat movers. With Dick Lester, you knew you were going to get to the end of the Olympic final. He was unflappable, which was the difference between him and Smallbone."

Wol—Yallop was like a hippy. He was laid back and played the part of being laid back. He was a really good 7 man, with natural length of stroke.

"Crooks at 6 was a nutter. He was mentally strong and just pulled and pulled and pulled and pulled. You think the rigger's going to get pulled off every stroke he takes. When he was stroking in '75 at Henley, he probably blew the crew up. They couldn't keep up with him."

Hugh Matheson at 5—"Was a pain in the arse, but he was probably the strongest on bow side, biggest guy in the boat. He was good, he was good."

"Maxwell at 4 was called 'Honest Dave' by Bob because he would give everything he'd got. He was solid and pulled the boat along, but didn't say a lot. He was a workhorse like Clark, without being moody."

Jim—"Clark in the 3 seat hated everyone inside the boat and outside the boat all the time. He was a horse, trained hard and rowed competitively."

Fred—"Smallbone was a kind of wheeler-dealer kind of person, an experienced racer and a tactician. He did a really good job as stroke in '74, but was very temperamental."

Lenny—"Robertson rowed the bow seat better than anyone else. He was clean, clever, with good timing at 54 or 24 strokes to the minute. He was very aggressive, loved racing. Always wore yellow socks to race. And he hated everybody outside the boat, which always helps."

Going on the water in Montreal.

On the morning of the final, we went for a paddle and there was a headwind on the course. We weren't a big crew, so a headwind wasn't ideal but what we had was flair, form and spirit. Baillieu and Hart, in their final in the double scull during the afternoon, were superb and earned the silver medal behind the Norwegians. That was the second Olympic rowing medal since 1948.

We gathered for Bob's pre-race briefing and he said he thought we'd come second, some of the lads said we'd blast off and race for the win but Bob told us that he'd watched the East Germans and he thought they were stronger than us. "Take them as far as you can down the track." Chris Dodd. Pieces of Eight.

Bob had finished his coaching work and some saw his emotion as he turned away. He'd already put in his resignation to the ARA and was to run his own boat-building business after the Games.

We were on the start in lane one, the headwind was coming off the far bank, which made it a little rougher on our side, New Zealand were next to us, the East Germans in lane three, then Australia, Czechoslovakia, and in lane six, the West Germans.

It was unfortunate that the start was delayed a few minutes as the wind was blowing the boats off line and I had an unfortunate flashback:

It wasn't good.
Another Olympic final.
Delafield and me in the double.
Munich, four years ago.
We had a cross headwind.
Rougher on this side.
The same as today.
In Munich, we led.
Then gradually died.
It hurt so much.
Physically and mentally.
Not again, not again.
We're straight and ready.
I'm frightened. Get a grip.
Go 70% power for the first ten.

Off we went and after the tenth stroke, I was giving my all, back in the race groove, accelerating hard to twenty. I'd given myself a break, it was a fix which put me back on top, but New Zealand were a little in front. Our burst at 750m felt good and put us into the lead.

Pat: "We burned at 1100 metres and opened up on the field. Only the East Germans hung on to us. At 1500 metres, looking across only the East Germans were there, half to three quarters of a length back. Everyone else was out of it." Chris Dodd. Pieces of Eight.

Many of us thought we could win it, but the crucial moment was going to be when Pat called our burst at 1500 metres to sprint for the finish. If it felt light at that point, it meant that we'd all jumped on it strongly and the boat speed had improved.

Pat called it,—but it was heavy.

[WE'VE GOT TO FIGHT FOR THIS, BUT WE CAN STILL DO IT.]

We pushed on, but the magic was slipping and the lactic acid building. Our lead was being eaten away and at 1700 metres, we had barely a quarter of a length, and everything had to go right. [WE CAN STILL DO IT.]

There was a huge roar from the grandstand. My young brother and sister were up there, shouting themselves hoarse, it was Christopher's sixteenth birthday, he said, "We were shouting, shouting. I hyperventilated so much I had to sit down, otherwise I would have fallen down."

The 'East' came up level and when they were past, the fight went out of our boat. We'd given all we had and more into the headwind, but we pressed on as best we could, struggling with acid and pain, to finish a length down. To be caught like that was so hard.

New Zealand were another length back. We sat, shattered, beaten, and down, but after ten seconds or so, Pat said, "They give consolation prizes here, let's go and get that silver medal."

At 1750m, the headwind can be seen.

A few moments later.

It was so disappointing but I was pleased with my silver medal in the end. If we'd had a tail-wind, we might have won as we were beaten by power, not skill. We were the fastest amateur crew in the race, the East Germans were in the army and trained full-time, three or four times per day, running, rowing, weight training, gym work and physio between. Their state-run drugs scheme across many sports was scientifically based and athletes had to swallow pills daily under supervision.

Vitamins, stimulants, and other drugs such as steroids, which were given to help build muscle mass, were taken as well as placebos where appropriate, in this huge scheme of scientific experimentation. The athletes didn't know what they were taking and many detailed records of this drugs scheme were found in filing cabinets after the Berlin wall came down thirteen years later.

Now, nearly fifty years later, the International Olympic Committee are close to stating that the East Germans who were considered to have been taking drugs in three Olympic Games including Montreal 1976 were cheating. It is a bit late, but to have had the gold would have been nice.

Brother Chris again, "That night, my sister and I went out with Tim, along with some girl he'd picked up. I assumed at the time that the medal round his neck may have helped there. We were treated like royalty in the restaurant where we ate, and the waiter even moved to one side some of the things on the table next to us so that he could stand on it to take a photograph of us. The table had people eating at it!"

Bob's project was finished, our three-year eight had twelve guys in it, eight Montreal oarsmen plus cox and coach, plus Bill Mason and Richard Ayling who had been in the eight in previous years. There were also the guys who were in the eight when we broke the Tideway HOR record in '75, but every member of Bob's squad contributed to the final result, as did many other oarsmen, coaches, rowing clubs, Leisuresport and many others who had helped us on our way.

This had been a big one and British rowing was back on the map following a quarter of a century in the doldrums and the long-term effort organised during the previous decade by those in the Amateur Rowing Association.

The eight started to fragment immediately in a subtle way, we were still physically there but the glue was gone. Some were talking about the future and Lenny asked me whether I'd row in a four with himself, Jim and Wol, which I recognised was a crew with medal potential, but I said, "Oh, we've done fours, I'm going to do the single."

Jim was the strongest from the Thames Tradesmen and he would go on to perform better than any of us from the eight. He won a silver medal with John Roberts in a pair in the World Championships in both 1977 and 1978. In 1979, he came fourth with Chris Baillieu in the double and the following year at the Moscow Olympics, he came fourth again in the double.

I was faced with the yawning pit of the 'Post-Championship Blues' after the Olympics, and needed something very strong indeed to hold me up. I needed an extreme personal challenge *straight away,* and I'd been given the opportunity of rowing a good four, somewhere, sometime soonish but without Bob coaching. However sensible it would have been, it simply didn't cut the mustard.

The dreadful chasm was open, I had one foot in it, and being on the edge of another awful mental crash, I had to take on a bigger challenge, the single sculling event. The decision was my lifeline and any alternative was an instant passage to hell.

I grasped my future with enthusiasm, *it was so unwise,* it was going to be so hard, but when faced with mental collapse, this was the positive action *which had to be taken immediately*.

Chapter 31
The Even Bigger Challenge

The second week of the Games would be a privileged expenses paid holiday for me but I'd been invited to go sailing again. I'd arranged to fly out on the day after our finals.

I wish I could have relaxed and enjoyed the opportunities I was offered in Montreal, but I knew I had to get out of it, while not understanding *why* it wouldn't work for me. Some of the men in the crew I would hardly ever see again, we were all moving on in some way but I'd chosen my own exit.

My flight to Gatwick was delayed and after arrival, I ran to the Monarch Airlines desk only to find that my flight to Greece had just closed. I said to the girl, "But I've come from the Olympics, I've got a silver medal."

She made a phone call, and the captain of my flight was willing to keep his doors open on condition that I ran with my suitcase to the plane. "Which gate?" And I was off. After a long run with my heavy case, I stepped into the isle in the plane, there was a loud cheer and rapturous applause, everyone looking up to me as a hero. My stress evaporated, I was off to Greece on holiday.

My friends were in Pireas harbour, Athens, waiting for me aboard Thyiatera again, congratulations from all and a big hug from Gail. We drank and talked, ate well, and drank more before crashing out into our snug ship's berths. Jon's father, Max, was the skipper and we set off the following morning in the sunshine and wind, four knots flat-out in our broad beamed craft. We were free in the sun, the wind and the sea.

There were two single girls on board, one about my age who I didn't feel chemistry with and the other was younger. I was introduced to everyone, we were eight in all. This promised to be a fantastic holiday despite my unstable mood, I'd had a good time, had a plan going forward and the old tactics for keeping my mood up worked.

I was the slightly crazy Tim that my friends knew well and it was all good fun and an adventure. How could anyone in my situation not be happy? While I was busy one afternoon some distance away making telephone calls, the crew met an attractive American girl and Max told her all about me and what a good chap I was. Later, I went walking with her and she asked me if I'd make love to her later on. Oh, alright then. Yes, of course, no problem.

One evening, our crew of eight had supper in a typical Greek taverna, and while on our way back to the yacht on a little boat in the dark, I was taken short with a desperate call of nature. As soon as we arrived at the stern of Thyiatera, I grasped the ladder, climbed up on deck, ran a few steps, shorts and pants off in one, jumped and dumped in mid-air, I swam away with a racing start. It had been a close call.

We had a day of stormy weather and all our clothes got wet, we had our 'windy day with the white clouds flying, and the flung spray and the blown spume, and the sea-gulls crying' (Masefield.)

It was fun, it was grand, it was blowing and crashing, we held on tight, all of us in the open cockpit, whipped by the wind and the sea. But the younger girl's clothes had all been soaked, she'd been caught by the storm in her swimsuit, she was cold and then freezing.

We had to ride out the storm and she refused the idea of going down below and wrapping up warmly. In the end, she was miserable and I could no longer ignore her plight. I beckoned her to sit next to me, we turned our backs to the spray and I put my jacket round both of us. She shivered on, but in the end, did warm up.

We became close despite my intention not to get involved. A smile here, a touch there and a helping hand. One day, we went for a walk on a deserted coast, we held hands and felt the force of attraction. I held her, looked into her eyes and kissed her.

It was a holiday romance and a beautiful thing. I had tried to avoid it because she was quite young, but the chemistry was strong.

The forces in my head reduced in those last few days, yearning and wanting are connected with passion, which is about the future and heavenly imaginings. Demons are challenged in that world and the future banishes the torments of the past and fortifies the mind. But the relationship went no further.

No wonder the human brain searches out the excitement of passion and the holiday romance, it's an elixir which rescues the mind and makes the future possible.

The time had come to travel back to England. On my arrival at work, and soon after the congratulations were over, I was asked for the paperwork about maritime engines. I'd completed a large pile of detailed handwritten pages but felt put upon by the request coming so soon, I simply said that I hadn't finished it, and they didn't get any of the work I'd done in the end.

I hadn't been sculling for over three years and I couldn't wait to get on the water. One evening at Leander, I wiped the worst of the dust off my boat with my hands and set off down the regatta course.

I was comfortable in my single sculling boat straight away, feeling so strong and going better than ever. I'd arrived at the river feeling OK, but was soon on a high, loving my boat, loving the Henley Regatta course, the wildlife, and life in general.

My plan was to improve the efficiency of my sculling boat by changing the geometry of the levers which drove it. My engineering background made me dissatisfied with the mechanical aspects of it all. I adjusted my riggers to make the span across them wider, which made the forces pushing the boat more directly in the direction of travel.

That alteration made it easier to pull, but I wanted to keep the overall gearing about the same, so I had a pair of sculls made three cm longer, at 3.01 metres, with larger blades, which hardened it up again, (normal sculls were about 2.98 m long in those days). None of these changes were scientifically trialled or tested, but I believed in what I'd done and it seemed to work for me. I had approached the oar and mast-making company, Collars of Dorchester in Oxfordshire, and they agreed to sponsor me by supplying sculls free of charge. They were happy to go along with a detail I asked for which was to make the scull handles oval instead of round. The handles were 3 mm fatter in the direction of pulling, so that if my scull hit a wave in rough water and spun in my hand, I would feel it straight away, and that's saved many shipwrecks since.

Although I sculled in different boats over the next two years, I never made any significant changes to the sculls.

Training at Henley.

Putting my boat into the water.

The ARA had lined up possible coaches for me and I arranged with John Pilgrim-Morris (JPM) that he and I would work together. JPM suggested that I should do the midweek land-training with the National Rowing Squad in Putney and that worked well.

The ARA had arranged with Bob Janousek, who was running his new boat-building business to run the squad land-training and it was good to see him again as well as some squad members who had stayed on after Montreal.

Bob joined us for our warm-up run one evening and was looking terribly stiff, I was running just behind Lenny, and Bob said, "I had to do something for my body, I got out my tracksuit."

Lenny said, "It's a pity you didn't take the coat-hanger out, Bob." Typical Tradesmen's humour. Love it.

JPM and I had only just got together and were making a good working relationship. His background was in rowing plus years of single sculling, and when coaching me, he was always well-organised, friendly and positive. His weekly training programmes were detailed and thorough.

I'd seen a few of the scullers abroad using what I thought was an odd technique. On each stroke, they used their legs first to drive their hips/body back on their sliding seat before using their back and then arm muscles. I didn't understand the reason for it and it simply looked like 'bum-shoving' to me. They were in fact using the Shubschlag style to move the slowest type of boat, the single scull, efficiently.

I'd been taught at school when rowing eights to drive with the legs at the beginning of the stroke but to use my back at the catch as well, 'to open the angle' between body and legs. If you move the shoulders back early in the stroke, the legs cannot extend as quickly, they're held under pressure for longer each stroke, particularly in a slower boat, and that causes leg fatigue.

In my single scull I was using the sitting up Kernschlag style, using a long leg drive, because that was how we'd been winning races in the eight and I knew nothing about these different styles of moving boats at the time. The Kernschlag is definitely not the style for slower boats, it's too hard on the legs.

I never discussed this matter of technique with JPM as I thought my leg fatigue was simply a failing of mine, however, it was the result of using my back early in the stroke to get a really strong catch.

I had a pile of long-playing vinyl records in my maisonette and there were a pair of loud speakers in the kitchen as well as the ones in the living room. When

Phil Gregory, my lodger, was doing the washing up one day, I thought I'd get him with some loud noise from my sound effects record.

I had the volume low in the living room and when the Spitfire flypast was coming, I switched to the speakers in the kitchen and wound the volume way up. *ROAR.* Phil charged in. "Fuckin' 'ell, did you see that aeroplane?"

The Boat Show at Earls Court was to be held during December '76, and was to include a stand for the ARA. I was one of those who volunteered to man it at times and our silver medal Empacher eight, which was fragile and nearly sixty feet long was hanging on a wall, I hate to think how they got it there.

The time I spent there was uneventful, just a little contact with the public, except that two blonde model girls had been taken on to do shifts, one at a time, possibly to add some interest to our stand (It was the 1970s). It became obvious that one of them had taken a shine to me, and yes, the inevitable did happen, she looked older than me despite what she said, but she was vivacious and fun and we struck up a relationship.

She lived in Chiswick, which was well placed for me after training at Putney or Hammersmith, and I didn't have much spare time, so my visits were usually overnight.

All National Squad members were released for three weeks during March to train in eights for the Tideway HOR and I went to row with Leander. We had five of Bob's winning 1975 GB Squad 'Grand' crew from two years previously, it was superb and we won by twenty seconds from Isis, which was the thinly disguised Oxford crew.

The Sculler's HOR race was two weeks later, the first two single scullers to start were Baillieu and then Hart, our Olympic silver medallists and I started among the new entries. I had a good race despite having to steer round many slower scullers, Baillieu finished first and Hart second and I was third equal.

Two weeks later, I won the Wingfield Sculls, which neither Baillieu nor Hart raced. It was raced over the championship (Boat Race) course as it had been since the race was first run in 1830. Grandfather was very pleased to see my win, sixty-three years after his own win, and fifteen years after he'd taught me to scull.

Life was going more smoothly, and with longer days and the light evenings, I was enjoying my outings on the water at Henley. My mood was high and fairly stable, but even then, I had to use my old strategies at times to keep the demons out.

My training, the pressure of everything and seeing my girlfriend were helping, but I was having trouble with the computing side of my work in engineering research and development. My life revolved around sport and my head was in the sand with regard to any work difficulties.

The winter land-training at Putney had finished, the weather had improved and I was training six days per week from Leander on my favourite piece of water, and on top of that, I lived and worked nearby. Pretty good, and it was. I was sorted.

JPM gave daily support, he met me after his work in London, gave a quick briefing which would include the day's training 'work' as well as a technical points to work on. I'd push off the landing stage, warm up and 'get the work done'. My winter training on the water had involved sculling longer distances but from this stage onwards the harder outings were highly intensive masochistic forays into the realms of anaerobic training and lactic acid.

JPM was thorough in his approach to hard patches of work followed by lighter periods for recovery, his training programs followed a wave form, and these waves were lightly drawn as a graph in the background of each written program.

Chapter 32
Superstars and Early Regattas 1977

While at Nottingham on a Sunday morning, I was about to go on the water and there was a phone call for me from Transworld International who were organising the 'Superstars' competitions for BBC television.

I'd been on the list of reserve sportsmen, someone had dropped out and I was asked whether I could 'arrive for lunch *TODAY*' at St Ives near Cambridge. The 'UK Superstars' competition was to be filmed over the next two days, Monday and Tuesday. I paused and said that I could come after lunch.

The training that weekend had been hard, I set off after lunch and on arrival at the hotel in St Ives, was offered coffee and a chance to meet the other competitors. I apologised, saying that all I could manage was bed, so I slept for three hours.

My early evening call came, we were issued with all the Superstars kit, and supper followed where introductions were made. We were a varied bunch.

- Malcolm MacDonald—Football
- Mike Channon—Football
- JPR Williams—Rugby
- Gerald Davies—Rugby
- Geoff Capes—Athletics (Shot put)
- Dave 'Boy' Green—Boxing
- Keith Remfry—Wrestling
- Tim Crooks—Rowing

There were ten different sports competitions, and no one could compete in their own sport. We each had to compete in eight of the following:

100 metre sprint
Swimming
Football skills
Weight lifting
Gym tests
Kayaking
Table tennis
Cycling
Pistol shooting
Steeple-chase

The two sports I wanted to drop were the table tennis and the 100 metre sprint, but I had to drop the gym tests because of a rib injury, so I ran the 100-metre sprint instead.

I was last in first event, the 100 metre sprint.

My boss was not happy when I rang him and told him why I wasn't at work, but at the end of the first day, I'd collected a good number of points from four events. On the second and final day, Geoff Capes was leading on points and in the last competition which he didn't contest, the steeple-chase, I had to come first or second to win the competition overall.

Geoff was filmed watching me with some exasperation as I overtook Dave 'Boy' Green at the water jump near the end, taking second place, which gave me enough points to become the BBC's 1977 UK Superstar. The result had to be kept quiet as the TV programme was to be shown six months later.

The prize of £2,500, if I'd taken it, would have made me a professional sportsman and I would no longer have been able to compete in my sport of amateur rowing, so the prize was sent to the ARA to be held until I had given up competing. I could however claim expenses from it.

That summer season was a good time for me, it was a whirlwind of work, training, top performance in competition and burning the candle at both ends. I was hyper-manic and was flying on pressure and hormones, but my mood never went too high into an episode of uncontrolled mania.

On my way from Chiswick to Maidenhead for work one morning on my motorbike, there was a long traffic jam on the M4. Two lanes of traffic moving very slowly and as I had no time to spare, I overtook everyone at speed. There was a space of about a metre on the right-hand side and riding on the paving slabs, I kept within the speed limit of 70 mph, but to have ridden on the hard shoulder on the left would have been illegal.

Mannheim, the source of free army cutlery, was the venue for our first regatta. Sculling on Saturday, I came third in my heat behind Dovgan the Russian and the Olympic Champion Karpinnen. In the final on the same day, I came second to Kolbe, the previous year's Olympic silver medallist, but I beat the Russian and the Olympic champion. I was on top form for the Sunday regatta, and won my heat and the final.

Salzgitter regatta was next and none of us been there before. On our arrival, we saw that I was to race Kolbe, the Olympic silver medallist again. On Saturday morning, both he and I qualified comfortably for the afternoon's final from separate heats but then, two things happened before lunch.

An old acquaintance, Simon Johnson, who had lived near Henley, greeted me and told me the best way to beat Kolbe. He explained that he and his brother Phillip were living in Germany and trained in a double, often alongside Kolbe. He said that I should push hard before halfway, keep going, and that Kolbe would crack.

The second thing. I was told that a woman was looking for me, and a few moments later, I saw a familiar face, this was the girl who had visited the flat where I'd been living at Mainz during my difficult days after the 1972 Games over four years earlier.

She was animated and rather forward, and it seemed she might be wanting to hook-up. I told her that I had to get back for our team's lunch and she insisted that she drive me to our hotel. We set off in her car but when she said, "Where shall we go? I mean, I want to do this somewhere nice," I realised what it was like to be driven around by a sexual predator. I wondered if she was a West German secret weapon. I made excuses and she dropped me off politely.

During the afternoon in the final, Kolbe took about three lengths early on but I charged from about 700 metres and when I came level with him, he gave up. It felt good finishing well in front. In Sunday's final, it was rough, I had a good start, and Kolbe didn't challenge me.

When I arrived at work on Monday morning, I was told by my immediate boss that the head of department wanted to see me in his office and he said, "Tim, if you don't resign by the end of the week, we're going to sack you."

I hadn't performed well at work. My downfall as far as I was concerned had been my difficulties with computers, but my head had been full of sculling and training instead of research and development. I simply hadn't been of much use to them.

Those were the days before workers had many rights and employers didn't have to follow procedures and give warnings before employees were sacked. I resigned and was rather suddenly out of a job.

Chapter 33
The 'Diamond Sculls' and Lucerne 1977

The Henley Brewery was a local employer and I managed to get a job as Electrician's Mate, variable hours and a low wage, to start immediately. My boat had never had a name but she became PIMMS No.1, because Leander Club had a new sponsor, Pimms, the drinks company.

At the beginning of the Henley Regatta week, I was on top form and knew I could go the distance.

Racing the single is straightforward, when it's going well, you can't beat it, but if you're struggling mentally, it's a different matter. In a crew, the camaraderie and team spirit makes for a wider and fuller experience and if I was struggling mentally in a crew, I was still able to perform.

So, which did I prefer, a crew or the single? The crew experience was the ultimate co-operative experience, it could be superb, very satisfying and it was safer mentally.

When the single went well, however, it was the very best.

The answer to the question is that they could both be my favourite.

The entries for the 'Diamonds' included three scullers from abroad. The Australian, Ted Hale, the New Zealander, John Alexander and Jim Dietz, the American. I'd seen Dietz, who was 6' 7" tall, win the single sculls at the first Junior World Championships ten years previously at Ratzeburg when we were 18-year-olds, and I'd watched him more recently competing among the world's top single scullers, he was good.

My first race at Henley was on the Friday against a British sculler and I was comfortably in the lead, passing the Steward's Enclosure and seeing Patrick Delafield (my double-sculls partner from 1972) with his wife in a skiff I called over, "Happy Birthday, Judy." They were amazed and we had a big smile. I was to race Ted Hale, the Australian, in the semi-final on the following day, Saturday.

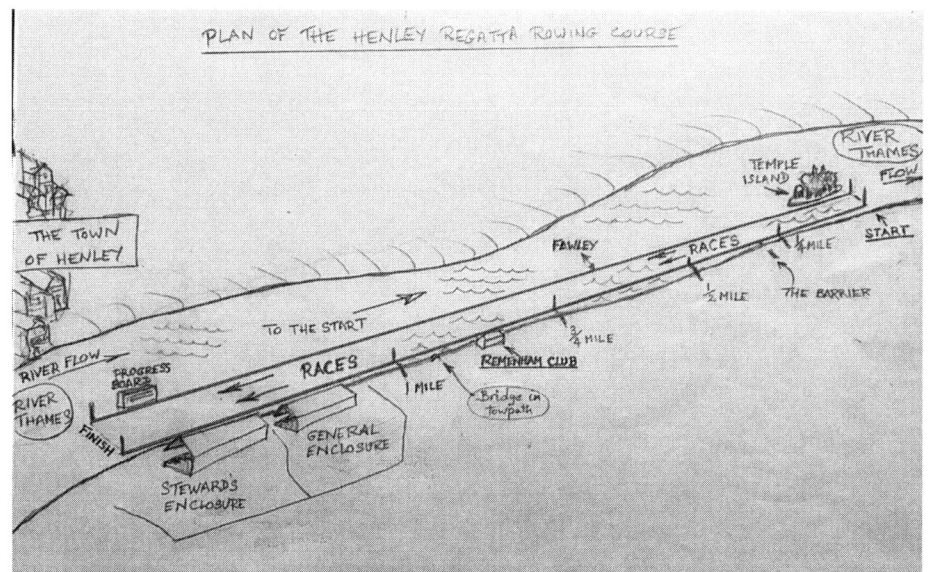

The Henley Regatta Course

On the start I didn't know that Ted Hale, the Australian champion, had won the Diamond Challenge Sculls during the previous year, I'd been in the squad eight, and we hadn't taken part in the Henley Regatta. As far as I was concerned he was simply an Australian lining up against me.

Off the start Hale took a few feet and along the island more. At the Quarter Mile, he was three quarters of a length up but I could see his stern out of the corner of my eye, our boat speed was identical. As we passed the Barrier the lactic acid was creeping into my legs, I shortened a little on the slide but by stretching for the catch and using my back and arms more, I maintained my boat speed.

Approaching the Half Mile post, with about one third of the course gone, was the time for my challenge, I'd never blown my back muscles when rowing or sculling. The back is so strong with its superb blood supply, I knew there was more potential.

Push on, and a little short on the slide, I went with my back and a bigger pull with the arms to add more run between strokes. Having initiated a challenge, the fight was on.

Good spring with the legs, still short on the slide. With my rate up a little, I unleashed the power with my back, then arms on each stroke, blades buried deep till the moment of release. The blood supply to the back is so good, I was using all that potential.

There was joy in the run of the boat as I flew between strokes, big steps up the river, and I had the satisfaction of seeing his stern coming into view. Gaining a few inches every stroke. A big one, and again, and again, inching up every time as I worked on accelerating the second half of each stroke.

My hands kept accelerating to the finish, and there had to be a 'follow through' like many other sporting movements to be sure the acceleration continued all of the way to the release of the stroke. We'd won our races in the squad eight by accelerating each stroke through the finish. The hands moved away fast, but had to slow down soon after, but watch a tennis player or the golfer who drives through the ball, and think of the number of runners who've lost because they didn't drive through the finish line.

We'd won our races in the eight with hands arriving at the finish at their absolute maximum speed, and that speed was maintained round the semi-circular movement of the hands at the finish, I believed in it, and it was working for me in the single. My hands only slowed after the blades were out of the water and had moved round most of a semi-circle.

The boat is moving at its fastest after the stroke, and if your body, or all the bodies in a crew, move immediately towards the stern at that point, the boat speed goes up to a higher maximum. There's a cost to that, because the resistance to the boat's movement, the friction in the water, rises with the square of the speed. It's most efficient to keep the maximum boat speed low (and constant, but that's not possible in rowing), but to win races we have to finish our strokes going faster than the other boat.

My commitment in sculling was to accelerate each stroke to the highest speed possible, in order to gain just a little, every stroke.

I've seen hands stop at the finish, and that begs a question: Do the hands start to slow down before the finish? That's no good, or do the hands crash into the body? That's no good either, but can the hands stop on the top of the thighs having executed a superb finish? Possibly, but an unrestricted follow-through from a high speed sporting movement was my aim.

Hale couldn't match the speed of my challenge and before Remenham Club, I'd taken the lead, I was through. The margin at the end was nearly three lengths and both the crowd and I were very happy with that.

Leading the Australian Champion Ted Hale in the semi-final.

On the following day, Sunday, I lined up to race the final. Jim Dietz was on my left and this was the big one. We didn't look at each other.

"WHEN I SEE YOU ARE STRAIGHT AND READY, etc."
The starter went through his instructions.
A few moments later—

"ARE YOU READY?"

He's gone, and me
the bell and the red flag are going
we stop, I slow the boat and turn
I'm facing Dietz and he smiles
so close, it's funny, the tension's gone
we go back, he's warned by the umpire
who goes through his start routine again

"ARE YOU READY?
GO."

at the Quarter Mile, both rating 36
he's got nearly a length on me
at the Barrier, both rating 32
we're locked a length apart
I see his stern with a twist of my head
I'm on top, focused and sharp
my puddles* are strong, sailing away
perfect technique today
working for speed but still relaxed
I need to do more, but not yet
the Half Mile post, and here's my challenge
push on, spring off my toes
drive with the legs but not too long
care for my spring all the way
committed now, it's a fight to the end
stretch from the shoulder, now catch
spring then body, pull with the arms
fly away puddles, clean
I'm moving up inches every stroke
I have the strength, this is pleasure
power unleashed and fly between strokes
I'm almost up to his stern
he's answering my challenge but I'm holding on
what will he do now?
Focus behind and keep it clean
spring and fly even further
this is flow, the mind with the body
gauging my absolute limits
speed of hands, balance, and flying
THERE IS NOTHING better than this
almost level, he can't hold me back
keep on, it's not over yet
totally focused, unleash my body
power and fly, we're level
I'm coming through relentlessly
I have the lead, push on

concentration, power and technique
it's crucial to continue to gain
he has to know he's beaten and losing
I have a quarter of a length
then half a length and I'm moving away
his pace is dropping, I'm through

*

Tom Boswell, a London Rowing Club friend of mine, as one of the commentary team for the regatta, took the trouble to record a special commentary on a tape cassette, just for me, from the launch. "And that, perhaps over the last half minute, was the most crucial stage of the race, the umpire's launch revs trailing away again after that heated portion of the race with both scullers doing a tremendous burst."

Dietz is trailing three lengths behind
we're passing the Milepost now
I know how crushed he must be feeling
but this is my moment, my time
the crowd are excited, loudly approving
they're my supporters and friends
clapping and cheering me along
I'm close to the progress board
and feeling the joy, I bounce my boat
a lift from the stands, they love it
so do I, just ten more strokes
I've done it. It's been a good week.

Verdict 3 and 2/3 lengths.

While changing, Jim Dietz said, "Anyone who can do that to me is good."
I smiled. "Thanks."
My income had dropped badly and my smart MG had to go, a Ford Cortina Estate car for £100 from an old friend was its replacement. High mileage with

peeling silver paint, a little body damage and a strong smell of dogs, but it went well.

I cleaned the car out as much as I could to get rid of the smell but in the end, drove down the M4 with all the windows, the tailgate and the driver's door wide open. I had to use my right foot hard against the door and my left foot on the accelerator, and that finished the job.

Lucerne Regatta the following weekend went well for me, I was fourth at 500m while racing the final, third at 1000m but pulled through over the second half to win from Dovgan the Russian. That went so well, it was almost easy.

[WHY ARE YOU GUYS SO SLOW?]

Chapter 34
Deja Vu

We flew home, knowing which crews would represent GB in the World Championships, to be held in Amsterdam six weeks later. I was to be the single sculler, but by the next morning, I was in trouble, the curtain had come down and my world was black.

I'd just been on the most superb ego trip ever, but it had all been too good to last, my hyper mood had evaporated, burned itself out, and my demons were in control.

This was an *exact replay* of my mood collapse exactly six years previously after Lucerne Regatta in 1971 when Glyn and I had been selected to row for GB in the pair. Perhaps I'd been living the dream a little too high, manic maybe, and that had triggered the mood collapse on each occasion.

Back to work at the brewery, I had a few days off training and spent some evenings with family and friends. I drove fast, took risks, was outrageous, drank too much, 'saw' my girlfriend and did all the things which might have saved me but nothing worked.

While training during the month before the World Championships, I felt no magic in the anticipation of the event and one day when trying to do too much in my lunch break (making sandwiches and eating them while driving and steering with my knees), I damaged my car all down the driver's side by hitting the mudguard of a truck going in the opposite direction. I never had repairs done as my trusty Ford still drove well.

My behaviour was totally unacceptable but I was unable to change anything, I could only keep going, simply to force myself on, I couldn't give up the sculling. That and any other intervention was subconsciously dismissed as it might have triggered unimaginable collapse. I was *SO LUCKY* I didn't hurt anyone on the roads.

I hated myself, how could I be so bad, so irresponsible? My self-esteem was regularly pushed down by events and situations. I wasn't in control, so I was out of control, and my only way forward was to ignore all symptoms and to press on.

My coach John (JPM) saw his role as helping to get the best out of me, he'd always accepted how I was and knew that my ups and downs were part of the package. Medical science in terms of psychology was not well developed and it would be twenty or thirty years before psychologists would be found in sports teams.

Sports coaches often didn't get very involved in personal psychology and JPM's approach was that he rationalised the situation as he always had as an officer in the RAF. He could see the pressures I was under and he always allowed for my recovery as needed. His approach was pragmatic, he advised and encouraged to get the best out of me.

At the 1977 World Championships in Amsterdam, I came second in my heat to Karpinnen, the Olympic champion, by a length and a half, the East German and the Russian were in other heats.

In my semi-final I beat Karpinnen by half a length and qualified for the final, but I had only needed third place. As always in a championship semi-final, could have qualified by keeping ahead of the fourth boat. I should have kept energy for the final but my computing power was thoroughly compromised.

At that time, I was so mentally incapacitated that much of my energy must have gone into pretending that I was Tim Crooks. All I could do was to be dressed and ready for racing when the time came.

On finals day, there was a cross headwind off the grandstand side, which favoured lane one, and many of the medals for small boats were won on that side. Of course, I got nothing for my fourth place in lane 5, but I knew, as did others that I hadn't realised my full potential.

At the boozy oarsman's party that night, I drank a few beers but couldn't join in the socialising, I left early, feeling terrible and set off running back to the hotel. Eventually, I was given a lift by a police car having been picked up on a dual-carriageway. They'd told me to get in their car because I was running away from my destination.

When we arrived at home, I was relieved it was all over and as I was cut off badly in my own little world, I didn't even know what medals our team had won.

[WHAT CAN I DO NOW? I HAVE NO CHOICE. I HAVE TO GO ON.]

JPM was supportive and happy to help me with my training for the 1978 season, I was working so hard to be OK, to act normal. He wasn't paid for coaching, this was his contribution to the GB rowing team, which was done for love of the sport. I needed further help but couldn't confide in anyone, not even JPM or my girlfriend, I was locked in my pit.

I'd been back into training at Henley for some weeks, Baillieu, Hart and myself were land-training two evenings per week at Putney with the rowing squad and during that time, various job proposals came to me through rowing connections. The word about my career situation must have got around but the details in my memory are very sketchy.

John Hall-Craggs who had coached at Leander was interested to employ me as a salesman, selling pumps, and I went for an interview in Reading. I was contacted by Lewmar Winches to sell their products. Loughborough University made contact with me, possibly to be involved in sports research but I was dragging myself through each day, unable to cope with the prospect of anything at all, and in my brain fog, I politely turned them all down.

[WHAT TO DO, I NEED HELP, I CAN'T GIVE UP. A SPONSOR!]

To find a major sponsor seemed to be the only way. I wrote details of the financial support I needed for three years to take me to the 1980 Moscow Olympics, which covered estimated expenses for three years to cover travel, training camps, equipment, clothing, food and medical expenses.

There was, of course, no pay included as I was an amateur. I went ahead with these plans despite having huge doubts about planning anything at all for my future. This effort was a private and desperate battle to save myself mentally. I didn't talk to anyone about it, not even JPM.

Having written it, my girlfriend was happy to type up the sponsorship proposal for me and she sent copies to a hundred and twenty companies. No alternatives presented themselves to me at the time and to give up would have sent me to hell.

In September '77 Collars, the oar makers, who had agreed to provide me with new sculls for the 1978 season needed the specification. I designed asymmetric blades, which I was sure would be more efficient but didn't go ahead with them. Being deep in a black pit, I wasn't in the mood to engage with people asking questions about funny blades. Ten years later, the Dreisigacker blades came along, just like my design. Totally normal now.

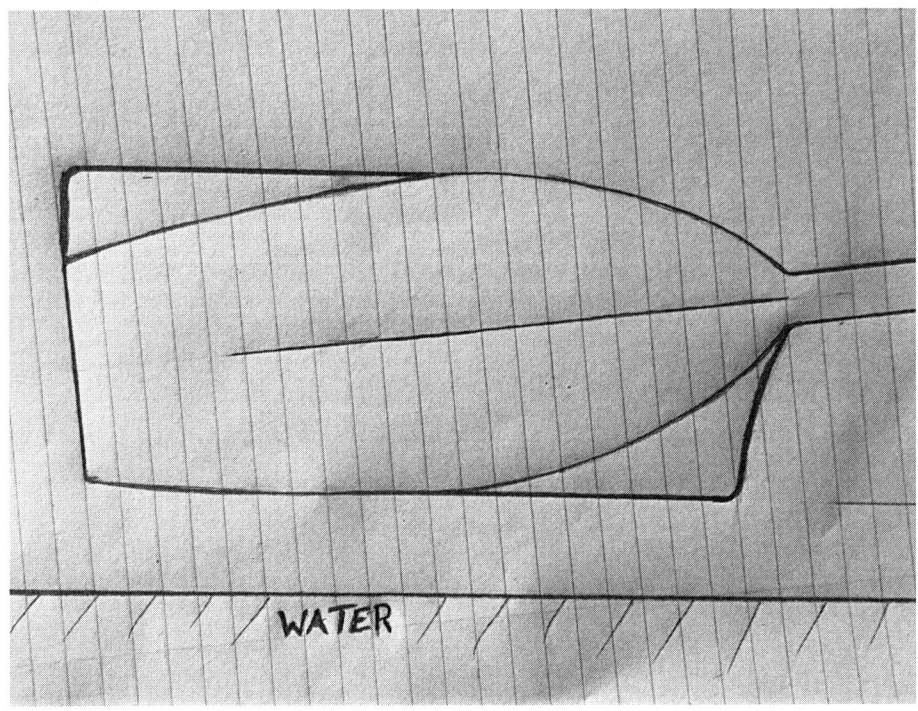

My normal blade with additions for my proposed new blades.

While thoroughly depressed and attending a social gathering in West London, a girl sitting next to me asked me to dance with her, and when I declined, she said, "You wouldn't dare." That triggered a loss of reason in me.

[ME? WOULDN'T DARE? WRONG PERSON. YOU CHOSE THE WRONG F—ING PERSON.]

I put a wine glass down on its side and smashed my fist down hard on it. Madness. I was tormented to hell. There was a shocked pause before my bloodied hand was wrapped in a napkin and I was driven to A & E by my girlfriend where a doctor stitched me up. He said that I'd been lucky as a tendon had been cut half through.

Three or four days later, I was asked by Chris Baillieu whether I would scull in a quad in the Fours HOR on the Tideway, the crew from bow would be Jim

Clark, myself, Mike Hart and Chris at stroke. I said yes and after a few practice outings, we raced and won comfortably.

On the face of it that could have been a medal prospect for the 1978 World Championships but we didn't try it again, partly because the crew contained team members who could potentially win medals in three different boats. The other possible factor was my brain.

What the others thought I'd never known until recently. Apparently, they were aware that I wasn't quite myself, but for me, everything was black, untold and unsaid. Of course, if I'd talked to my friends, coach, or a doctor about psychological matters, I might have been helped, but it was taboo, I couldn't do that.

A World-Class quad. Baillieu, Hart, Crooks and Clark.

Only one reply was received from all the sponsorship letters and that was from the South of England Building Society whose head offices were in Maidenhead, not far from my place of work. I visited the managing director in his office, he was positive and agreed to support me to the tune of £25,000 over three years, which was a lot of money in 1977. We shook hands on the deal and I went on my way.

I rang a senior officer of the ARA that afternoon, told him what I'd arranged and asked him if he could liaise with the building society and organise how the funds would be paid. He agreed, I sent a copy of my breakdown of costs to him at the ARA but two weeks later, I'd heard nothing.

I rang the ARA and asked what had happened. "Oh, haven't they been in touch with you?"

Apparently, two men had gone from the ARA to the building society's head office in Maidenhead and had discussed the sponsorship with the managing director. The decision had been made that the sponsorship money would go to the Junior Rowing Team because the senior men's team, which included myself, was sponsored already by the Nat. West Bank.

The bank's sponsorship money was mostly spent on airline tickets and hotels, but in my position, I hadn't known about any of that. I'd been looking for a lifeline and the ARA had shut the door in my face, cut off my future. I ended my phone call to the ARA, shocked, and with few words, as I wasn't well enough to fight that.

My sporting body, the ARA, had taken my lifeline. The only way I could go on from there at all was to block the whole sponsorship thing out of my mind.

It had never happened. My girlfriend was the only person I told, and about ten or twelve years later, I felt free to mention it in the bar at Kingston RC and at first there was shocked disbelief. My hurt had dissipated a little by then.

I had used my initiative to find a sponsor but at least two men from the top of the ARA had felt it appropriate to arrange for 'my' sponsorship money to be used for the junior rowing team. If there was justification for their actions, the way they did it was wrong.

They said nothing to me, ever. No explanation, no excuse, no thank you, not a word. Where did that leave me? It did my head in. It was the last straw. What could I do? Go to the newspapers? I was too far down to do that. No, I had to put the whole affair behind me and scull my nuts off at Henley to stay sane.

I needed a career, made enquiries about sports courses and started on a sports teacher's course at the West London Institute, Borough Road in Isleworth. I remember little from that time but applied for a student grant and had to wait for their reply. I was nearly ten years older than most of the other students and was surrounded by happy and fit girls and boys.

Out of the blue two potential sponsors presented themselves in quick succession. Peter Sly, a rowing man and owner of a night club in Chiswick was one, the other was the Guardian Royal Exchange, and I attended a meeting/interview with both. I attempted to promote myself but failed to talk about the future with any purpose and confidence.

I didn't say that I was going to be a champion because, being on my road of short-term mental survival, I never said that. But it needed to be said to a potential sponsor, they wanted to see my intensity and determination but they probably saw my illness. My future didn't exist for me, so it didn't for them.

The idea came to me that it would help me through the winter if I could train within the National Rowing Squad and row in their crews. Chris Blackwall, the new national coach, allowed me to join his squad, they were mostly fairly new to the squad but Lenny Robertson, Richard Ayling, and Phil Gregory, my lodger, were the ones I knew best.

There were new coaching launches at the Hammersmith boathouse with 'SOUTH OF ENGLAND' painted boldly on them, along with new outboard engines, but I was the only person who knew the history of that.

Having the camaraderie of the squad kept me going, we trained in fours most of the time but I was struggling and the rowing wasn't up to the standards of the 1973–1976 years. The guys put up with me well and included me in fun and games but on two occasions, I threw weights discs at squad members, but making sure that they were watching (so, it was kind of alright, as they could dodge.) The weights always made a dent in the wall. The anger came from trauma, the mental pain in my head and the fear of what was happening to me.

My girlfriend and I decided that I should live with her as my life was very busy and both my college course and squad training were in London. Her flat was on the top floor of a block of flats next to a railway line in Chiswick and the building swayed at night when the freight trains went past, but we made it sway anyway. Sex is on the long list, with alcohol, drugs, risk-taking, self-harm, and all of these can be used by people to escape their torments.

My girlfriend and I seldom had relaxed times together, we were generally hyped-up or sleeping, and I'm sure that she had her own problems. We were both simply trying to find our way on our individual and lonely paths.

Those days were hectic and it was the rushing which was keeping me going each day until sleep took me over at night. I was still taking 5 mg Diazepam and a Mogodon sleeping pill every night and I slept deeply but could have slept longer.

I was late to college one day and told not to be late again, but I overslept for the same lecture a week later, jumped up, dressed, rushed out and drove off between parked cars in the narrow street.

I crashed head-on into a car coming the other way on a bend between parked cars. Head in hands.

[OH GOD, OH GOD, OH GOD, IRRESPONSIBLE HATEFUL IDIOT. WHY CAN'T I JUST BEHAVE? F—F—F—F—F—]

Insurance paid for his car. Mine had its front pushed in but it drove courageously on.

The BBC's UK Superstars programme was shown on the TV, I'd told my parents beforehand, but rang them immediately afterwards, they were muted considering my win but my mother was very ill with depression.

The following morning, I went to college to attend my sports course, I had things on my mind including my parents but nearly all of the sports students had seen the Superstars TV programme. While waiting in the coffee queue in the large canteen, three lovely girls came up to me, all smiles, and said, "Excuse me, but didn't you win the Superstars last night?" I laughed and said that I had. It was a delightful moment.

[OH MY, OH MY. BEAUTIFUL GIRLS.]

But I couldn't cope with it. I'd have loved to have been spontaneous and fun, and to have taken the moment wherever it could have gone. Meeting girls when I was 'high' tended to produce chemistry, cheeky conversations and possibilities.

If my brain was in a 'mixed mood'*, the whole thing was just bloody difficult but on awful depressed days, I felt only sadness and loss because of what might have been. I'd had good eye contact with one of the girls that lunchtime and as I turned away, I saw disappointment in her eyes. Sadness and confusion for me *yet again*.

---

* see Appendix

I was shocked when my girlfriend mentioned that she and one or two of her girl-friends had on a few occasions avoided difficult Sundays after drinking and partying through the night by taking two 'Moggies' (which turned out to be mogodon sleeping pills) in the morning and sleeping through.

I was invited with a partner to the Sports Personality of the Year dinner. We sat almost opposite Sebastian Coe who was a young 'up-and-coming' runner, but despite real efforts, my low mood didn't allow me to hold a proper conversation.

My finances were in poor shape as I had outgoings, including the mortgage in Maidenhead, but no income. There was no rent coming in from my property because I no longer had a lodger and my application for a student grant was turned down because I'd been receiving a grant as an engineering student only three years previously.

The squad eight was invited to an 'International Regatta' to race on the Nile at Luxor and then Cairo in Egypt over Christmas. I was in the six seat in the eight and in many ways, the trip was a great success. It *was* a success, we raced well, won things and had a couple of booze-ups. We visited the Valley of the Kings, Karnak and the pyramids and I nearly enjoyed it, but it was badly spoiled by my brain.

Chapter 35
The 1978 Season

Early in 1978, I was offered an engineering job by Mike Fothergill, a London rowing club member who I knew a little, his proposition was both very well-timed and it was a great offer to a fellow sportsman. Mike owned a construction engineering consultancy in Richmond and needed a draughtsman.

I'd done plenty of mechanical engineering drawing and I quit the sports course at college to take up his offer. I was surprised to find my friend Mike Hart from the British rowing team in the office, we'd both been members of the team for five years and knew each other well.

The engineering drawing work, although relating to buildings rather than mechanical engineering, was straightforward, the offices were over the foyer of the Odeon cinema, looking out along Richmond Bridge and it was particularly good to be earning a wage just then.

My relationship with my girlfriend ended when I found that I wasn't the only man in her life. After I moved out of her Chiswick flat I lodged with Tim and Rose Bramfitt in Teddington and looked for a house in Kingston while my Maidenhead property went on the market.

After a bad outing in the squad eight one evening, my key wouldn't open Tim and Rose's front door, and apparently, I kicked the door in, it's funny how selective my memory is. I was told later that they were in the kitchen drinking tea and when they heard the crash, Bramfitt said, "It must be Tim, quick out the back." They went to the pub.

They had Benny, a half-Labrador, half-Ridgeback who was very friendly but I wasn't told about his aggressive side. One evening, I challenged him with a growl and my forearm. He snatched my forearm in his mouth but luckily, didn't do the biting and tearing thing. His reaction was quite restrained, so I'm sure he sensed that it was just a 'play-fight'. Tim was amused.

One Saturday, I was unable to face the evening, I was in an awful depressed state. I couldn't go on without taking some action to distract myself from the pain. There were the many options, including alcohol, drugs, sex, crime, self-harm, and as a last resort, suicide.

I was feeling very bad indeed, but at least I chose a responsible course of action. My mission was to find a girl, and I drove to Barnes where I'd lived as a student, parked, and could see lights spilling out of a door onto the road. Suddenly: "Tim!". I'd bumped into a friend, a girl who I knew quite well, and had always liked, she was happy and excited to see me. Oh my goodness, it was incredible, hearing such a warm welcome, and from someone who cared for me.

The relief was superb, but the strength of my emotional release took me by surprise. I was about to collapse, sobbing in the street, on my hands and knees. But my masculine pride took over. I couldn't be seen to break down, and I walked away. It all happened in a moment. My split-second reaction showed that there'd been no time to think. I just walked away. Kelly, I'm so sorry. You could perhaps have saved me, you might have helped me out of that terrible pit, and it was horrible of me to turn my back on you.

As I walked, and then drove, my mind was blanked by the shock of what had happened. I wasn't saved, but the events had subdued the pain that had forced me out that evening. I was safe, and I slept.

The Sunday morning training, rowing in the eight, saved me, temporarily of course, but that crisis was over.

One afternoon, my boss, Mike Fothergill, suggested that he and I should go for a walk. It turned out that he was on the ARA committee and they were offering to pay for me to see a psychiatrist. My reaction was, "Thank you, but no."

Most people at the time were ignorant about psychiatrists and I thought you had to be mad before seeing one, and I knew I wasn't that. The ARA's offer was significant in that it had huge potential to improve my life, it was an opportunity missed, I wish someone had taken me by the scruff of the neck. I've wondered since if Mike's job offer had resulted from the ARA's handling of my sponsorship, as he had a position within the ARA and might have heard about it.

For the Tideway Head of the River Race, I sat in the stroke seat of the squad eight, my sport lifted my mood, so that I could perform every time. We had to start near the back among the new entries because as a composite eight from different clubs we were a new crew, and we came second behind the Lightweight Squad Eight.

Racing between the slower boats in the 'New entries'.

After the race I was back to sculling, and in the Scullers HOR two weeks later, started number three.

In the race I was on a high, went fast early on, overtook Mike Hart and had closed up significantly on Chris Baillieu before I blew out badly with just two minutes to go. I felt ill, was unable to look round to check steering, but forced myself to finish the race and was lucky to win from Chris by one second. Ten days later, I won the Wingfield Sculls for the second time.

My Maidenhead property had a buyer, I'd found a house in Kingston and when my move day came, Bramfitt helped me move from Maidenhead to Kingston. I'd hired a Luton van, which was full for the journey, and on the elevated section of the M4 at Chiswick, taking a right-hand bend quite steadily, we had a scare when the engine revs suddenly climbed.

We were looking down over the Armco barrier at the houses below and one of our back wheels was spinning in the air. I was thinking about our modest speed but also how high our centre of gravity must have been.

It was time to start sculling from Kingston RC, so I brought my boat to Kingston RC from Henley, my house was a little over half a mile from the rowing club and was close to Kingston Gate of Richmond Park.

One dark evening while running in the park, I came to the exit gates on Park Road, found them locked, and finding myself trapped inside, I grabbed two of the vertical bars of the gate and shook them violently while letting out an extended King Kong shout of rage.

One of the bars had rusted to nothing at both top and bottom, it broke off and I found myself with the heavy square steel bar in my hand. While putting it down on the side of the road, I noticed the pedestrian gate, so I came out feeling foolish though slightly amused. There was no one around.

On working days, parking was difficult in Richmond; often, I used to park on the tidal slope on the river on the far side of Richmond Bridge but it was essential to keep close tabs on the tides to avoid the car being submerged by the incoming water.

After work one day, I walked towards the bridge and saw that the water was high, a crowd on the far side of the bridge were looking down to the left and my estate car was being flooded. I'd parked facing up the slope away from me and as I got closer, I could see that the water was over the seats and almost up to the steering wheel.

[OH NO, FOR GOD'S SAKE, STUPID.]

Adrenaline is building as I walk across
I come to the back of the crowd
no thinking, no nothing, the primate again
shoes and trousers off
shoes and trousers on briefcase to a stranger
"Could you hold these things?"
off down the steps in shirt, pants and socks
into the river I stride
unlock and open the doors my side
then deeper, to open the back
the water's almost lapping the back window
lift the tailgate up
totally committed, here I go

shoulder to the door pillar
release the handbrake and really shove
the car rocks sideways, that's all
much more force than that is needed
an Olympic Push, she moves
tiny steps with massive force
my socks are gripping well
head down, push harder, do not stop
water running out everywhere
keep going, more force all the way
check steering, head down, don't stop
more force, MORE force, MORE force still
a way to go, more force
tiny steps and pushing harder
socks aren't slipping at all
nearly there, above the tideline
three feet more relax
gallons of water trapped in the footwells
lean in, handbrake, dunnit

The distributor might well have been underwater, so no sparks for the engine but I locked up anyway and walked towards the silent onlookers who must have been impressed, I thought they could have clapped or *something*. My belongings were returned to me, people watched as I took my socks but not pants off, put trousers and shoes on, and we all walked away. I stopped at a phone box, rang Bramfitt to beg a lift and he collected me.

The next day, the engine wouldn't go, but I dried out the distributor and eventually she started. It was at least two months before the windows stopped steaming up, I had to put up with soggy carpets and black sacks on the driver's seat. The car had been cheap, the paint was peeling, I'd crashed her twice, had no repairs done, she was faithful, reliable and willing, and for my part, I'd checked her water, oil and tyres and we understood each other.

Every day, I woke up feeling awful but set out to have a good day. My engineering drawing work was OK, though I had to force myself at times to do it and the pressure of physical training always perked me up later on. My sculling was done on the river at Kingston, I went running regularly and ran hill-sprints up a grassy slope in Richmond Park near my home.

JPM followed me on the river for my outings but it was years before I appreciated the pressures on JPM, family man, Squadron Leader John Pilgrim-Morris, working at the Ministry of Defence in Whitehall, commuting from Maidenhead to work and travelling to Kingston Rowing Club on trains and his folding bike.

The job with Fothergill Associates had enabled me to get a mortgage and my Kingston home gave me so much, it was my refuge and security, and with lodgers from Kingston RC, it was a happy home.

I was animated often, having a laugh particularly at home, but my world, my outlook and my activities had shrunk in many ways, I was a shadow of my former self, with no long-term plans for a career, life or future.

My Superstars prize of £2,500 had been held by the ARA for nearly a year and as I could use the money 'for expenses', I ordered a sculling boat, which was to cost £1,305 from Empacher. The wooden boat arrived a month before Mannheim regatta, it was difficult to balance it between strokes and I found that whatever I did at the finish of the stroke, it fell unpredictably to one side or other on the way forward for the next stroke.

At Mannheim on the first day, I wasn't far behind the leaders, but on the second day, I was second to Kolbe but in front of the Olympic champion, Karpinnen. I could not get the Empacher to run level between strokes and in the end at home, went back to using my ten-year-old Sims boat.

Ratzeburg and Nottingham International regattas came and went, but I missed them as I had a chest infection and was training very gently. After two courses of antibiotics, my chest was finally clear and I was to race at Henley.

JPM decided later that my immune system had been compromised by overtraining, and it's known now that cortisol, the hormone produced by extreme stress, suppresses the immune system.

Quoting from the internet, "Burn-out, or overtraining syndrome, is a condition in which an athlete experiences fatigue and declining performance in sport despite continuing or increased training. Overtraining can result in mood changes, decreased motivation, frequent injuries and even infections."

There was overtraining and cortisol, but there was also the issue of bipolar disorder, which we didn't know about, I know I needed help, and it was given by various people. Thank you again to those people. If you are one of those who helped me or were 'put upon' and never repaid, please feel free to remind me.

Chapter 36
The 'Diamonds' and Lucerne 1978

Henley Royal Regatta 1978 was my twelfth Henley Regatta, and during the previous year when I was on top form, I'd won the 'Diamond Sculls' but my second season of sculling as Great Britain's single sculler was proving most difficult.

On Monday of the Henley Regatta week, just days before racing started, while talking to my coach JPM and others outside Leander, I could hear my voice but was strangely detached. Tim Crooks was two people, everyone looked to me and expected so much, and yes, Tim was there.

I had control of that person but I was outside my body, looking down from above my left shoulder, I could see him but how could I, that person, possibly live up to all that was expected of me with a blanket in my brain, a clamp on my head, depressed, stressed, incapable and weak.

That person seemed to be an impostor, acting a part, but I witnessed it, it was me, I felt terrible, guilty and ashamed. It's impossible to convey the feeling of profound clinical depression to others, the only way to know what it's like is to experience it.

I've heard doubt thrown on the phrase 'the pain of depression' but I came to know that depression can overwhelm the brain, it can be excruciating, control of facial expression can be lost. Many things can result including bellowing into a storm. There can be careering and tearing torments too, oh no, 'the pain of depression' simply doesn't cut it, it's worse than that.

Later on that day, I told JPM that I was too depressed to race in the regatta, he thought for a few moments and said, "You've been drawn against the Italian, Cavalieri on Thursday, he's a club sculler, you can beat him easily, let's just work towards that."

[OH GOD.]

A pause while I wondered if I could do it. "*Ok*," I said. It was a good call, John, you got me to my first race. As always, JPM had used a professional's logic to manage his sportsman while neither of us knew what my underlying problem was.

On the Thursday, paddling down to the start, I stopped to watch a race coming up while feeling dazed and lonely and wishing I could be somewhere else, anywhere else. I arrived at the start without any formal warm-up and rather out of touch with everything.

Off the start, I felt weird but pulled ahead, the crowd gave me support but my head wasn't there. I was watching the race on a narrow screen with the sound muffled and it was most odd, but straightforward in that I was in front.

On the Friday, my quarterfinal was against Dan Topolski, the ex-Oxford University oarsman and World Champion in the British Lightweight Eight as well as coach of many Oxford crews who'd won the Boat Race.

I set off down to the start rather late on purpose to use the tension of the tight schedule to keep my mood from crashing. [I SHOULD WIN, JUST DO IT.] The water was flat, I turned 300 metres below the island, set off towards the start and did a short sprint with a line of buoys on my right.

Ten strokes towards the start to get warm
it's good, going well, I'm flying
I square my blades to take the last stroke
my right blade hits a buoy
the handle flies out of my hand
it's going away from me
the blade skims along the water
the long way round
and hits my boat behind me, whack
I'm still going flat out
my right blade's under my left rigger
with a stream of bubbles behind it
it's square, a one blade emergency stop
my left scull's perfectly fine
but my right scull handle is pointing away

I come to a standstill, upright
and both my blades are on my left
precarious. [OH MY GOD]

I took my right scull loom* in my right hand and eased the scull out from under my boat, threw it away from me hard and it skimmed the water all the way round, the handle coming into my hand. Looking to the start, they seemed to be waiting, and as soon as I paddled, my right blade went deep, the rigger was badly twisted.

I arrived on the start in a world of stress, I couldn't face a delay, the challenge of this race might save my mind but I didn't know what would happen.

The starter went through his routine:

*

"WHEN I SEE YOU ARE STRAIGHT AND READY," etc.

"ARE YOU READY?
GO"

In order to compensate for the bent rigger, I had to drive back hard off centre to the left on each stroke, and when moving forwards on that diagonal angle to the centre for the next stroke, my left scull dragged heavily on the water. I gripped my scull handles tightly and made it up as I went, but gradually pulled in front, we raced up the Henley course, (over a mile and a quarter, about 2,100 metres, upstream), and by halfway, my left shoulder was screaming with the pain of the lactic acid. After every stroke I had to lean on my left scull before coming to the centre-line, and it seemed to go on forever but I won the race.

I'd taken on that challenge and had given two fingers to my demons. Afterwards, I had to adjust my rigger a long way to compensate for the twist in it, and having won, for an hour or so I felt OK till my demons dragged me back into the pit. No one ever asked me about that untidy race apart from JPM.

I saw young women at Henley and wished I could get to know them but the Henley scene was too charged already without added complications. There was a serious block keeping me from contact with those beautiful girls, especially when my mood was mixed or down.

If I was on a high, I could initiate a relationship but it was never straightforward because I knew my rollercoaster moods would fuck it up sooner or later.

My emotional turmoils were incomprehensible to me, there was a screaming conflict between wanting, knowing that on one hand, I could attract girls, but knowing that I was flawed and that sooner or later, I'd be found out. You can't have a close relationship without being open, so these girls were out of reach.

Seeing beauty in a young woman just made me sad because I knew I couldn't cope with it. If I had opened my heart to anyone, I would have fallen apart. The semi-finals were on the Saturday and I was to race Nicolov, the Bulgarian champion who I'd beaten on the continent during the previous year.

On the other side of the draw was Hugh Matheson, my ex-crew-mate and friend. He was to race his semi-final against Kolbe, that Olympic silver medallist before my race, and Kolbe led, but at the half mile post, the scullers were level. Matheson took the lead soon after and he tells me now that his race was a bluff, Kolbe could have come back if he'd tried because he, Matheson, was shot. Kolbe didn't challenge and Hugh won the race.

JPM and I were approaching Henley in my VW campervan for my race against Nicolov, the police had closed Remenham Lane, which was the route we wanted to take. The traffic was solid down the hill towards Leander and Henley and we inched forward until we agreed that time had run out.

I asked John to drive, changed in the back of the campervan and set off running down the hill to Leander. I knew I had enough time to paddle to the start as it was only about four minutes to run.

The club captain, Chris Etherington, was waiting for me outside the club, looking distressed; usually unflappable, he blurted, "TIM, WHERE HAVE YOU BEEN? COME ON. QUICK, QUICK."

So, there I was, trying to be calm and to stay on top of the situation. "Ethers, it's OK, there's time, it's fine, there really is time." I got boated and while paddling down to the start, I was thinking calm thoughts, no proper warm-up, but no panic.

Ethers went down on his bike and near the start, he saw me appear from behind the island, he was gesticulating for me to go over to him on the riverbank and he shouted across, "Give me your tracksuit bottoms, quick, or you'll be late, come on, quick."

So, I took my bottoms off, I'd have been quite happy to race with my bottoms loose in the boat or pushed down around my ankles but I took them off, threw them to the bank and by the time I got on the start, I was late and thoroughly rattled. My focus was gone.

Umpire's preamble. Followed by:

"ARE YOU READY? GO."

We steam off and at the end of the island
I have half a length
at the Quarter Mile more
but five strokes later it's all over
my thighs are engulfed in lactic acid
I've blown, Nicolov sculls past and my mood crashes.

[OH GOD, HENLEY '78. WHAT A WAY TO GO.]

Here I am, the holder of the Diamond Sculls, trailing and broken
I feel a blanket of depression bedding into my brain
the pressure in my head's getting worse
there are calls from the bank
"Come on, Tim."
I look round and I'm three lengths down, it's a bad trip
in my own little world, wishing it could be over
I don't want to be here, but it goes on and on
"Come on, Tim," but it hurts my body and mind

[THERE'S NO ESCAPE FROM THIS, NO WAY OUT, I HAVE TO GO ON]

I feel terrible
at Remenham Club they try to rally me, but it's no good
I'm in a black hole, hating it, really hating it
"Come on, Tim."
Then by the little bridge in the towpath near the mile post, I look round
it's still 3 lengths, but I realise my legs are better
the lactic acid has been flushed away

[I CAN GO, BUT MY BRAIN'S BAD, SO I CAN'T]

no adrenaline, no spirit, no drive, no nothing
I make the decision to go
and the drugs flood in, like injections everywhere
testosterone here, adrenaline there
a dose of dopamine, another of adrenaline
it's like nothing I've ever felt before, the surge of energy and power
my brain's clearing, the changes are rapid and my strength is flooding back
mood changes everything
I'm on a big up-swing from terrible down
to somewhere exciting and wonderful
I'll sprint from the bottom of the enclosures
but he mustn't know
I know where I am, so I don't look again
putting power into my finishes, I keep sculling steady
the adrenaline's pumping and I'm nearly there
two more strokes, one more, [**GO**]
my rating jumps from 26 to 36 and the crowd reacts.
This is my home stretch, 1½ minutes to go,
like interval training again, but just one
I'm steaming now and counting
after 30 strokes, I'm overlapping, it's going to be close
I'm on a high, hunting and sprinting
the crowd are loving it, hear their roar
it's half a length, I'm clawing back
nearly a foot every stroke, and not far now
at the progress board there's ten strokes to go
we're level and I know I have it
two more strokes and it's done
his charge dies and I get there first
I was beaten, but not any more

I'm on the far side, and nearly there.

Hugh Matheson was sitting in the crew amenities tent with a cup of tea while my race was coming up, he'd beaten my opponent Nicolov at Ratzeburg and was pleased to hear the race commentary saying that I was trailing by three lengths. His afternoon was soon spoiled however by the crescendo of noise, the roar, the applause and the result.

Hugh and I had knocked out the two foreign champions in our semi-finals, so Sunday's final was to be between two British scullers, very much appreciated by the crowd.

Apparently, I'd been invited to a Bar-B-Q and was to follow JPM's car in my VW bus, so we could be independent at the end. As we were driving out of the main car park, the policemen were setting up the one-way system past Leander and back through Remenham village.

JPM drove out as the 'No Exit' sign was placed near Leander but a policeman indicated STOP to me with a flat hand, my VW campervan vertical windscreen was close to him and I shouted out of the side window, "I've got to follow that car." The policeman shook his head.

He doesn't know what he's dealing with

I shout, "I'm following him."
saying no, he puts his hand on my windscreen
stuff you
I rev my engine and push him back, then rev and push harder
he staggers, and falls
his one hand on the ground keeps him up
"If you do that again, I'll arrest you."
My anger subsides, and I
see the funny side of it
acknowledge his authority
back away with a smile
and comply with their one-way system.

I had no way of knowing where the Bar-B-Q was, and couldn't contact JPM as mobile phones were yet to be invented, so I drove back and ended up having a quiet evening at my place. My mood was still down and I didn't want to stand around pretending to enjoy myself. Parties are so crap when your brain's bad.

Hugh and I were to race each other in the final of the 'Diamonds' in the middle of Sunday afternoon, we'd been the 'engine room' of the eight for three years, had trained on land and water and had been team members together, so we knew each other well.

He was a good athlete but I'd performed a little better than him in most tests during those squad days; however, I felt that in the circumstances of this week, our race was to be a real challenge.

On the start for the final, the umpire's preamble,
    then; "ARE YOU READY? ….GO."
We power off together and he pulls ahead
careful today not to blow it
I'm pacing myself and he's still gaining
but now our speed's the same
he's got over a length and we're moving together
my challenge will come when I'm ready
the Half Mile post is where I'll go
push, my rate is up
my boat speed lifts, my power is on
spring and a surge with my back

bench pulls, power it, make the boat fly
accelerate each stroke all the way
bench heaves, smoothly released are effective
the boat runs further now
the spaced out puddles are bigger steps
the footprints further apart
the race pattern's familiar, I'm moving up
we're side-by-side and stuck
be patient, strong, more power, more run
still gaining, I'm now in the lead
big ones, inches, that's all I need
and he can't answer this

[ANGER, WHERE DID THAT COME FROM?]

pulling further away

[HOW DARE YOU CHALLENGE ME?
THAT'S MY ANGER, YES]

    I keep on pushing, feeling good and pulling steadily away, the support from the crowd was superb, I was loving 'my' crowd and I finished comfortably in front. I'd done it again. The right thing for me to do after this finish would have been to wait for Hugh and to shake his hand, it would have made a good photo, 'Diamonds' finalists, old friends and mutual respect, with sculls and boats tangled, but my emotions were messed up and I couldn't do it.

    I sculled away, feeling shame that I couldn't even shake Hugh's hand, too messed up to do any acting. I went to the prize-giving in the Steward's Enclosure, dressed smartly with shirt and tie, blazer and white trousers but no socks and wearing World War One moccasins (don't ask.) It had been an odd week.

    Everyone around me at the prize-giving was happy, I'd won the Diamonds again, and yes, I was relieved, but *happy*, what's that? I was in the pit. *How* in the *hell* did I win the Diamonds, stressed to bollocks, lonely, in a world of my own, with a blanket in my brain and a clamp on my head? The challenge allowed me to perform, that's how.

Afterwards, I was pretending to be Tim Crooks, smiling, positive and fun in that public world.

Yes, I go well when faced with a race
you see, the old magic still works
the pressure lifts my mood for the event
and I'm fine, it's always been so.

The stress and challenges keep lifting me up
but I'm right on the edge just now
the fact that I'm having to 'act' confirms it
my demons are holding me down

What's wrong, it's no way to be going on
I'm not *enjoying things*
come on, chin up, I'm the man,
it's Lucerne Regatta next

Back to work and training, and at the end of the week, I was off to Lucerne with the team as usual, there isn't much I can say as I have no memory of it but they say I came fifth and I was selected to race in the World Rowing Championships.

Chapter 37
The Boston Marathon on the River Witham, Lincolnshire

Following that weekend, there were nearly three months until the World Championships, to be held in New Zealand, the finals to be at the beginning of November. JPM was coaching the quad, (the sculling four), as well as myself and his strategy to extend our season was to steady our pace for two months before building our speed again. He provided variation and interest to keep us focussed too.

We were to race in the Boston Marathon in Lincolnshire, a 30½ mile rowing/sculling race on the River Witham, starting from Lincoln and finishing at Boston RC. The emphasis until the marathon would be long distances at maximum power, aerobic training at low ratings, combined with improving our technique.

I'd been invited to compete in the UK Superstars again to defend my UK title, and this came up during that period. On my arrival at the venue, I met Dave 'Boy' Green, the professional boxer, who I'd got on well with the previous year, and within a few minutes, he said quietly to me, "I hope you don't mind me saying, but you're half the man you were last year."

[OH MY GOD, YOU'RE SO RIGHT.]

My acting skills obviously weren't doing the job and I told him that things weren't too good. My sporting performances over the two days of competitions were fairly poor, I didn't enjoy it and I came sixth out of eight competitors.

JPM took me to the Farnborough Air Show, which was good of him, but I wasn't well and missed a noisy demonstration by an early vertical take-off jet aircraft just metres away. JPM and I weren't together and I was fast asleep on the ground.

He organised a training camp for me combined with a camping holiday for himself, his wife and two children at Lake Bala in Wales. I drove, taking my young brother, Christopher, in my VW campervan with three boats on the roof rack, my single, JPM's single, and a double.

Chris had sculled at university and he and I had a few outings in the double at Bala, the weather was fine, I trained hard, mostly sculling, but I ran, worked with weights and one day, I swam the length of the lake, 3.7 miles. It was good and my mood improved.

My VW campervan at Lake Bala in Wales.

The Boston Marathon race in Lincolnshire was during September, a week before leaving for our three-week training camp in Australia. The race has been run annually since 1946 and is organised as a head of the rive race (HOR), with crews and scullers being set off individually. Start and finish times are recorded and results given afterwards.

The marathon day was warm with a tail breeze, I was advised to take at least three pints of water in the boat but I'd never taken any water in a boat and took just a pint. About twenty-five minutes into the race, there was a lock which was avoided by having assistants who helped carry sculls and boats around it.

I drank my water there. After another hour, I felt weak, and very soon, I was sitting, unable to use my legs at all and I thought that maybe I needed water. There was nowhere to get out of the boat, a quick decision, to drink from the river, my pint container had a large diameter opening, so I filled it and drank quickly twice, two pints before paddling on as best I could.

My strength came back so fast, twenty strokes later, I was as good as new, steaming. Sculling with power, I pushed it along, powerful strokes, clever and clean, beautiful day, going well. About an hour later, it seemed wise to take on more water, I planned it, and with a pause and in virtually one sweep, I took on a pint while the boat ran on.

Its relentless, it's good
there's a school four ahead
and I'm closing slowly
inching up
focus on balance
clean and clear
focus on the balance
between effort and gain
conserve the effort
optimise gain
I'm coming up now
pushing the four
and angry, I shout
"COME ON—RACE ME"
no change, I'm moving
inches each stroke
push till I'm clear
legs and power
it's great, I love it
big steps down the river

Later, I took on water again, pause, fill, drink, while the boat ran on, I was getting tired but came to a bridge and I knew where I was, I'd been there years before from Boston RC, maybe less than half an hour to go.

Sculling in the later stages of the Boston Marathon.

Head up and focus
legs down, big finishes
sharp and clean
blades carried clear
let her run free
cover is everything
focus on balance
step up the effort
feel the run
not far now
legs down, big pull
fly between strokes
stride out more
go all the way
the last bit, push
it's over, knackered.

[THAT WAS GREAT!]

Into the bar, my goodness I was thirsty, and I'm asked, "What can I get you?" Me: "Two pints of bitter."

It became all very sociable, two pints on an empty stomach and I was happy, then another pint, and one more. That was four pints of the river plus four in the bar. What's a gallon between friends?

When the race results came through, myself and the quad had won, both breaking records. We were given our prizes and headed off home. JPM driving, not me.

The quad's time was about three hours, mine was under three and a half hours, which was satisfying and I'd broken the existing record set by Nick Cooper, another Radley man, by about six minutes. I got the violent shits two days later on Tuesday evening and wondered whether it could have been related to drinking the river on Sunday, but surely not.

Years later, I heard about Weil's disease in the river. It's a concern as it can kill when in your blood, it's not such a risk in your stomach, they say. Recently, I was told that my record still stood, so no tailwinds at Boston in September please.

Something which came to me after the Boston race was that I'd felt that sudden and awful loss of power before. It was earlier in the year at the Scullers HOR on the Tideway. Dehydration had almost certainly been my problem in the last two minutes of that race too as I'd had a total power failure. I'd been lucky to win it.

I'd met up with my Chiswick girlfriend two or three times through the summer months but the relationship was all wrong. Two days before I was due to travel away for the World Championships in New Zealand, I finished it firmly but as kindly as I could. She drove off in a state, flat out in first gear with valve bounce all the way down the road. Upset all round.

Chapter 38
Training Camp and New Zealand

The team flew to Australia for our three-week 'training camp', our accommodation was not far from Sydney Rowing Club and the Parramatta River where we trained. It was a superb place to train but I was badly isolated, not by the others but in myself.

Hugh Matheson and other old friends were on the team but I couldn't socialise with anyone. My training and building up to race pace went really quite well in the hot sun, JPM followed in an inflatable coaching launch but nearly three weeks later, I raced Matheson, Ted Hale, the Australian, and others in a regatta but didn't finish the race.

We had a few days before travelling to New Zealand but I'd started coughing, my chest was infected again. I'd never been susceptible to chest infections before that summer, it seems that my immune system was still compromised. The team doctor put me on antibiotics again and our physiotherapist, a new addition to the team, pummelled my back while I lay on my front, to dislodge phlegm.

Ian McNuff, from the coxless four, remembers me as, "an athlete who wasn't well, coughing up all sorts of shit." JPM was careful not to leave me on my own and he continued to be supportive and positive as always. Meanwhile, I was driving myself to keep going.

The fear of the consequences of giving up and falling unrestrained into the bottomless pit was the strongest motivation ever. I felt terrible mentally and of course, the competition ended badly.

Last in my heat. Fifth in my semi, so I didn't qualify for the grand final. Fifth in the small final, which placed me in eleventh position overall.

I remember very little from those World Championships at Karapiro in New Zealand. After the battle to get to the finishing line in my last race, I lay back

with my head on the splashboard, I'd pushed my seat off the end of its runners,
my knees were up and feet still in the shoes.
The whole thing's over, nothing left
how to escape this torture
roll over, disappear, Oh God, I need help
save me, lift me up please

Profound depression, nothing but black
and dreadful muscular pain

[COME ON, GET UP, GET UP, GET BACK]

I try to sit up, oh no

I try, there's no way that's going to happen
but I need to get back, [JUST DO IT]
I did do it finally, climbed on my seat

[THIS REALLY IS THE END]

The end.

    Back at the landing stage, everyone acted as if nothing had happened, it was a huge effort to put my boat away. I was in the worst pit of all.

Chapter 39
Six Months in Sydney

The team flew back to London via Sydney and I jumped ship there, my plan being to stop over for six months, have a break to try to recover. My sporting days were over as I could see no way forward with any of it. I had no understanding of what had gone wrong, all I knew was it was dreadful.

I said only one goodbye before walking away at Sydney airport and that was to JPM, I thanked him for everything and told him I could be contacted through Sydney RC. I couldn't say goodbye to anyone else as I had to get out of there.

I went to Sydney RC where we'd had our training camp and it may be that someone organised accommodation for me. I don't remember much of the first few weeks except that Athol McDonald, one of the Sydney RC members, sold me a Holden HR car for 400 dollars. It was good transport.

On the water, I'd been put at six in their top club eight and was able to perform well in the boat despite everything and I joined in the drinking sessions with enthusiasm. My glass was always empty, a round was bought and my glass was then empty.

I answered job adverts and had interviews, one of them with two young men who ran a company selling welding equipment, I was to be a travelling salesman selling welding rods to companies and workshops. My car had no air-conditioning, it was the beginning of the Australian summer and the young men interviewing me were concerned, saying it would be tough, but I was enthusiastic and was given the job.

I went back the next day to sort out details but my mood had collapsed. They were sympathetic that evidently I wasn't well, but the job didn't happen. I went to Manley beach, laid down to sun-bathe and the sun went the wrong bloody way.

JPM had made an enquiry on my behalf to see whether I could work for a local boat-building firm, S & B Boats, who were a well-respected manufacturer of wooden racing boats in Sydney. I went along for an interview, was employed and became the 'Pommy bastard' who got all the bum jobs, but that was fine.

What a relief to have purpose every day and what a good bunch of guys they were, I stacked timber, cut batches of components on machines, finished them on the sanding machine, swept the floor and made tea.

There was plenty of work and a lot of good-natured banter, and I gave as good as I got, but was acting of course, pretending. Life was sweaty and dusty but in many ways, satisfying, even if I did have a clamp on my head and a blanket in my brain.

I worked, trained and drank beer to escape. I found a rowing girl and we were close for two or three months but it didn't last, and of course, she never really got to know me, nothing had changed for me and every activity was an escape. The lads at the rowing club drank beer from the half pint 'midi' glasses but my preferred glass size was the biggest, the 'schooner', which was just a little bigger at twelve fluid ounces.

"Ah, you're on the schooners then." A statement which went up at the end and sounded like a question.

The depressive episode was relieved briefly many times by training and drinking with the rowing crowd right through the Australian summer, and I was invited to a few parties with all the animated young people around me. It should have been very good but was completely and very badly ruined by my mental state.

I sent my Sydney RC address to the ARA and to my parents. No one contacted me apart from family, JPM and a letter from the new warden of Radley College, Denis Silk who I'd never met. It was evident that Denis had followed my 'Diamonds' final in the umpires launch at Henley and was intent on supporting me, an old Radleian, on the river. I was touched by his letter, which reached me via the ARA office and Sydney RC.

During April '79, the Australian National Championships were held in Adelaide, I was in the Sydney eight and we won the Kings Cup.'

The Kings Cup was the impressive trophy given by King George Vth to be raced for by crews from the services at the Peace Regatta in 1919 at Henley. My grandfather had rowed for Thames RC and had won the Fawley Cup, the top eights event for non-services crews,

The Australians had taken the King's Cup to Australia, and it was subsequently awarded annually to the winning eight in the Australian National Championships every year for a hundred years until it was returned to the Henley Regatta in 2019.

Sixty years after Grandfather had won the Fawley Cup, I was in the crew which won the Kings Cup at the Australian National Championships. He would have liked that, but I didn't know the significance of it at the time so I didn't tell him.

Following the Peace Regatta in 1919 the Grand Challenge Cup was again the top event for eights at Henley, as it had been previously.

I'd been in Australia for six months and had been missing the UK, our temperate climate and all things green. I was looking forward to getting back. I wrote a postcard to my old friend, Tim Bramfitt, letting him know when my flight would arrive at Heathrow and asked him whether, if he was 'by any chance free', whether he could pick me up.

I'd moved out of his house a year before and we hadn't been in touch since, and there was barely time for the postcard to get to him before I flew. After the World Rowing Championships, held in New Zealand six months previously, I'd stayed away from home, having been fearful of the yawning void for me in England.

I'd resigned from my draughtsman's job before leaving and had no plans for my future. My rowing and sculling was now finished and this Australian venture had softened the blow of my return.

I'd lost my career, my sport, my identity, and my life. I was an empty shell, but how far do you have to go before you're broken? Was this whole episode some form of breakdown? My self-imposed exile was all but over, I wanted relief from mental pain and somewhere secure to recover. I wanted home and was prepared to start anew.

The Sydney rowing club guys told me they were having a drink at the club and 'you must come', I turned up feeling really crap but found that all the men were there and this turned out to be a send-off for me. I did try to join in and after an hour or so, I knew I owed it to them to be more enthusiastic.

Having downed my schooner of beer, I ate my huge portion of fish and chips and downed another beer but at that very moment, one of the men came out with 'half a yard of ale' and the guys gathered round. Some very generous words were said by way of a farewell to me but I was concerned about the 'half yard' and the fact that I'd just filled my stomach.

I made a fair attempt at the beer but its shape is designed to deliver a tidal wave about halfway through, yes, all good fun. I had a go, got wet and there were laughs all round.

They were good mates, really very good mates, seeing me off in style and I enjoyed my evening in the end with those friends who must have seen my disappointment after the World Championships.

They saw me joining in socially for six months but also my body language with my arms folded across my chest and with my empty glass. We had lots of good chats, but I couldn't let anyone in, they were as close as anyone could be.

Two Sydney RC eights had raced to a dead heat in the final at the Napean Regatta (me at bottom left).

Chapter 40
A New Career

At the beginning of May 1979, I got on a Jumbo to come home, my body was there, it was OK but *my self, my inner person*, was on hold, I was flying, seated, jam-packed in a long, narrow brain-fogged corridor. On arrival at Heathrow, I was relieved to be back, but jet-lagged, dazed, and mentally unable.
I felt I might not manage public transport to get to my home in Kingston. At the 'Arrivals' gate, a happy Bramfitt was waiting, what a man, such a relief, I'd been saved. He drove me back to my house and I invited him in for a cup of tea but he dropped me off quietly to start my recovery.

I looked at my home, my blessings and my belongings. My world was small and didn't extend outwards. It was my all-important world.

[THIS IS MY HOUSE, WITH ITS CHARACTER AND SECLUDED GARDEN. THANK GOD FOR MY HOME.]

My lodgers were out at work and they had looked after No 32, although my collection of long-playing records was gone, but that was no big deal in the scheme of things.

My VW campervan was sitting in the garage and started immediately after my absence of eight months, the long roof rack scraped gently as I drove out just as it had scraped all of the way in. While driving down the road in thick brain fog to buy a few supplies, I was there, but not there, feeling irresponsible in charge of a motor vehicle.

I needed a new career and having talked to JPM about it months before, I decided to look into teaching design technology in secondary schools.

How can I
any new career is too much
life is crowded in on me
but I'm empty
I don't deserve to be this fucked up
there's something wrong in my head
I'm starting anew, but confused, and my confidence is gone
why is it so impossibly hard, but God, I have to go on
"You must go on. I can't go on. I'll go on." (Samuel Beckett, the maestro of failure)
I'm struggling now but I'll be back
as I was OK and will be again. I was founded on stone
but I need to get my feet on the ground.

Remembering the letter I'd had from Denis Silk, the warden at Radley College, I made a telephone enquiry, wanting to speak to him about teaching as a career. When I visited, I ended up being offered a job, I was to help in the design technology department and to coach rowing.

On my arrival at Radley, my old friend Jock Mullard gave me the Boat Club Landrover key and said that I was to coach the First Eight, I felt unable, not well, I was the impostor, but everyone looked up to me and I tried. My time at Radley was short, just the second half of the summer term as I'd secured a place to get qualified as a teacher, so I said my goodbyes at Radley at the end of term.

I had to defer my start at college for a year, so that I could receive a second student grant and ended up teaching technical drawing, paid as an instructor as I was unqualified, at Glyn School, Ewell, near Epsom.

During the school summer holiday, I worked on my house as there was much to be done, and one day, I bumped into a rowing girl who I'd known for years but was married. Almost the first thing she said was, "What went wrong?"

As I didn't really know, I couldn't answer that properly. We talked briefly and it came out that I was unwell and lonely, she was sorry but surprised by the 'lonely' bit. She said, "But whenever you walked into a room, there was electricity in the air, the girls were always interested."

I felt the same old sadness, but we, just old friends, parted and went on our way. I joined a cycling club, was made welcome and covered some mileage on my £3 racing bike, which was not that special. The training always picked me up and a few weeks later, I covered a 25-mile time-trial in a respectable time.

My world was very small, just my house, my little garden, and cycling. I'd turned my back on the river and everything else. During the autumn in '79, the technical drawing teaching started at Glyn School, Ewell. It was formerly a grammar school but had been a comprehensive for three years and I found dealing with the adolescent boys difficult.

I still didn't know what was wrong with me and at the end of the school days, I took to having a stiff drink as soon as I got home. Half a tumbler of gin topped up with tonic, straight down, the same again and maybe another, I always sat in the living room to enjoy the last one. This was the winding down process.

One evening, I was knocked off my bike by a car and went flying, no helmet, a forward roll on tarmac again, but luckily, wasn't badly hurt. I decided to try the sport of running, joined a running club on Wimbledon Common and I found the running style of runners very different to us heavy-footed rowers. By working on it, I improved and they said that considering my size, I was good up hills!

Whatever kind of training I did made me feel better, and during one of my visits to the doctor when depressed, was told that I was treating myself through physical training. This rang true with me but was still so far from the whole story.

At work, I asked the two strictest teachers how they managed the worst fifteen and sixteen-year-olds. The older Maths teacher dressed in his suit said that you just had to keep on top of them, which wasn't helpful, but the woodwork teacher had his own method which he said 'works a treat'.

All you had to do about once every four or five years was to take one of the worst boys, ask him to help you in the woodwork stores and hit him hard. There had to be no witnesses and you had to hit him in the stomach, so there'd be no bruises. "You won't have any trouble after that." Well, I thought that was totally unacceptable and that I hadn't been helped at all.

The funny thing was that one of my worst trouble-makers ended up in a detention with me in my classroom, he was totally unrepentant and spent the whole time tapping his pencil on his desk. Eventually, I resorted to the unacceptable method but was then shocked and upset at what I'd done.

[OH GOD, THAT'S THE END OF ANOTHER CAREER.]

But in fact, I'd done it well and it worked.

Through coincidence he and I met years later, and there was no bad feeling directed at me at all. I did feel grateful that the chapter was closed in that way.

It seemed to me that my best career path in the long term might be in rowing coaching and I signed up for the ARA bronze level coaching course to be held at Nottingham in January 1980 during the school holiday.

I met a few familiar faces from the rowing world, I was missing rowing and sculling and about two weeks later, I drove to Kingston RC and approached the club on foot.

[IS THIS A MISTAKE? ROWING DOES YOUR HEAD IN, DOESN'T IT?]

I joined in with a fairly unfit veteran bunch in an eight. It was great to be on the river again and I made a whole bunch of new friends in the bar afterwards. One Thursday evening, I was on a high, the bar was packed and I bought a round for everyone. Just the one.

During a Thursday evening outing, I was in the stroke seat of the eight and we did some impressive bursts rating about 32. The guys were used to rating much higher (bash and batty rowing), but they were able to produce a surprisingly good rhythm and boat speed at a lower rate.

We met up with a school eight towards Hampton Court, agreed to row a burst alongside them and when we got the word 'Go', I set off exactly as we had practiced but the rest of the crew bashed off, rating higher. It was the most syncopated and worst burst ever, and at the end we stopped, I turned and shouted up our boat, "What the fuck was that?"

Unfortunately, I couldn't see the funny side and being frustrated and messed up as ever, something had to give. I was livid but wasn't going to punch anyone, certainly not Angela, facing me, who was coxing. I took my seat off its runners and slung it high along the river but when we backed down to collect it, there was no trace. It had sunk.

I couldn't row, so I bailed out, swam across to Dittons Skiff and Punting Club and ran the couple of miles back to the rowing club in my wet socks. I arrived at the same time as the crew and having showered, we had a few beers and put the world to rights. Something which comes up in conversation occasionally even now is 'Tim's Triathlon'.

During March I collected Pimms No.1 from Leander, brought her to Kingston RC and came second in the Sculler's HOR on the Tideway. Ten days later, I raced in the Wingfield Sculls and in the end, won comfortably. This was 1980, the 150th anniversary of the inauguration of the Wingfield Sculls. My grandfather couldn't attend due to his health but was very pleased to hear that I'd won it again. He was the oldest previous holder at the time.

Some months later, I started going out with a rowing girl who travelled to Kingston RC on a motorbike from London. She proved to be a good and loyal friend and she helped me in many ways, we went out together for about two years although she was convalescing after a motorbike accident with her parents for nearly half of that time.

I was usually reliable but could take on too much when I was on a high, and couldn't cope when depressed. One time, this girlfriend started a sentence with, "I knew your feet were made of clay when—" [OH GOD, I KNOW, I KNOW.]

At one stage when I wanted to settle down, she was not willing to commit because, though she gave so much, she thought she could never make me happy, and in the end, I finished the relationship. By the end of the school summer term, the teaching had mentally exhausted me, but I had achieved my aim of teaching for the year.

I was invited to compete in a 'Challenge of the Champions' Superstars competition. All of the previous winners of the UK Superstars competitions were there, many outstanding sportsmen. There were names we knew but I was badly off form, hoping the sporting challenges would perk me up, but they didn't.

I had good conversations with David Hemery and Lynn Davies, two exceptional sportsmen and easy conversationalists. During the summer break, I got help to move the staircase and water tanks in my house and I built another bedroom on the landing, which gave space for another lodger. My mood improved, I was to start at Teacher's Training College at Shoreditch College in Egham in the autumn.

In September, I took part in the Weybridge Silver Sculls, which was an old favourite of mine, winning the men's event aged thirty-one but an eighteen-year-old Steve Redgrave won the junior event, beating my time by five seconds. We met at the prize-giving for the first time and were destined to meet again.

The three winners, myself, Pauline Bird and Steven Redgrave. We'd won respectively, the Senior, Women's and Junior events.

While at college and had an opportunity to run sometimes, my mood had deteriorated but I had confidence that running would pick me up. I'd set off with purpose and usually, I'd feel good, but a few times it didn't work at all and had to walk back.

During January '81, there was the ARA's 'Silver' coaching course in Nottingham, which I had signed up for and on arrival was asked if I would deliver the classroom session on sculling. I was happy to do that, it went well and some years later, one of that audience said he'd been surprised how much I knew about sculling as he and his mates thought I'd won all my races on 'motivation and adrenaline'. Ha!

During early March, I was near the old Thames Tradesmen's RC, which was upstream from Chiswick Bridge and I saw Steve Redgrave and members of the ARA's British Sculling Squad with their coach, Mike Spracklen. Mike had put together a crew of single scullers in an eight to enter the Eights Tideway HOR but they were short of a man. I was asked if I would join them, Steve was at stroke and he put me at six, so I was happy.

I joined in with their outings on the Tideway and at Marlow for a few weeks up to the race and I'm told by Eric Sims that one evening, I threw my oar at Mike Spracklen, but that's one of those embellished stories.

In fact, at Marlow one evening, Mike was following us in a launch and it was well past my deadline for going elsewhere, and I was frustrated. It was rough, my oar blade hit a wave, the oar sprang out of my rigger, and still holding the oar handle, I slung it out to the side. There was no anger directed directly at Mike. Our race went well on the Tideway and we beat the British Rowing Squad Eight by nearly ten seconds, with all the other four hundred or so crews behind.

Rowing with National Sculling Squad members, Steve Redgrave at stroke and me at six, winning the Tideway HOR 1981.

During my college course, I worked as a trainee teacher on teaching practice for a few weeks in two schools, one of which was Eton College. The head of department suggested that I should go for the design and technology metalwork job, which was becoming vacant. I went for an interview with the headmaster and was offered the job, which I accepted, to start in September.

While walking out across that famous Eton College quad, something was fearfully wrong. I was stressed to the extreme and had *a loud roaring* inside my head, it was a one-off life event, a natural warning, I'm sure. It was frightening and sounded like a diesel generator inside my head.

[I MUST BE MAKING A MISTAKE. DON'T DO THIS, IT'S ALL WRONG.]

This job seemed to be a wonderful opportunity, more than I could have hoped for as a teacher, I couldn't go back and say that I'd changed my mind. The 'roaring experience' was shocking but I had to take a 'next step' of some sort in my career. I kept walking.

During the summer term at Teachers Training College, I was invited to a Superteams competition to compete in a team of 'Watersports' men where we narrowly beat the 'Rugby team' but were beaten in the final by the 'Athletes'. The teams were packed with famous names, we spent those four busy days in the city of Bath and then my year at college finished with myself as a qualified teacher.

During the summer school holidays, I was busy with my house, went to Devon and Cornwall where I saw Bucknall and then family on holiday and I spent time on the sea in Cornwall, racing in heavy sea-going rowing boats.

All of this wonderful life was badly spoiled by the background mood. When I was back in Surrey one evening at the Kingston RC bar, I was talking to a guy I'd only just met and he said, "Didn't you used to be Tim Crooks?"

Chapter 41
Out of the Woods? Not Yet

There was no alternative to making the best of things and trying to make a life, just forging on. I started in September of 1981 as one of three teachers at Eton in the design technology department, known (quaintly) as 'The School of Mechanics' and we had to dress in a dark suit, white shirt with wing collar and white bow tie.

This was hardly appropriate for me as I was metalworking, using oily machines as well as blacksmithing, welding and casting molten metal. Also the daily routine didn't work well for me. I was expected to be in the department, on duty for long hours, to help any boys who wanted to come in and 'make things' but my predecessor had killed off any interest in metalworking, so I worked hard to improve the workshop facilities.

With regard to coaching on the river, it was hopeless as I wasn't available regularly enough to make anything of it. One Saturday, I took time off to race in the Weybridge Silver Sculls, and finishing in second place in the Senior Division was OK, but thirty-five seconds behind Steve Redgrave!

At Eton I was looked up to, and when asked out to dinner by other members of staff (Beaks), I was asked about the Olympics and Superstars, which was sometimes fine. The folks were interested and well-meaning but it could be stressful because too often, there were questions about my rowing and sculling such as, 'Why did you stop? Surely you could have gone on to the next Olympics?' I was careful to be polite while feeling cornered and angry.

[WHY DID I FUCKING STOP? FOR GOD'S SAKE, YOU KNOW NOTHING, I CAN'T EVEN TALK ABOUT THAT, YOU POSH TWATS.]

In the end, the stress of everything was doing my head in.

[YES, THE WARNING ROAR AFTER MY INTERVIEW HAD BEEN SPOT ON. F-, F-, F-, F-.]

I had to turn down social invitations, which was a shame, it was mental survival. Everyone meant well and were so polite but the conflicts made me want to scream.

The last day of term was Christmas Eve and I got away from Eton in the late morning. My young brother Christopher and sister Dee were coming that evening to my house for Christmas. I drove to Kingston to do all my shopping and the parking situation was awful.

There was a long line of cars parked on a yellow line about half a mile from my house and I parked there while thinking about 'safety in numbers'. An hour and a half later, I returned very stressed with a Christmas tree under one arm and many heavy bags with all the food, drink and presents.

What I had achieved was too much to attempt but I'd done it. There were no cars in the street. Every one towed away.

The disbelief, the anger's arrived
one option I have, that's all
I stride out for home at a fast walking pace,
and soon, my shoulders are shot
this load has become desperately heavy
five hundred metres more
the bags are bumping against my legs
my anger's supporting my shoulders
lactic acid, and bracing my frame
I'm livid, won't stop now
push on, *angry,* last two fifty
how *dare* you take my car
shoulders screaming, push on again
the last bit down my road

Having arrived at home, what was needed was intervention and probably sedation but my lodgers were away for Christmas and there was no intervention to be had. I dumped everything through my front door, shut it and set off running hard, back the way I'd come, my destination was the police station, that half mile which I'd just walked plus a fair bit.

I know I've lost it, running hard
this is going to happen
striding long and cutting corners
my quickest route is straight
I charge through gaps, surprising drivers
focused, going well
I tire but keep my form by lifting
legs and lengthening stride
across the market place at speed
someone's about to get it
I burst through doors, the desk is high
the bar 'gainst mad and drunk

"I WANT MY CAR BACK, AND I WANT IT BACK NOW"

There's a silence, quite a pause.

Four policemen rushed out and surrounded me, one tried to push my right arm up my back to immobilise me. [HA, YOU'RE WASTING YOUR TIME.] I held it forcefully down and after seven or eight seconds, they ran away round a corner out of sight. They'd been well rehearsed, another pause and I bellowed, "THAT'S GREAT, FIRST THEY NICK YER CAR, AND THEN THEY ASSAULT YER."

Another, longer pause, then one of the two lady officers at their desks asked me what the registration number of my car was, and if I had the means of paying a fine at the police pound. [SO THAT'S THE DEAL.] I nodded and she gave me a card bearing the address of the pound.

My anger was gone and she was close to me, just the other side of the desk, we had a little eye to eye connection and a slight smile, which confirmed the end of the afternoon's entertainment. Christmas went well after that.

At the beginning of March 1982, Steve Redgrave phoned me, asking whether I'd row in his eight for the Tideway HOR. The race was less than three weeks away. I said, "Steve, I'm not fit."

"You're *always* fit. Six-thirty, Tuesday night, Marlow. You're at six."

A pause before I replied, "OK, see you then."

[OH HELL, I'M *NOT* FIT. I'VE BEEN TRAINING, BUT NOT AS MUCH AS BEFORE.]

We went out on Tuesday, it was almost the same crew as the previous year and during the hard training, I had to be economical. A sharp catch, a bold finish with not too much in between. We lost the Tideway HOR by three point eight seconds to the British Rowing Squad Eight. Sorry, guys.

During the summer term at Eton, I was looking at advertisements for design technology posts to teach elsewhere, I went for interviews and was appointed to start in September at a boys' comprehensive in Cheam near Sutton. This was a case of looking for something, almost anything to move on, but I had jumped out of the frying pan into a different one.

I was invited to another Superteams competition in Bath, and in the first round, the 'Watersports' team, competed against 'Rugby' and in the other heat, 'Athletics' were up against 'Soccer'. I was on form physically and we beat the Rugby men narrowly but lost to the Athletes in the final. There were just two more weeks of the term at Eton, but I had very much switched off the job.

I took a girl I'd fallen for to see the film *Chariots of Fire* about runners in the 1924 Paris Olympics and there's a scene where the steeple-chase runner was failing, unable to keep up the pace coming into the water jump. It was a slow-motion scene, along with the atmospheric Vangelis soundtrack, and it took me straight back ten years to 'our failure' in the double scull final in Munich '72. Tears ran down my face in an involuntary reaction.

Later that evening, I tried to kiss my girl who seemed to be very close, but was shocked at the jerk of her recoil. I dropped her off quietly at her home, disappointed but feeling that I was doing the right thing. I regretted much later, when wiser, that I didn't/couldn't open a line of communication with her as she seemed to be a sensitive and lovely person. I know now that there's so much can happen to people, and so much going on in many people's minds.

When I went to the doctor during those years, it was because I was depressed, stressed and not functioning. They never saw me when I was on a high because at those times, I was definitely not ill, I was FINE. This made it difficult for them to recognise what was wrong with me and they treated me for what they saw, which was depression, stress and insomnia, so I was given antidepressants, plus the Valium (diazepam) and sleeping pills which I knew well.

Now that medical science has moved on, doctors are able to treat sufferers of bipolar disorder more efficiently. One of the results of giving antidepressants to a bipolar person (rather than a mood stabiliser, which has been shown in general to be more effective), is that mood swings can become shorter and more frequent with possible worsening of the depression. My antidepressants didn't help me.

I was invited to compete in World Superteams, this was to be 'Great Britain' against 'North America' and a 'Rest of the World' team. When the sportsmen began to arrive, it was superb to see the faces, some of whom I had never expected to meet in real life, and to be living alongside and competing with them was a privilege. I was physically fit, performed quite well but my 'brain fog' spoiled it badly and we lost narrowly on points to North America.

My teaching job in Cheam started in September '82, the pupil's behaviour was poor and it was a difficult environment. I pushed myself to do it but week after week, it got harder. The training at Kingston RC continued and I sculled in a quad with three Kingston RC lightweights.

In the Fours HOR on the Tideway, we were pleased to come second, only eleven seconds behind the National Sculling Squad crew, and I carried on single sculling about three times per week through the winter.

Kingston RC coming second in the Fours HOR.

Stroke: Graham Pratt, then me, Tony Lutz and Maurice Hayes who steered us round many slower boats.

The discipline at the school was poor, and there were two serious incidents involving me which I reported. The first was a half brick thrown at me by a thirteen-year-old in the playground, and the second was being told to f... off publicly by a sixteen-year-old. The school didn't take any action at all regarding the two boys who I'd reported, and the end result was that an already looming depression gripped me, and during January '83, the doctor signed me off work. I spent my time, not well, at home but continued training on the river, which helped to pick me up. It was the only thing I was enjoying. Thank God for the river and sculling.

Chapter 42
Fire and Muscle, and That Race

The Kingston eight for the Tideway HOR in '83 was strong as it included Andy Holmes (who went on to win two Olympic medals with Steve Redgrave, one in a four and the other in a pair.) There was myself and most of the others had rowed at some time in the Kingston RC coxed four which rowed for the country in '79 and '81, and had won the Britannia Cup at Henley. We trained for five weeks with Richard Ayling as our coach and in the Tideway HOR, finished fourth.

At the rowing club, I was introduced to Terry Clarke, the artist blacksmith, he and I enjoyed a discussion about blacksmithing over a beer or two, and my mind went back to the metalworking and welding I'd done fifteen years previously as an apprentice. Terry saw my interest and offered to help me get started as a self-employed blacksmith.

I resigned the teaching job and after Easter, went on a blacksmithing course and came away fired with enthusiasm. Second-hand blacksmithing equipment was easily available, I set up a forge and sound-proofed my garage. I found both gas and arc-welding equipment, but the extractor fan to expel the fumes wasn't adequate, so I worked in a smoky atmosphere.

These skills had inspired me as an apprentice in Birmingham and I was loving working metal using fire and muscle. I'd read that historically, the blacksmith was the 'king's right-hand man'. It was said that the king couldn't do without his blacksmith, so his place was on the king's right and the Man of God had to stand on the left.

In days gone by, there was respect for the magical skills of the blacksmith, but distrust also because of his 'pact with the devil' to use fire to work his wonders; he had to live out on the edge of town.

I had four lodgers in my home, all members of Kingston RC. Maurice Hayes who I sculled with in the quad, Andy Turnbull, John Wilson and Steve Trebble.

Andy reminded me that those were such happy years, and, "You were working as a blacksmith in your garage and one day, you had a large electricity bill."

"You brought it into the living room where all four of us were sitting and told us that we'd divide the bill equally between us. After you'd gone, we weren't happy as the lights used to go dim when you were welding. John stood up and said, 'I'm going to talk to Tim. I may not be back'."

The release from the stress of teaching, along with my exciting new life put me back on top. I was living the dream, working metal at home. During the early summer of 1983, life was good. I was happy.

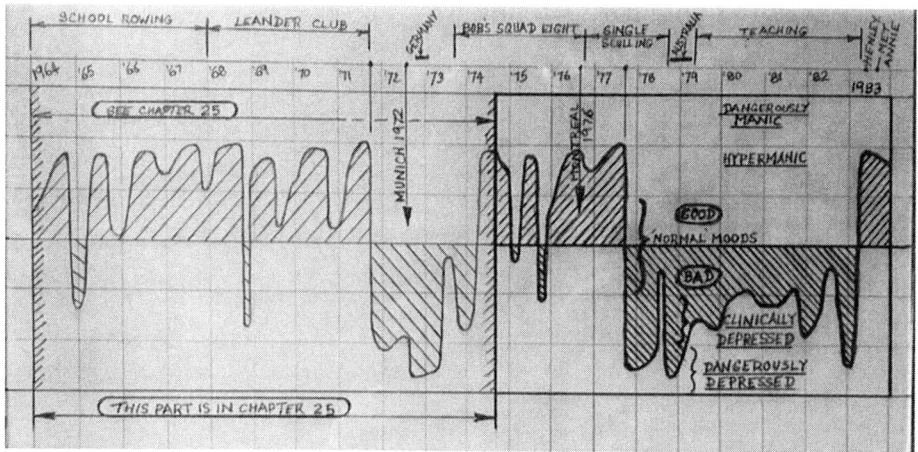

Graph of moods 1964 to 1984.
The first ten years of this ('64–'74) featured in Chapter 25.

During my working days, I was forging sets of fire-irons, plant hanging brackets, all sorts of traditional wrought-iron style items and it wasn't long before I was commissioned to designed and make garden gates and heavy driveway gates.

At Kingston RC during April, we re-formed the quad, which had come second in the Fours Head the previous autumn, I was training in the single as well and was to race both the quad and the single at the Henley Regatta. I raced the single at Marlow Regatta two weeks before Henley to tune up, met Steve Redgrave and he beat me by four lengths.

Two weeks later at Henley, my form was excellent, I qualified for finals in both the 'Diamonds' in the single, and the 'Queen Mother Cup' in the quad scull. In the single, I was to race Steve Redgrave again who was at the time Britain's sculler, though I didn't know it. I really had turned away from the top of the sport and knew nothing about our squads.

In the quad, we were to race a Hamburg crew and I asked the regatta organisers if this race could be in the morning. I felt it could give me a psychological advantage over Steve in that he might assume that I'd be tired after a morning race, also my three crew mates could have a drink after their race and enjoy their day. In the race, we pulled ahead early on, I didn't work hard for most of the way but pushed on for the last twenty strokes.

My first race on finals day. Winning the Queen Mother Cup.

Afterwards, we were changing in Leander, I was feeling on top form for the afternoon and said that I didn't want to beat Redgrave. Maurice asked *why?* I said that I felt it was *his time*. He said, "Bugger that. You don't get in a Henley final and not try to win it."

At three pm, I'm on the start
Steve and I line up
off the start he pulls ahead

but he won't get away
efficiency's my watchword now
a length he gets, not more
he's stuck on my bow, I'll push when I'm ready
the Half Mile post, I go
he responds, we're committed now
the challenge, the fight is on
till one of us can give no more
I'm taking back his lead
the 'Remenham Roar' is deafening
I'm clawing steadily back
spring and lift, send each puddle
taking bigger steps
almost level with his stern
needing more each stroke
side-by-side at Remenham Club
level and still I'm gaining
he's struggling, I can see he's shot
and now, my bow's in front
we've covered a mile, I have the lead
half a length in front
the crowd noise grows tumultuous
he should give up now
in the 'home stretch', hanging on
just quit now Steve it's time
but Steve doesn't quit, he just keeps going
coming to the Stewards' enclosure
but still, I have a decent lead
focus on total efficiency
my tank's on empty, another world
and still I am in front
now, Steve's gone through and I collapse
with nothing, nothing left

 The crowd went silent except for the scream which pierced the air so high.
 …Pause

[OH GOD, COME ON]

I sit up suddenly, steam off hard
the crowd support my charge
cheers rip the air and cage us in
this isn't over yet
a few strong strokes, but now I'm weak
can't win this race, I'm done
we paddle in with claps and cheers
the crowd just loved our race

The Verdict: Winner of the 1983 Diamond Challenge Sculls, Steven Redgrave, by one length.

I was happy for Steve and for myself. Both of us won a medal that day.

The race is over, paddling light to the finish.

Recovery.

Epilogue

Three months later, I received a phone call from the new national rowing coach, Penny Chuter. I hadn't seen her for five years since the 1978 World Championship in New Zealand where I'd been sculling and she'd been coaching Jim Clark and John Roberts who won the silver medal in the pair.

She asked whether I'd be interested in joining the National Squad with Redgrave and others to form a crew for the Olympics in Los Angeles, less than a year away. My hesitation was short, I politely declined as I knew my demons well.

Some weeks later, I met a girl called Annie at a party. Later that evening, she told me she had a ten-year-old daughter and an eight-year-old son at home and within weeks, I knew that this was the family I wanted.

The following spring (1984), saw me metalworking in my garage making decorative items and gates, I was loving the life but not earning much. Unfortunately my photo album showing all that work has gone astray, but Jock Mullard asked me to make a boat trailer for Radley College and I went on to produce others.

Hugh Matheson contacted me and asked if I would scull in the double sculls event with him at Henley.

I agreed, and having turned my back on all rowing except what I was doing at Kingston, assumed wrongly that he'd given up competing at top level as I had during 1978. In fact, he'd gone on to win the 'Diamonds' in 1979 and had come sixth the following year in the Moscow Olympic final in his single.

My new way of life; blacksmithing, training from Kingston RC and my personal circumstances had put me firmly back into a hyper mood. I entered two events at Henley, the 'Diamond Sculls' in my single as well as the double sculls with Matheson. I had responsibilities, however, with Annie and two children and these challenges at Henley were was over-ambitious. This was another case of thinking, when my mood was high, that I could conquer the world. During the regatta, my mood collapsed and I didn't perform well in either of the events. I'd made a bad mistake as Hugh and I lost the doubles final which we could have won.

My boat trailers.

A few weeks later, during that summer of 1984, I was pleased to hear that at Los Angeles, Steve Redgrave's four had won the Olympic gold medal. That was the first of five golds which Steve would win in successive Olympics.

I began to have serious doubts about inflicting myself on Annie and her young family; meanwhile, although my anger wasn't with me as it had been, she had recognised flaws in me, but we married two years later. She helped me find a new design technology teaching position as a head of department at St Johns School in Leatherhead, to start in January '86. This was away from the Thames and rowing, and we moved to a large but slightly run-down house not far from the school in Leatherhead.

We went on to have two baby boys, so as they grew up with two young teenagers, there were six in our home and there were wonderful times with the family. I struggled with long hours in my department at the school, took on many extra responsibilities including being an assistant housemaster, running the naval section of the CCF, being master in charge of swimming, playing in the school wind band and then starting a jazz band. I was pushing myself too hard, using my old tactics of using pressure and training to maintain my mood but was finally diagnosed with bipolar disorder during 1993. Since that time it has become clear that I suffer from bipolar 2, commonly written bipolar II ***

From that time onwards, I was helped by medication and counselling, but taking medication wasn't straightforward to begin with. There were side-effects from the mood stabiliser, lithium, which removed not only the worst depressions but also the euphoria I had lived with, and had loved, for so many years.

The absence of the highs seemed intolerable, my brain felt dulled, and twice within the first year, I did what others have done, and discontinued taking the pills. I was persuaded to take the medication, however, and the quality of my life improved, but I was under extreme pressure, and consider that I was in a 'mixed state' for much, if not most, of the time. That was evidenced by the characteristic torments which raged in my brain.*

I continued with the busy teaching life for six more years but in 2000, had to find less stressful work, firstly in quality control in engineering manufacturing, and then in a DIY shop. The medication had reduced the severity of my moods at the cost of feeling mentally dulled, but I then benefitted from the calmer life.

** See Glossary
* See details of bipolar disorder and its treatment in the Appendix.

Tim Bucknall with my Annie, some of his family and our two boys.

During 2006 I bought a van, went self-employed and took on wood-working and home-improvement jobs, but in the longer run I enjoyed outdoor work and landscaping of all sorts which was creative as well as thoroughly physical. I still suffered with moods, found life difficult and drank too much, the end result being that Annie and I separated. We were apart for nearly two years but missed each other, I'd stopped drinking and we were beginning to get together when Covid hit. That was the event which threw us together and two years later we remarried.

My moods are now very much moderated, but cannot be cured, and I have learnt that whatever happens to me mentally, I can relax because bad times always pass. We live in Dorking in Surrey, the children are all grown up, most of them live nearby, there are six grandchildren and my rowing and sculling continues from Kingston RC.

Annie and I are blessed to have a lovely family, she has been my anchor, and I consider Annie to have saved me. We've had many, many good times but she and all the family have put up with the bad. Annie deserves more than I can ever repay.

Annie

***

I've spent most of my life pushing on, trying endlessly to escape, but have been seeing a counsellor. We've made great strides, and she's teaching me how to live without pressure, to accept space and time, and to enjoy relaxation.

I hope that this book will help others who relate to my story. The importance of knowledge and understanding of mental illnesses is paramount in order to break down the taboos surrounding it, but particularly to improve treatment. Too much fear and misery exists.

Please help to pass on understanding and knowledge of mental illness.

Glossary of Rowing Terms

'Single sculler': A person in a racing boat on his own with two oars, known as sculls, when a pair of them are used by one person.

'Clinker-built': Traditional wooden boats were built with hulls made from overlapping planks fixed to a wooden frame. The boats were strong but heavy.

'Stroke': The person who sets the pace from the stern. Everyone can see his oar, he must be reliable, strong mentally and physically and must lead boldly, so that all the others can follow.

'Sliding seats': The most basic racing boats have fixed seats but the leg muscles can be much better utilised by the addition of sliding seats, which run on wheels, back and forth within the boat on tracks. Using the power of the legs gives longer strokes and more speed.

'Coxswain': The person who steers the boat and gives orders and encouragement to the crew is the 'cox'. Some boats have the cox lying down in the bows but traditionally, the cox sits in the back of the boat, facing in the direction of travel, the main disadvantage of that is their limited view, as all the rowers are in the way.

'Paddle light': This is one of the different pressures to row at. There are different speeds at which the boat can be propelled, and rowing clubs sometimes have different names for these pressures, but commonly, 'paddling light' means relaxed rowing at a low rating (not many strokes per minute).

'Stroke-side': When rowing with an oar on one's right-hand side that is rowing on stroke-side. When rowing with the oar on one's left, that is rowing on bow side. (See diagram at the beginning of the book.)

'HOR' race: 'Head of the River' races are for large numbers of boats. Each boat is started individually with a time gap before the next boat, usually ten-second gaps, and a time is taken for each crew at a start line and again at a finish line. In this way, the finish order of the crews can be worked out and published on a results sheet. Most courses take between ten and twenty-five minutes to complete. These events are known by the location followed by HOR, typically the 'Tideway HOR' or the 'Reading HOR'.

'Double scull': Two scullers can scull together in a boat called a double scull.

'National Rowing Squad': The Amateur Rowing Association (ARA) took three major steps during the 1960s to oversee the improvement in GB rowing performance.

(1) 'Chief National Rowing Coach': During 1969, the ARA appointed a chief coach to deliver courses all around the country with the aim of teaching coaches how to coach a modern/winning style of rowing. This strategy was not effective but it led ultimately to the first national coach, Bohumil (Bob) Janousek, coaching a hand-picked squad of his own which was successful during the mid-1970s.

(2) 'National Watersports Centre': The ARA arranged for a water-sports centre, which included a 2,000-metre rowing course, to be designed and built near Nottingham.

(3) 'National Rowing Squad': The ARA gathered initially about thirty of the best oarsmen and scullers in the country to be trained by Bob Janousek and other top coaches. Most of the rowing was done in pairs to start with, but individuals from different clubs were selected to row together in crews.

'Repechage': After heats have taken place at a regatta, there are sometimes another set of races called repechages where those who have not already qualified for the next round will have another chance to qualify.

'Puddles': When a boat is moving and the oars or sculls are taken out of the water at the end of a stroke, there are sets of swirls or 'puddles' in the water where the strokes have been taken as the boat moves away.

'Loom': Every oar or scull has a handle on one end and a blade on the other, and the straight section between is called the loom.

Appendix

1 Sports psychology research
2 Information about bipolar disorder
3 Treatment and management of the illness

1. Sports Psychology Research

Research into the performance of athletes across many sports has been carried out, much of which is easily available on the internet. The following is particularly relevant to my story: 'The Dark Side of Top Level Sport' published by Newman, Hannah, Howells & Fletcher at Loughborough University (2016).

The paper makes interesting reading and the athletes whose autobiographies were selected for the analysis (below) made substantial intellectual contributions and gave approval for publication.

- Graeme Obree-Cycling
- Marcus Trescothic-Cricket
- Andre Agassi-Tennis
- Serena Williams-Tennis
- Graeme Dot-Snooker
- Jonny Wilkinson-Rugby Union
- Leon McKenzie-Soccer
- Victoria Pendleton-Cycling
- Ian Thorpe-Swimming
- Amanda Beard-Swimming
- Clarke Carlisle-Soccer
- Ricky Hatton-Boxing

Taken from the 'abstract' at the top of the paper: "The purpose of this study was to explain the depressive experiences of top level athletes and the relationship of such experiences with sports performance. Initially, sport represented a form of **escape from the depressive symptoms,** which had been exacerbated both by external stressors (e.g. experiencing bereavement) and internal stressors (e.g. low self-esteem)."

"However, in time, the athletes typically reached a stage when the demands of their sport shifted from being facilitative to being debilitative in nature **with an intensification of their depressive symptoms.** This was accompanied by deliberations about continuing their sport and an acceptance that they **could no longer escape their symptoms, with or without sport.**"

The above abstract struck me immediately because for years, sport very much helped me to **'escape from depressive symptoms'**, but during July 1971 and again during July 1977, following periods of particularly high mood and superb performance at Henley and Lucerne regattas, my mood collapsed and I **'could no longer escape symptoms, with or without sport'.**

In the end, during 1978, I had to walk away from the sport because of extended episodes of depression. I could no longer perform and needed to move into other aspects of life as well as to make a career for myself.

2. Information About Bipolar Disorder

General Considerations

- Statistics have shown that sufferers are well for most of the time.
- The illness can be effectively treated.
- The illness can be moderate to severe, and can affect individuals differently.
- There can be a hereditary element leading to an individual suffering from the disease.
- The illness will not develop in an individual simply through 'having the gene'.
- Rarely, the illness can be triggered by trauma or life events.

- A normal life can be lived by sufferers of the illness. (See 'Management' at the end)
- The illness is a chronic one, meaning that it cannot be cured.
- After an episode of the illness, it can 'sleep' for years.
- Relapses may occur when people think themselves 'cured' and stop their medication.

What is Bipolar Disorder?

From 'The Disordered Mind' by Eric Kandel: "Bipolar disorder is characterised by extreme changes in mood, thought, energy and behaviour. These episodes are often associated with high risk behaviours such as substance abuse, sexual promiscuity, excessive spending, or even violence."

"During a manic episode, people may say or do things that strain their relationship with others. They may get into trouble with the law or at work. Manic episodes can be frightening, both for people with bipolar disorder and for people close to them."

The original name given to bipolar disorder was manic depression. Both names are recognised but both are misleading in that neither describes the illness well. The symptoms are wide ranging as well as differing from one sufferer to another.

Highs and lows are generally easy to recognise, but there are many symptoms, so this illness isn't a case, as some have said, of being 'happy or sad, which we all get', but one with a wide range of sometimes devastating symptoms, which can claim lives.

Lives can be lost, but not only when sufferers are depressed. Moods can be anywhere in the range from extremely high ('manic'), through somewhere in the middle (a 'mixed state') to extreme low ('depressed'). Any of these states of mind can be strong enough to convince previously 'normal' people that to end their lives is the *preferable option*. Family members and innocent bystanders sometimes die too.

A healthy person's moods are usually affected by their surroundings but the moods of a person suffering from bipolar disorder are often disconnected from their environment. We are all affected by moods on a daily basis and the change from healthy to unhealthy moods is often not recognised.

From the book, 'Bipolar Disorder. A Guide to Patients and Families' by Francis Mondimore: "In mood disorders, the mood becomes disconnected from the individual's environment, and 'happy' and 'sad' feelings take on rhythms and fluctuations of their own."

Also: "Sometimes, though, the mood states are so extremely abnormal that a person's ability to judge reality is shattered; his behaviour can be bizarre and frightening."

Another useful book is 'The Bipolar Survival Guide' by David Miklowitz who says that suffering from bipolar disorder: "Is not a life sentence, and feelings are based on painful experiences from the past and understandable fears and uncertainties about the future. But having a bipolar illness doesn't mean you have to give up your identity, hopes and aspirations."

"Try to think of bipolar disorder in the same way you would think of diabetes or high blood pressure. That is, you have a chronic medical illness that requires you to take medication regularly. Taking medication over the long term markedly reduces the chances that the illness will interfere with your life."

The Different Moods

Please note that there are books written by well qualified medical physicians which give fuller information. My descriptions below come from these books as well as from my experience and should help give a broad, if rather basic, level of understanding.

Mania

Mania is the most dangerous symptom of bipolar disorder.

There are three levels of mania generally recognised. The first is an enthusiastic or excited mood, but falling within 'normal' levels for the general population. This can build over a period of time, weeks perhaps to the second stage, which is hypomania.

This can promote feelings of exuberance, high spirits, confidence and well-being among other things. One patient's description: "The world was filled with pleasure and promise; I felt great. Not just great, I felt really great. I felt I could do anything, that no task was too difficult."

Another patient: "If I'm ill, this is the most wonderful illness I've ever had." (* Mondimore)

If a patient's mania increases further, the mind races, speech may not be able to keep up with their mind, creative thoughts and ideas race by, sufferers may have grandiose delusions of self-importance. This may culminate in the state of 'madness'. Behaviour can be bizarre and people can become so fearful and traumatised by the racing of their own mind that they wish to end their lives.

Depression

There are many symptoms of depression, which include feelings of intense sadness, hopelessness, shame and guilt, as well as loss of appetite and sexual drive, unexplained pain, angry outbursts or irritability often over small matters, feelings of brain fog and forgetfulness, loss of interest or inability to gain pleasure from normal activities which usually have given pleasure.

Other symptoms are inability to concentrate, and simple decisions may be impossibly difficult, also reasoning and memory may fail. The sufferer may also have low energy, poor sleep, feelings of worthlessness, withdrawal from social interaction, they may lose their temper but then feel intense guilt.

When in surroundings or circumstances which should stimulate joy, the sufferer may feel grief and sadness because they cannot feel happiness.

There are three levels of depression recognised clinically. The first is felt by many and is not a clinical illness as it is within the range of normal moods. The second is a clinical depression, and sufferers will usually feel a range of symptoms. Medication can be of great help as well as talking therapies.

The most severe depressions can be totally debilitating, resulting in indescribable suffering and clinical intervention is important as the sufferer may see no hope for their future and may wish to end their lives.

Mixed States

Also from Francis Mondimore's book 'Bipolar. A Guide for Patients and Families': "Some people experience symptoms of both mania and depression at the same time, a condition known as a mixed state."

The sufferer is subjected to mental conflict and torment, which can be as debilitating as any manic or depressive episode and the description continues: "The accelerated thinking and hyperactivity typical of the manic state remain its most striking feature, but instead of a euphoric mood, these changes become combined with a depressed, despairing, desperate mood."

Also: "There is some evidence that this mood state does not occur in all patients with bipolar disorder and that, when it does occur, a different treatment approach may be necessary." *Mondimore

Note: These 'mixed episodes' can vary both in one sufferer and between sufferers, but the torment and effects of them can, in my experience, be recognised by facial grimaces among other symptoms.

'Mixed episodes' can also drive people to take their own lives. I would like to be able to convey how these states of mind feel to others, but it can't be done. The only people who know these feelings have personal experience of them.

The Four Types of Bipolar Disorders Generally Recognised

Bipolar 1

These bipolar sufferers experience the most extreme mood swings from severe 'mania' to severe 'depression' and are classed as suffering from Bipolar 1. It is common for people to become manic (extremely high) first, this then 'burns itself out' and depression follows.

These are the group of people who can be most severely manic and on occasion, forcibly taken to hospital, which is known as being 'sectioned'. All sufferers of bipolar disorder are likely to respond to treatment given and they may then be well for extended periods.

It is not possible to say either how long an episode of illness will be, or what length of time may elapse before a subsequent episode, as these are so variable, but the illness can be managed. Approximately one percent of the population is thought to suffer from Bipolar 1.

Bipolar 2 (usually written Bipolar II)

Note: My diagnosis was simply 'bipolar disorder'; however, my symptoms indicate clearly that bipolar II is the condition from which I suffer most.

Bipolar II is sometimes erroneously characterised as a milder form of Bipolar 1. Although patients with bipolar II tend not to develop the most severe symptoms of full-blown mania, they tend to be symptomatic more of the time, and their long periods of depression can be more debilitating than the dramatic, but short-lived, episodes of Bipolar 1 illness.

The depressions also tend to include more phobias, eating disorders, feelings of guilt and tendency towards suicide. About five percent of the population are thought to suffer from this form of the illness, which is harder to treat than Bipolar 1. The time scales involved are again variable.

Cyclothymia

This is where mood swings are never extreme but they deviate out of the 'normal' range into both manic and depressive moods. "Cyclothymic disorder is characterised by frequent short periods (days to weeks) of depressive symptoms and of hypomania separated by periods (which also tend to be short, in the order of days to weeks) of fairly normal mood. By definition, the patient does not have either fully developed major depressive episodes or fully developed manic episodes." (*Mondimore)

Those with cyclothymic symptoms may have frequent ups and downs, and approximately six percent of the population are thought to suffer from cyclothymia.

NOS ('Not Otherwise Classified')

There is an odd category of bipolar types, which is referred to as NOC Bipolar. This is sometimes classified as bipolar NES. (Not Elsewhere Classified). This is where "there are patients who seem to have some kind of bipolar disorder but who don't meet the diagnostic criteria for bipolar 1 or II or cyclothymia." (*Mondimore)

3. Treatment and Management of the Illness

Diagnosis and Medication

The first step is diagnosis but there are many with the illness who are moody, who have racing minds and are often angry who don't even get to see a doctor. The medical profession are now much more experienced and know the illness well, but there is still stigma about mental illness and this acts as a deterrent to seek medical help.

This stigma is being slowly eroded as knowledge expands and it is realised how large a percentage of the population suffer the serious effects of mental illnesses.

The first stage of treatment is often medication. This may be a mood stabiliser and often, an antidepressant. When the drugs take effect and the moods become much less pronounced, a large number of people miss their moods, particularly those wonderful moods which they have lived with, and enjoyed, possibly for years.

The temptation is to discontinue taking the medication and many patients overlook the threat of depression. There may also be undesirable side-effects to the medication(s) which affect patients badly. Both these factors can combine as a powerful deterrent to comply with the doctor's orders.

Note: Many people stop taking their pills. I know this, having done it twice during my early treatment. This most usually happens because mood stabilisers, lithium in particular, dulls the senses and although moods may be less severe, the patient can feel worse on their medication.

In this situation, it is important for the patient to continue with the medication for a period of some months at least until they realise that they have become better overall. Support from outside is often needed here. The fact that most sufferers become well on their medication leads to a percentage of them considering themselves 'cured' and thence to discontinue taking medication.

This almost inevitably leads to relapse, and as the illness is a chronic one which means for life. Medications should not be discontinued as the illness can lead to death.

Anyone who is concerned about their mental health should go to the doctor first, they may be referred to a psychiatrist, but if the patient is given medication for a mental illness, my advice is that the patient should research the illness by reading about it widely, so that a fuller understanding can be gained. My research has enabled me to improve the quality of my life.

Psychotherapy or Talking Treatments

Patients need help to process the thoughts and difficulties which they experience and this can be done through talking and discussion in a number of ways, the best being one-to-one counselling; however, group therapy is widely practiced and can be most useful. This is a broad topic, doctors will advise and the internet is a useful source of information.

Drugs, Including Alcohol

Many bipolar sufferers 'self-medicate' by using mind-altering substances in their attempts to relieve their mental problems. The best first step for anyone with an alcohol or drugs problem is to go to the doctor. Alcoholics Anonymous may be recommended as well as other groups for users of other drugs.

Although A. A. is not strictly a talking treatment for bipolar illness, it can be a most effective talking therapy, as well as getting to grips with an alcohol problem. There are many effective ways forward to be found on the internet for those dependent on mind-altering substances.

It is understood that those with mental suffering may want to use mind-altering substances, but in the longer term, anything other than professionally prescribed drugs is likely to be harmful.

There are meetings to give up alcohol (AA) and other drugs every day throughout the country. They are free and there is no pressure to contribute verbally. Someone who's been invited in may talk about their 'journey', this is most useful as group members recognise their own difficulties through what is being recounted.

The members of the group can then share their difficulties and feelings. The honesty and openness in these meetings is refreshing, but newcomers are not pressured to believe in God or to say or do anything in particular. In time, they almost always make many friends and understand that to follow the simple actions of millions of others can transform their lives.

Management of the Illness

Fool-proof reminders should be used to make sure that medication is not missed. An example is that the pills, or a reminder, be placed where they will be seen without fail, both morning and evening, maybe on the kitchen table.

Another is that at bedtime, pills are placed on clothing to be worn in the morning, and in the morning, they are placed on the bed ready for the evening. If travel is undertaken, some additional measures should be taken, as the distractions of travel too often lead to forgetting the all-important medication.

Triggers: It is most useful to write a list of triggers for your illness because the process of doing it increases awareness and understanding. To live a well moderated life helps stability of the mind. Some triggers to be avoided are:

Alcohol and/or drugs. Best avoided *completely* by sufferers of bipolar illness. (Mondimore)

Heavy or irregular eating.

Getting overtired (too much professional work, partying late, physical work or overtraining).

Procrastinating and working to tight deadlines.

Disorganisation.

Lack of direction/purpose/routine.

Driving fast. It is wise to set off early (and imagine providing comfort and relaxation for a special passenger)

Travel (unless essential).

Financial difficulties.

Too much of anything.

Allowing relationships to deteriorate.

Arguments.

Crowds of people.

Great challenges, risks, excitement or being outrageous.

Discontinuing medication.

Also: For many people it can be very useful to use a written:

1) Seven-day schedule of events, to include exercise.
2) Record of mood, which can give advance warning of relapse.

3) Plan for severe mood emergencies. Imagine scenarios and plan your actions which may involve family, trusted friends and the doctor.
4) Support system of family and close friends who should be told that that you are taking this illness seriously because it is dangerous. They will be more able to help if you explain to them how you are managing your illness and if you show them your written work above.